Israel, the Impossible Land

STANFORD STUDIES IN JEWISH HISTORY AND CULTURE

EDITED BY *Aron Rodrigue and Steven J. Zipperstein*

Israel, the Impossible Land

Jean-Christophe Attias and Esther Benbassa

TRANSLATED BY
Susan Emanuel

STANFORD UNIVERSITY PRESS
STANFORD, CALIFORNIA
2003

Stanford University Press
Stanford, California

Israel, the Impossible Land was originally published in French in
1998 as *Israël Imaginaire*, © 1998, Flammarion.

Assistance for the translation was provided by the Lucius N.
Littauer Foundation.

Cet ouvrage, publié dans le cadre d'un programme d'aide à la
publication, bénéficie du soutien du Ministère des Affaires
Étrangères et du Service Culturel de l'Ambassade de France aux
États-Unis, ainsi que du Ministère français chargé de la culture—
Centre national du livre.

This work, published as part of a program of assistance to publi-
cation, received support from the French Ministry of Foreign
Affairs and the Cultural Services of the French Embassy in the
United States, as well as from the French Ministry of Culture—
National Center for the Book.

Printed in the United States of America
on acid-free, archival-quality paper

Library of Congress Cataloging-in-Publication Data
Attias, Jean-Christophe.
  [Israël imaginaire. English]
  Israel, the impossible land / Jean-Christophe Attias and Esther
Benbassa ; translated by Susan Emanuel.
     p. cm. — (Stanford studies in Jewish history and culture)
  Includes bibliographical references and index.
  ISBN 0-8047-4112-3 (hc) — ISBN 0-8047-4166-2 (pbk.)
  1. Palestine in Judaism. 2. Zionism and Judaism. I. Benbassa,
Esther. II. Title. III. Series.
BM729.P3 A8813 2003
296.3'1173—dc21   2002013518

Original Printing 2003

Last figure below indicates year of this printing:
12   11   10   09   08   07   06   05   04   03

Designed by Janet Wood
Typeset by Classic Typography in 10.5/14 Galliard

Contents

Acknowledgments

This book would not have taken the form it has today without the advice and stimulating suggestions of several of our colleagues, especially Israelis, such as Israel Bartal, Simon Epstein, Harvey Goldberg, Galit Hasan Rokem, Ruth Kark, and many others, whose encouragement was valuable during our research trip to the Hebrew University of Jerusalem in October 1996. Our gratitude also goes to our friend Sarah Palmor, then librarian of the Zionist Archives of Jerusalem, who was always available to help us in our bibliographical searches, as well as to Yoram Mayorek, then director of those archives, who lent us some of his still unpublished work. Thanks, too, to Tom Segev for his bibliographical references. Of course, we alone are responsible for our text and the points of view it expresses.

We cannot forget the inestimable assistance of our friend and colleague, Aron Rodrigue of Stanford University, who generously followed the difficult maturation of this project and attentively read both the earlier and final drafts of our manuscript, in French as well as in English, with the critical sense and tact that characterize him.

Finally, we would like to thank our translator into English, Susan Emanuel, our copy editor, Peter Dreyer, and our Stanford University Press editors, Aron Rodrigue and Steven Zipperstein.

Nota bene: We have quite deliberately kept the critical apparatus of this book to a strict minimum. Curious readers and specialists will find a selective bibliography sufficiently abundant and diverse to guide their respective searches at the end of the book. The notes gathered at the end are intended only to signal the sources of information, concepts, or analyses that have nourished our thinking; when a work is mentioned for the first time in a chapter, it is generally not mentioned there a second time, even if we have drawn upon it in other passages in the same chapter.

Translator's Note

I have relied as much as possible for English translations of Scripture on the works published by the Jewish Publication Society of America, and for the translation of the Mishnah on *The Mishnah: A New Translation* by Jacob Neusner (New Haven, Conn.: Yale University Press, 1991). Spelling of proper and topographic names follows the Encyclopedia Judaica wherever possible. The English translations of bibliographical citations originally published in Hebrew have been checked by the authors.

I would like to thank Nadine Lindzen for her copious assistance; as an insider to both Jewish and French thought, she was able to help make this book more lucid for an anglophone readership. I would also like to thank Rabbi Howard Jaffe of Temple Isaiah in my hometown, Lexington, Massachusetts, for answering specialized queries.

The series editor and the authors themselves lent their help in the latter stages of refining this translation.

SUSAN EMANUEL

Introduction

> K constantly felt he was lost or had wandered farther into foreign
> lands than any human being before him, so foreign that even the air
> hadn't a single component of the air in his homeland and where
> one would inevitably suffocate from the foreignness but where the
> meaningless enticements were such that one had no alternative but
> to go on and get even more lost.
>
> —Franz Kafka, *The Castle*

Through so many centuries of exile, what has the land of Israel represented to the Jewish imagination? The memory of ancient glory. The horizon of an expectation. The improbable site onto which a hope for better days is projected. Somewhere between heaven and earth, and more often nearer heaven than earth, Zion beckons and gives meaning. One realizes, then, unlike Kafka's hero, that going on does not mean continuing to get lost, and that there, one day, the restoration of this fractured world will be completed, that there, one day, the Jews will see the end of their tribulations.

There, or perhaps here, one day, or perhaps starting today. While waiting for the dream to be realized, it is always possible to imagine that the place where one lives is already like a Jerusalem in exile, like a provisional extension of a land of Israel that is inaccessible.[1] Amsterdam is the Jerusalem of the North, Sarajevo the Jerusalem of the Balkans, Tlemcen the Jerusalem of North Africa, Vilna the Jerusalem of eastern Europe. . . . One person's Jerusalem is not another's. Each Jewish group has its own, which it places above all others. Of course, such a land does not replace the real, distant land, but rather makes it possible to be patient, to bear an exile that is internalized but never totally accepted.

Not far from Istanbul, two Jewish villages face each other, one on the European shore of the Bosphorus and the other on the Asian shore. Each still has its own cemetery. The most pious and devout folk of the European village preferred to be buried with their neighbors on the Asian side of the Bosphorus. And so their bodies crossed the narrow strait to rest over there, opposite, in almost holy soil, just a little nearer Jerusalem. Did they imagine that they would thus reach the land of Israel more quickly and surely on the day of resurrection? Was this, then, a shortcut? In any case, that's how the legend has it.

Israel, Promised Land, Holy Land, the consolation of exile. How can it be described? How can we touch the dream without distorting it, decode it without being submerged by the emotions that mention of it always arouses; how can we understand these emotions? To do so seems hard indeed, and even more so these days, now that the dream has been incarnated and become reality—a reality that has, moreover, by no means killed the imperturbable, age-old dream, which has not ceased, albeit in a different form, to haunt the minds both of the Jews of the Diaspora and of Israelis.

Israel is the land of the Book, first and foremost, of a Book that unites around it a dispersed people, a Book that itself serves as a land for those who no longer have one. Far, very far, from the real Palestine, which had long since ceased to be the place of residence of a gathered people, which was not even any longer the real center of the Diaspora, the Torah—the Land/book that was ritually read and untiringly interpreted, the primary material of liturgy—had replaced the lost land, while supplying everyone with the pretext and opportunity to evoke that land without cease. But does evoking it amount to really thinking about it? Did yesterday's Jews have the means to visualize a land that, due to its distance from them in space and time, had become for them almost impalpable? Sliding gently into the imaginary, becoming embedded in the Book, it ended up no longer existing in and of itself, instead becoming an idea or a metaphor.

In the nineteenth century, a turning point occurred. While the West experienced a vogue for Orientalism, and bitterly debated the "Eastern Question," there was a renewal of interest in this piece of earth that had been almost forgotten since the Crusades. The Jews themselves were not indifferent to this, since a new era of citizenship had opened up for them, at a time when some were proclaiming that Jerusalem was wherever they happened to be, and that for them there was no Zion other than the countries that had emancipated them. The nationalisms on the rise in Europe in those years began to influence people, at least in certain circles.

Yet neither Zionism nor the foundation of a state would totally strip the dreamed-of and recreated land of its legendary attributes. Zionists would work the land in all directions and dig deep furrows in it. They would have no less need of myths, as if the myths alone could really make it nearer and more concrete. Did the real and the concrete ever succeed in overcoming the idea of the land? This question remains open and lies at the very heart of the debate that agitates Israelis today, more than fifty years after the foundation of the state.

Investing the ancient myths with modern meanings, sometimes substituting new myths, have the Zionists been able to do no more than transform yesterday's Land/book into today's Book/land? No less than formerly, the land of Israel today remains haunted by the Book. One has merely to think of the emotions that the conquest of the "territories" (the heart of ancient Israel) after the Six Day War aroused throughout the Israeli population, extending well beyond ultra-Orthodox or extremist milieux. The land of the Book was finally taken into Israel's bosom. A symbolic land, charged with the imagination of centuries, with ancestors' rituals, with the weight of the Book, became the stake in passionate debates and the prize in a controversial settlement. Today, how can one negotiate over a symbol? All the efforts made toward a normalization of the Jews' relationship with their land run up against the obstacle of its sacralization. Each square inch of the territory is converted into an absolute—by the Jews, of course, but just as much in reaction by the Palestinians. Why can this particular land never resemble others, or become for those who inhabit it as natural as the air they breathe? On top of this, the Christian West has afterthoughts about this little disputed corner of the Middle East. The Holy Land remains holy, and holy for everyone.

This is the strange territory that we, the authors of this book, want to explore, undertaking a long voyage into the Jewish imagination from biblical times to the dawn of modernity, tracing the first steps of Zionism, then the return and the restoration of Jewish sovereignty on the ancestral soil. We ourselves came to the land of Israel by different routes; we want to answer the questions it poses in two voices that remain distinct, even though our ideas intersect and our conclusions are similar. One of us came to the land of Israel through the Book, sojourning there to master a land unknown to him; only then did he make contact with the real land, the one that seizes you bodily. The other author came to the Book after having passed through the land. By its very structure, this book echoes these two intersecting routes: it leaves the Book to go to the land, and from the land it comes back to the Book. The writers' respective experiences undoubtedly influenced each's choice of themes and periods to treat. We could not help reacting to diverse fragments of images that are sometimes contradictory and sometimes coherent, and respond to a plural reading of Zion by means of our own plural kind of writing.

To pierce the mystery of these images, to deconstruct them in order to grasp their meaning and function, their origins and history, to resituate in historical terms the fertile mythology that has peopled and continues to people the Jewish imagination of the land of Israel—this is the aim of this book. This by no means makes it a Diasporist or post-Zionist book. We do not believe that describing the real is sufficient to disqualify the myths once and for all. "Things are not so simple. Myth is not opposed to the real as the false to the true; myth accompanies the real. . . ."[2] Which people does not have its myths? The Jewish people have their own, whether they live outside this land or on its soil. The time has perhaps come to demythologize so as to better apprehend that which interposes a screen between a people and its land. Israel is an undeniable fact; Israel exists and no longer has to legitimize its existence. Its horizons are no longer limited to Zionism alone. It is in the midst of living through the crises of adulthood, but crises that will probably open up new perspectives. The authors simply want to restitute and trace the genealogies of these contemporary crises. Only upon a clear understanding of this present and this past can a future be constructed someday: the future of two peoples, and of an irreducibly multiple land.

Part One   Genealogies

One The Promised Land

In 1939, Zionist demonstrators, marching against a recent British White Paper that imposed new restrictions on the purchase of land by the Jews of Palestine, carried banners stating: "Our right to this land comes not from the British Mandate but the Bible."[1] This simple argument, while recurrent in Zionist discourse,[2] has not always succeeded in winning the adherence of its adversaries—far from it. We should not be surprised. There is no shortage of reasons to acknowledge the legitimacy of territorial claims by the Jewish people, but despite what one might think, the biblical argument is perhaps not the most convincing one. To what extent is a book actually in a position to establish a right? It does not matter that this is a sacred book, since a majority of Zionists themselves did not hold it to be such. God's attribution of this land to Israel as an everlasting legacy would only count for something in the mind of a believer, and only a Jewish believer. What would a Christian think of it, to say nothing of a Muslim? For Christians, the Old Testament was overtaken by the New and so has limited authority. On top of that, Christians have long ago replaced the challenge of Jewish territorial particularism with the deterritorialized challenge of the Incarnation; to life "on the land," they now prefer life "in Christ," independent of any condition in space and time.[3] Moreover, in contrast to what is often asserted, the Bible is not merely the literary monument of a people residing on its land, the cultural fruit of the natural osmosis between this people and this land: a large part of it was produced in exile. Besides, the place that the Bible occupies in Jewish consciousness is far from simple. One might even maintain that, as fundamental as it may be, traditionally this place is not absolutely central; the return to the Bible, and the Zionist return to the Bible in particular, constituted a break with the traditional attitude. In fact, the Talmud,[4] and in particular the Babylonian Talmud, the book of exile par excellence, disputes (in general, successfully) this centrality of Scripture.

Finally, what does the Bible itself say? In truth, it does speak of the land. It has been asserted that it speaks of nothing else.[5] But demonstrating the centrality of a theme is one thing, while grasping the significance of how it is treated is something else again. Far from simply reflecting the link between a people and its land, the Bible mediates that link, and to a large extent creates it. Far from being the clear expression of a rooted culture, Scripture is a book of promise and expectation, of dispossession as much as of conquest, of nostalgia as much as of possession. In fact, from its first verses, the text partakes of an ambiguity that it never escapes.

No doubt this ambiguity can be perceived as a natural result of the history of this text's construction. The Bible is not a homogeneous ensemble, and the books that compose it are themselves the result of sedimentation and selection, a gathering and rewriting of diverse traditions, emanating from the milieux that secreted and transmitted them, as well as from the historical moments (sometimes far removed from each other) that fostered their crystallization. However variable the hypotheses and conclusions of historico-critical exegesis over the past century may have been, and however profound some of the revisions that it has undergone, no serious discussion of ancient Israel can ignore them. A history of texts obviously illuminates the history of the men and women who have used them, and vice versa. However, one cannot repudiate the status that these texts have acquired in the traditional Jewish world, as a closed corpus, validated by its canonization, divinely inspired, and thus a priori held to be noncontradictory. Classical Jewish exegesis has more than once proved attentive to the problems that biblical writings themselves—their disjointed structure, their repetitions, their inconsistencies—seem to pose, which might challenge the status that has been granted them. But that status has not been undermined. For centuries, the perception that the Jews have had of their written tradition has remained modeled on what their oral tradition told them about it. The never-completed study of Scripture and its long-lasting integration into liturgy (weekly reading of the Pentateuch and of certain passages from the prophets, recitation of the Psalms, etc.) have guaranteed it a considerable power over consciousness—as well as over the unconscious.

It is precisely this to which the historian of representations must be sensitive, trying in each instance to be more concerned with the *effects* than with the origins of the materials being examined. A "naïve" approach, a properly literary analysis that is not necessarily dependent on simple textual criticism, offers a good way of grasping these effects. But on the question of the land, as on other subjects, the final editors of the different biblical books, as well as those who fixed the limits of the scriptural corpus, have clearly chosen not to eliminate but to *assume* certain tensions, certain ambiguities, in the messages delivered by these books and by that corpus. The possibilities of reinterpretation, the reconciliations imposed by the idea one has of the texts can change nothing about these tensions and ambiguities, which are clearly preserved and can only be constantly reactivated in the minds of readers of these texts when they study them, through liturgical practice, and even, dialectically, through the efforts at reinterpretation and at reconciliation among commentators. So let us begin at the beginning.

"In the Beginning," Ambiguity

Hebrew is not lacking in words for land/earth. The most charged with meaning and the most general is also the oldest: *erets*. In the first chapter of Genesis, the word is used, by opposition to heaven, to refer to the earth, which along with heaven is the product of the first creative act of the Godhead. Then, by opposition to the sea, it refers to the dry land that appears through another initial act of separation. Finally, by opposition to uncultivated earth, it refers to the fertile land that sprouts seed-bearing plants and trees, the fecund earth that gives birth to the animal world. It is this land/earth that God gives as an inheritance to those whom He has created, male and female, in His image and resembling Him, and that He commands them to fill and conquer.[6]

But this first picture of beginnings is not the only one. Another follows immediately and markedly inflects its meaning. At the start of the second chapter of Genesis, in fact, the earth created by God is presented in a very different light. It does not yet give any fruit, because God has not yet sent rain upon the earth, and there is no man to till the soil. This earth, which must be cultivated, has a different name: it is no longer *erets*, but *adama*. From it, from a little "dust of the earth," God fashions man and blows into his nostrils the breath of life. Then the Eternal One plants a garden in Eden and in it places the man, who at this point is only male, or androgynous, to till and tend it. In this telling of the story, it is only later that, in the same way as man has been drawn from the earth, woman is in turn drawn from the man. Here, words signify the history of the beings they name. In Hebrew, man, in the generic sense, will be called *adam*, the masculine of *adama*, earth— just as woman will be called *isha*, the feminine of *ish*, man, in the sexed sense of this word.[7] Another linguistic echo signifying this kinship with the earth as constitutive of human identity is that the same term (*zera*) in Hebrew designates grain, the plant seed, and human offspring.[8]

Taken together, the first two chapters of Genesis depict, therefore, a complex and rather contradictory image of the relation between man and the land/earth. In Genesis 1, this relation seems one of pure otherness and subjection: created after the earth, but not issued from it, man is called upon to subject it, and the earth seems naturally bound to offer him the nourishment he needs. This relation is quickly transformed, though, in Genesis 2: now born of the earth and of God, as from a mother[9] and a father, man must work the earth and tend it in order to draw his sustenance from it, and what the earth gives him, he owes to himself and to God, who plants vegetation and makes the rain fall. First, there is domination, then a strange intimacy follows, in a kinship that associates God, man, and the earth in a common enterprise. This sliding together soon ends in a reversal: on account of the first sin, the earth is cursed: it is with toil that man will now draw forth his nourishment; the earth-mother becomes a tomb, "for dust you are, and to dust you shall return"; in the end she shrinks from the footfall of the one born from her, who is sent out of the Garden of

Eden for having contravened the divine interdiction regarding the fruit of the tree of the knowledge of Good and Evil.[10]

Thus, from its opening pages, the Bible is truly "the book of the place"[11]—a place that is both strange and familiar, speaking of life and death, of rootedness and exile, of transgression and punishment. Not a word has yet been said about the people of the Bible, the people of Israel for whom the Bible is the Book; not a word about this people's land, either, this "land of Israel" whose Book is the Bible. The argument is still strictly speaking universal, since the story of Abraham, father of the nation, does not begin until chapter 12—and yet everything seems already to have been said.

Reading what follows next merely strengthens this first impression. God gives the earth and takes it back, places man there and drives him away. A three-scene scenario seems to repeat itself indefinitely: the intimacy of a union between man and his earth; a violation of the Law that perverts this relationship; an expulsion, a dispersion, a wandering that is a sanction against the sin. Cain, the farmer, man of the earth, sees his offering disdained by the Lord and kills his rival brother, Abel, the shepherd. God then says: "What have you done? Hark, your brother's blood cries out to Me from the ground! Therefore, you shall be cursed because of the ground which opened its mouth to receive your brother's blood from your hand. If you till the soil, it shall no longer yield its strength to you. You shall become a ceaseless wanderer on earth."[12] Some generations later, judging that the earth is corrupt and that all living creatures on it have perverted His way, God undertakes with the Flood to erase man, whom He has created, "from the face of the earth." Finally, when men try to erect in Babel a tower whose summit reaches heaven, He disperses and "scatters them over the whole face of the earth." Each new alteration of the relation to place, moreover, is preceded or followed by a displacement toward the East, with negative connotations. Cain leaves the presence of the Lord and settles in the land of Nod, east of Eden, and it is by migrating east that men reach the valley where they build their tower.[13]

A Heritage Deferred

It is the Abrahamic venture that initiates a reversal of this negative dynamic, but without removing the ambiguity. It opens with a migration, but this time toward the South and the West. When God intimates to Abraham the order to leave, it is at first a tearing away and an exile that He prescribes: "Go forth from your native land and from your father's house. . . ."[14] The rupture thus commanded is local and geographic as well as familial and genealogical. It is an uprooting, an unfaithfulness to place, a necessity of becoming foreign to it that at first glance defines the Abrahamic condition. In addition, the land toward which Abraham heads does not yet have a name, and is not even located; it is just the land that God will show him when the time comes. The patriarch is thus a man who is going from a known land, with which he breaks ties, toward a mysterious land, of which he knows nothing yet. He gives himself up to the voyage, but the divine promise of descendants, of blessing and renown, as yet does not give a particular place to this land toward which he is heading. It does have a name, but we only discover it later: "the land of Canaan," because the Canaanites are living there. It is only once he has arrived that Abraham hears God promise him: "I will give this land to your offspring."[15] So it is a doubly foreign land for Abraham, since others are its permanent residents for the time being, and since only his offspring are called to inherit it. The Promised Land is not yet possessed, and its status still quite uncertain. It is a temporal reality more than a spatial one, the future of a family much more than its location.

However, the words are certainly more charged with meaning and more precise than a cursory reading suggests. When God gives the land, it is not a simple, gracious gift. Here "to give" is a technical legal term, evoking the legal transfer of a title deed. Similarly, Abraham's descendants, who will benefit from this transfer, are by no means any offspring issued from him, but only a favored lineage, a preferred line.[16] There is also a lineage without rights: Ishmael, Isaac's brother, will inherit the desert, and as for Esau, he will emigrate to a land other than Canaan on account of his brother Jacob.[17] But here what matters most is that the announcement of the appropriation is not dissociated from the announcement of a dispossession; Abraham's posterity will not be entering Canaan until after four hundred years of exile in a foreign land; the heritage is thus indefinitely deferred, always thought of in the future. It will be so for Isaac, too, and still so for Jacob.[18] If the patriarchs are now virtually the legitimate owners of Canaan, they still, in fact, continue to reside there as strangers—when they reside there at all! Only just arrived, Abraham is constrained by famine to sojourn in Egypt, and when he comes back from Egypt to Canaan, God orders him to walk through the length and breadth of the land, "for I will give it to you."[19] And, finally, the Book of Genesis closes with the establishment of Jacob and his family in Egypt.

Over this land of Canaan through which they are still just passing, the patriarchs ultimately have no other right than that for which they pay in currency. When Abraham wants to bury Sarah, his deceased wife, a native Hittite offers him his field and the cave it contains. But Abraham rejects this free offer and insists on paying the four hundred shekels of silver this place is worth. Thus he buys at a high price a fragment of this land even though it had been given him by God. To the legitimacy of the promise, he joins that of acquisition. Two generations later, Jacob will not hesitate to repeat this gesture when he acquires the portion of land where he sets up his tent—besides, this will be the place where the children of Israel, having conquered the country under Joshua's leadership, will bury the bones of Joseph, brought back from Egypt. King David himself will buy the threshing floor of Araunah the Jebusite for fifty shekels, where he will build an altar and sacrifice burnt offerings, and where his son Solomon will have the Temple built.[20]

Canaan is a strange land that scarcely seems to have any natural frontier except the sea; only deserts (the Syrian desert to the northeast, the Sinai to the southwest) separate it from Abraham's land of origin, Mesopotamia, and from his descendants' land of exile, the Egypt of the pharaohs. Canaan is a strange land that is devoid of precise limits and itself figures as a frontier territory, as a simple passage route, torn between two great rival poles of attraction.[21] It is especially strange in that the natives are not the legitimate heirs and the legitimate heirs are not natives, for Canaan is an inhabited land when Abraham, Isaac, and Jacob establish themselves there. People and kingdoms seem solidly implanted there, whereas the installation of the patriarchs has all the appearance of precariousness. A total of ten ethnic groups at this juncture are sharing the promised territory.[22] Numerous kings confront one another, and if it happens that a Hebrew intervenes in a conflict or provokes one, it is in order to protect one of his kin or to cleanse his honor, as when Abraham delivers his relative Lot, kidnapped by the victors of Sodom and Gomorrah, or when Simeon and Levi carry out a merciless vendetta against those responsible for the rape of their sister Dinah.[23] This latter action does not please their father Jacob at all, moreover, for he fears that it will make him "odious among the inhabitants of the land," and that since his "men are few in number," they will exterminate him and his house. As a general rule, confrontations with indigenous peoples are avoided, and some alliances are even made.

A stranger in this land that is destined for him, the biblical patriarch is aware of his fragile status. He is already there without really being there, while still being from elsewhere. He shows this clearly by his fidelity to the endogamous principle. When he wants to marry off his son, Abraham sends one of his servants on a mission into what he calls "his country," the "land of his birth," that is, into Chaldea, asking the servant to find a wife for Isaac there and bring her back.[24] His son must neither marry a wife from the place where he lives, Canaan, nor go to live where his wife is going to be found, Mesopotamia. Rebekah, the designated partner, is a close relative of Abraham; she is "of the house of his father," of "his family," and she must accomplish the same journey as her future father-in-law—that is, follow the servant and come to Canaan. The principle of rupture with the old place is thus maintained—but the principle of consanguinity and the maintenance of the ethnic frontier prevail over the attachment to the new place. Isaac, in turn, looking askance at Esau's Hittite wives, will send his son Jacob to find a wife in the home of his brother-in-law, Laban, in the land of Aram.[25] Thus it is he who marries within the clan outside the land who will inherit the land, while he who marries women of the land outside the clan will not inherit it.

But then what is the status of the actual masters of the land? All of them, Canaanites and patriarchs, descend from the same common ancestor, Noah. As we know, he had three sons—Shem, Ham, and Japheth—and "from these the nations branched out . . . by their lands, each with its language—their clans and nations."[26] The patriarchs are the descendants of Shem, by Eber, while the Canaanite peoples descend from Ham. The natural territory of each, Semites and Canaanites, is clearly defined in the biblical text.[27] And so the migration of Abraham, willed by God, appears to introduce a confusion into the normal geographic distribution of nations after the Flood. Thus the land occupied by the Canaanites is manifestly not a land like others; it is basically the natural place of no tribe and merely the natural site of virtue and right conduct in the eyes of the Eternal One.

The tragic episode of Sodom and Gomorrah is the best illustration of this.[28] On the one hand, there are two cities, about which there is great outcry and that are given to extreme perversity. On the other hand, there is God, who appears particularly interested in the doings of the peoples who reside on this land. Situated between God and the sinful towns, finally, there is Abraham, to whom this land has been promised and from whom God does not hide His intentions. So despite the intercession of the patriarch, Sodom and Gomorrah and the plain surrounding them and the very vegetation on it will disappear under a rain of sulfurous fire on account of the impious acts perpetrated by their inhabitants. The lesson in these events is clear: Abraham's descendants will not eventually have a chance to become and remain the heirs of this land unless they themselves practice virtue and justice. But in order for the virtue and justice of Abraham and his posterity effectively to earn them this inheritance, it will also be necessary for the vice and injustice of the Canaanites to reach their full measure. This explains the delay imposed on the effective transfer of the property: for four hundred years, the patriarch's posterity will sojourn in a strange land, where they will be subservient and oppressed, and only then will they be able to come back to Canaan, because only then will the perversity of its first occupants be complete.[29]

What a strange land this land of Canaan is, always under God's gaze, a land inhabited by men, but also, perhaps more than others, inhabited by God. This is the meaning of the discovery made by Jacob, not without surprise, exactly as he leaves Canaan for Chaldea when he is fleeing the anger of Esau, from whom he has stolen the paternal blessing. Night overtakes him en route and he lies down where he happens to find himself. There he has a dream, the famous dream of Jacob's Ladder. At the top of this ladder, God reiterates the promise made to Abraham and tells Jacob that the land on which he is lying will truly be given to him and his posterity. When he wakes up, Jacob cries out: "Surely the Lord is present in this place, and I did not know it!" He calls this awesome place "the abode of God" (Bethel) and "the gateway to heaven."[30] This striking discovery, however, in no way deters him from following his route and leaving Bethel for a foreign land. He leaves because his survival is at stake and because the place he is going to is where he will find the wife his father has destined for him. He abandons this land inhabited by God because he knows that elsewhere, too, in exile far from this land, the Lord will not abandon him.

Exile and the Desert

The first five books of the Bible, the Pentateuch, called the Torah (Teaching) in Hebrew,[31] are also those which the rabbinical tradition has invested with the highest legal authority. Divided into some fifty sections, they are ritually read, each week, over the course of a year during synagogue services. Abundantly studied and commented upon, they have largely contributed to fashioning Jewish self-consciousness. But of what do they speak? First of all, as we have seen, of the beginnings of a history of humanity, largely a story of the erosion of its relations with the ground that bears it and from which it is born. Then, as we have just noted, it speaks of the promise of a restoration of these relations for a particular family and for a particular land—a promise whose realization is deferred, however. The third and final part of this history, quantitatively by far the largest (in fact, it covers the last four books), evokes the beginnings of the realization of this promise, but the action still unfolds entirely outside the frontiers of the land. In effect, the story stops on the eve of the entry of Israel into

Canaan. And so each year, in the autumn, the course of the narration is suspended and the ritual reading starts again, "at the beginning," for yet another year. The presumed author of this text is Moses, born in Egypt and raised as an Egyptian. He lifts his people out of servitude, transmits to them the divine Law called to govern their life in Canaan, and leads them across the desert, but Moses himself will not tread upon the soil of the Promised Land; he can only see it in the distance from the top of Mount Nebo. In fact, with the exception of Caleb and Joshua, none of the Hebrews who came out of Egypt will escape alive from the desert; their bodies will remain there, and only their children will inherit the land.[32]

A veritable biography of the nation,[33] the history told in the final four books of the Pentateuch is thus set against a tension among three places: first there is Egypt, the place that is left, the land of exile, but also the land of gestation and childhood, where the house of Jacob has become a numerous nation; then Canaan, the place toward which one goes, land of promise and of maturity, the destination of this nation that is on the move; and finally the desert, the place that is crossed, neither land of exile nor land of promise, the non-place of adolescence, rebellion, and also initiation. None of these places is a permanent place, a place where one stays. In addition, the place one leaves, exile, is a place that is missed, and the place toward which one is traveling is a place that is feared. The history of the forty years in the desert is woven of nostalgia, hesitations, and infinite detours. Barely freed from the house of servitude, the people of Israel, who fear dying of hunger in the desert, grow angry at Moses and Aaron and sadly recall the pots of meat and the bread they had back in Egypt. When they are given manna, they grow tired of it and long for the fish, cucumbers, melons, pears, onions, and garlic they ate gratis in the land of the Pharaoh.[34] Conversely, when they are nearly there, they draw back in fear. The report of the scouts sent out by Moses is ambiguous. The Promised Land does flow with milk and honey; it gives magnificent fruit, but the people living there are powerful, of huge stature, and its towns are fortified and very large. The Promised Land is a land that "devours its settlers,"[35] and Israel does not feel either the strength or the courage to undertake its conquest. Wouldn't it have been better to die in the desert or in Egypt than to perish by the sword for a thankless land?

This lack of confidence, this incapacity to break free of the memory of an Egypt suddenly perceived as maternal and nourishing, this refusal to recognize Canaan as its true fatherland (the land of ancestors), this tendency to see it instead as a voracious stepmother[36]—all of this is what God decides to penalize with forty years of wandering in the desert. Nevertheless, in the same way that Egypt, land of exile and servitude, is also a positive place in which Jacob's house grows and multiplies in order to become a great nation, and where God, by the miracles He accomplishes, manifests His power, so the desert is not solely a land of sin, punishment, and wandering. A liminary space, an in-between territory, the desert is simultaneously a site both of infidelity and revolt (the Golden Calf) and of revelation and submission, where Israel, by receiving the Law, is constituted as a free people and a holy nation. The sole and unique piece of territory that the Pentateuch expressly designates as "holy" is precisely situated deep in the desert, on Mount Horeb: this is the ground where the burning bush appears to Moses. When he wants to approach it to see it better, God speaks in these terms: "Do not come closer. Remove your sandals from your feet, for the place on which you stand is holy ground."[37] It is the visible presence of God in this corner of the desert that transforms it into a holy site. This sacralization is ephemeral, though, and lasts only during this presence, and in fact the place is never even mentioned in what follows, either as a holy site or a fortiori as a site of pilgrimage. This is a status very comparable to the one later enjoyed by the Sinai, where God also appears, this time to all of Israel. Its sacralization is manifested by the establishment of a frontier, which only some people at certain moments can cross without danger: on the eve of theophany, on God's command, Moses confines the people to one area and establishes a boundary around the mountain, which thereby becomes holy.[38]

As a general rule, if the desert appears as the privileged site of the irruption of the sacred, the sacredness that this irruption confers on it is both localized and temporary. Like the people who cross it, the holy site in the desert is an essentially nomadic site. Any Israelite encamp-

ment establishes a provisional sacred space that contains three concentric zones. At the core, there is the tabernacle, mobile and capable
of being dismantled, that contains the tablets of the Law, the care of
which is entrusted to the Levites alone. Surrounding and facing the
tabernacle, there are the children of Israel, each placed under a distinct
banner according to his paternal tribe. Beyond, there is the rest of the
desert, the world, with no limits, home of the impure, where menstruating women, lepers, and those afflicted with a discharge or who
have been in contact with a cadaver are sent—so that they will not soil
the enclosure in the midst of which God resides. However, it is sufficient for Israel to raise camp and establish itself a little farther away in
order for these frontiers of the sacred to move along with it.

The fundamental experience of wandering in the desert is no less
central in Jewish memory than is possessing and then losing the land.
The three great festivals of pilgrimage in the liturgical calendar are
agricultural festivals that would later guarantee the centrality of the
fixed site, Jerusalem, by bringing to it three times a year a flood of the
faithful; but at the same time they are directly linked to the memory
of the nomadic existence of Israel in the desert, an existence that the
very rite of pilgrimage, which gives them that specific cachet, tries in
part to revive. Passover in the spring commemorates the exodus from
Egypt. The Festival of Weeks (Shavuot), fifty days later, commemorates the giving of the Law at Sinai. The Festival of Booths (Sukkoth)
at the start of autumn is meant to lead to a rediscovery of the precariousness of life in the desert; it clearly signifies a refusal to rest, a liberation from subservience to place: for seven days, Israel must quit its
stone houses and live in tents, in remembrance of the tents God gave
the Hebrews as homes when they left Egypt.

The crossing of the desert in fact keeps alive in the memory of a settled Israel a taste for a freshness and virginity that are evoked with
nostalgia: it was the time of youth and blossoming love, the time of
the betrothal between Israel and its God. The desert, moreover, does
not cease being a temptation, perceived as an ever-open possibility of
starting again; beyond exile, the desert is the site of an ultimate judgment and purification, before the ultimate reconquest of the land.[39]
The desert has an incontestably positive quality, as a moment, if not as

a place. Rootedness never effaces the trace of the voyage, and the sedentary is born of the nomad; a person from here knows that he or she comes from back there. Thus Joshua reminds Israel at the end of the conquest, and on the eve of his death, that their ancestors formerly lived beyond the River.[40] In the same way, when the farmer presents God with the firstfruits of his crop and expresses his gratitude toward the One who allowed him to inherit this land and to enjoy its fruits, his confession begins with these words: "My father was a fugitive Aramean. He went down to Egypt with meager numbers and sojourned there. . . ."[41]

The Memory of an Initial Expropriation

It is revealing that the Hebrews have thus kept and cultivated so pregnant a memory of their existence as a people before their arrival in the land of promise. The possession of land by Israel is never perceived as a self-evident fact, as a natural given. The land's very name suffices to perpetuate the memory of initial difficulty. At first, and long thereafter, it was known as the "land of Canaan" or "land of the Canaanite." Then it became more generally "the land" (ha-arets), meaning both an anonymous land and The land par excellence.[42] In the corpus of Scripture, it only latterly and rather exceptionally became known as "the land of Israel" (Erets Yisrael) in 1 Samuel.[43] Biblical literature testifies in fact to a never-relaxed tension around a recurrent question: what is the exact nature of the right of the children of Israel over the land that God gave them? Far from being presented as a tranquil affirmation of this right, Scripture is instead its anxious meditation.

The tragic events of Israel's ancient history could not help but reinforce this fundamental disquiet. Around 931 B.C.E., upon the death of Solomon, the kingdom's unity had been broken by a schism. In 722 B.C.E., the kingdom of Israel in the north was destroyed and its inhabitants deported to Assyria. And in 586 B.C.E., it was the turn of the kingdom of Judah in the south to fall, with a portion of the Judeans exiled to Babylonia. Had God abandoned his people? Had Israel therefore lost any right over the land from which it had just been expelled?

In effect, how one answered these questions determined the legitimacy of a hope and the possibility of a return. The promises made to the patriarchs implied "perpetual" possession; and God had assured David of an eternal kingdom.[44] But subsequent events demanded rethinking these divine guarantees more in terms of conditional promises: Abraham's posterity could not exercise an effective right over its land except to the extent that it proved worthy of this right. When they wrote the history of the monarchic period, the biblical writers took on the task of explaining why Israel and then Judah had been chased out of their land. And when they looked back at the previous period, that of Joshua and the Judges, they especially invited an examination of the meaning and conditions of what one must really call an initial expropriation.[45]

This may be why an exegete of the eleventh century like Rashi, commenting on the very first verse of Genesis, asks why the Torah, which to him is essentially the Law transmitted by God to His people, does not open with the first of the commandments given to Israel as a nation (the Passover sacrifice)[46]—rather than with the story of the origin of the world. A modern reader would have no difficulty whatsoever in answering such a question. You might invoke a chronological logic (you have to begin with the beginning) or a logical exposition (you have to progress from the general to the particular, from the creation of man to the election of Israel). But this is not the argument given by Rashi or by the older exegetical tradition on which he drew. If the Torah starts with the story of God's creation of heaven and earth, it is in order that Israel may have the wherewithal to answer other nations should they accuse it someday of being a "thief" and having wrongfully deprived the Canaanites of their inheritance. In effect, the affirmation of a divine right over the earth, in a general sense, was the only way to justify the way in which God subsequently disposed of the land, this time, a particular land. Establishing from the start that He is the creator of the world, the Torah establishes by the same token that God is its unique legitimate owner. He is free then to use it as He pleases. It is He who gives the nations their lots, He who fixes the boundaries of various peoples.[47] Thus He could, at a particular moment in history, decide to offer a particular land to the posterity of a particular man (Abraham), notwithstanding the fact that such a promise implied the dispossession of its preceding occupants. Similarly, He could, at another moment in history, in the time of Joshua and the Judges, realize His promise by means of a violent expropriation. Moreover, it is by this very expropriation that God's generosity with respect to Israel can be measured.

Israel does not inherit only soil or space, but rather a country, all it contains, all that its first holders built and sowed there—cities that Israel did not build, vineyards and olive trees that others have planted for it.[48] But is it possible to justify solely by divine arbitrary will, by the exclusive love of the Lord for His people, an expropriation that is accompanied by the physical destruction of the expropriated? For the divine orders are clear and forbid any compromise. The peoples that Israel must dispossess are fated to annihilation, and not a soul must survive. In fact, none of the cities to be taken (with a single exception) chooses to give itself up peacefully to the aggressor, so all of them must be conquered *manu militari*. And this is how the divine project can be fully accomplished: it is necessary for the enemy to resist in order for Israel to destroy them without mercy, "as the Lord had commanded Moses."[49]

As cruel as it may appear to the modern reader, this war of conquest that turns into a war of extermination is certainly not the fruit of supreme divine arbitrariness. It is undoubtedly because He loves Israel that God offers it this land as inheritance, as He had promised it to Abraham, and there really is some overflowing grace at work, some gratuitousness in the gift. However, there is nothing gratuitous in the dispossession. The crimes of the Canaanites have in fact reached their full measure and now amply justify their annihilation. On account of the abominations they have committed, the country has become impure, and God has demanded that they account for their iniquity and so has thrown the inhabitants out. And if Israel were in turn to give itself over to similar schemes, an identical sanction would necessarily fall upon it: "So let not the land spew you out for defiling it, as it spewed out the nation that came before you."[50] By vocation the residence of virtue and justice, this land naturally expels vice and iniquity from its bosom, like an organism throwing up noxious food. It seems that the identity of the people whose conduct is at issue makes no difference.

The fate reserved for the first occupants of the land is the patent sign of the conditional character of this grant to Israel. The parallel is not absolute, however. In effect, while the punishment of the Canaanites is extermination, that of the sons of Israel, on the day they do sin against the Law, will be exile. Of course, they "shall be left a scant few,"[51] but they will not by any means be annihilated. The path of repentance will remain open to them, and it will suffice for them to return to God in order for God ultimately to let them return to their land. Here is the whole ambiguity of the Covenant, in which the attribution of the land is an essential clause. Israel enters into possession of the land in order to accomplish God's Law there. As the Covenant is eternal, eternal also is the ownership of the land by Israel. On the other hand, because the Covenant is a contract, if Israel fails to fulfill its obligations to God, then the right of residence on the land is withdrawn. But this does not imply the annulment of its right of ownership, which is imprescriptible. Once the transgression has been expiated, God will remember the Covenant and the land once more and will let His people return.[52]

This coexistence of the principle of imprescriptibility and the principle of conditionality underlines the fundamental ambiguity of God's relation to His people, as well as of the people's relation to its land. In what sense, then, can the people be called proprietors of the land? Sometimes the land really seems to belong to itself alone, and to be endowed with an autonomy characteristic of living organisms, such that it naturally vomits out those who do not agree with it. Most often, though, it appears as the inalienable possession of God alone: "for the land is Mine; you are but strangers resident with Me."[53] Basically, Israel has only the usufruct of the land. Biblical agricultural legislation signals this constantly: the exploitation of the soil is subject to restrictions. Every seven years, during the sabbatical year, all land must be left fallow, and after seven sabbatical cycles, during the jubilee year, the land sold in the course of the preceding forty-nine years comes back to its first owners. The enjoyment of the products of the land is neither immediately nor totally granted: these products come from God and must be partly restored to Him. The first three years' harvest from newly planted fruit trees cannot be consumed; the fruits of the fourth year must be eaten in Jerusalem in the Lord's honor, and it is only in the fifth year that they can be freely used. Any crop gives rise to diverse levies that are the shares of God, the priests, and the Levites, a tribe who are forbidden to possess land. Thus the fruits of the land never belong totally to the one who owns and works that land. They also belong to the poor, to those who have no land of their own. Thus one abandons to the needy the ears of corn and grapes that have fallen, the small bunches left unpicked, the sheaves forgotten in the fields during the harvest. In the same way, it will be forbidden to reap the corner of the field, again for the benefit of the poor.[54]

A Dismembered Land

If biblical agricultural legislation firmly stressed the limitations to Israel's hold on cultivated ground, history, for its part, objectively undertook to limit its hold on the territory for a long time. The conquest carried out by Joshua and the Judges in fact remains incomplete, because from the beginning of its history, Israel has shown itself unworthy of having it all. An ambiguous dynamic is set up that whittles away at the territory effectively placed under tribal authority. God has expressly made the success of Israel's campaigns subject to an intangible rule: He will not help it in its battles except to the exact extent that it shows itself determined to wage war to the end, not to contract any alliance with the peoples that it must expropriate, and not to bow to any of their gods. Inversely, any temptation to compromise, any imitation of the behavior of the natives, will lead God to stop dispossessing them on Israel's behalf, so that they will become a trap and a pitfall for Israel, even to the point where it will end up disappearing from the land that has been given to it. Manifestly, the Hebrews quickly failed at their task. This was why a great part of the country still remained to be conquered when Joshua, very advanced in years, undertook to divide the territory already taken among the different tribes. So the children of Israel henceforth inherited a whittled-down land. The Canaanite enclaves with whom they had allied themselves, and which occasionally paid them tribute, in fact made the Hebrews' hold over the country forever fragile. God had decided to use these enclaves to test them and to judge whether or not they would keep to His ways as their ancestors had before them.[55]

The indirect, conditional, and fundamentally unstable character of Israel's relation to its land thus dates from the earliest days of its establishment and will never totally disappear. So we should not be surprised to find that the frontiers of the land of Israel, including its ideal frontiers, vary sometimes considerably from one biblical text to another. The frontiers of what the patriarchs were promised do not coincide exactly with those drawn by Moses on the eve of the conquest.[56] In the era of Joshua and the Judges, the "land of Israel" was a territory extending from "Dan to Beersheba," but even under Solomon, when the conquered area tended to approach the ideal boundaries of the promise, the land of Israel basically remained the territory effectively inhabited by Israel: still from Dan to Beersheba. It is remarkable to note that with the exception of Ezekiel (who was dreaming of the future),[57] no prophet appears to have been concerned with the question of frontiers, or ever to have reproached any sovereign for being content with a reduced territory or for not having realized the project of fulfilling the larger sense of the promise.

Paradoxically, the land of Israel was both limited and indefinitely extendable.[58] Its eastern frontier does seem to be the Jordan River, which has to be crossed to enter the country. Not to cross it, as witness Moses' desire to do so and God's refusal to answer him, is to remain outside the land.[59] And yet don't Reuben, Gad, and the semi-tribe of Manasseh ask to settle precisely across the Jordan, on the eastern bank of the river, and therefore outside this symbolic limit? And since this request is granted, doesn't the Jordan on this occasion cease to be a frontier? In fact, the status of Transjordania remains distinctly ambiguous. It is Moses who grants it to the two and a half tribes who want to settle there, whereas the rest of the people receive the "land" proper, to wit, the whole area situated to the west of the Jordan, from God himself.[60] Reuben, Gad, and the half-tribe of Manasseh, who live in Transjordania, actually fear that their brothers will someday regard them as foreigners on the grounds that God has placed a "boundary," the Jordan, between them, and that they thus have "no share in the Lord" (Josh. 22:25). They are therefore tempted to erect their own altar, which immediately evokes a bellicose reaction from the rest of Israel. The conflict is finally resolved peacefully, but the ambiguous status of Transjordania is confirmed by the proposal made by Israel to those who prefer to remain on the other side of the Jordan: if the country in their possession seems impure to them, they are always at liberty to cross the river, to cross back "into the Lord's land, where the Lord's tabernacle stands," and settle there.[61]

On top of the scars of an imperfect conquest can be added what we might call internal frontiers. From this standpoint, the reigns of David and Solomon are a brief bright spot. Because Solomon has married a large number of women from the peoples with whom the Lord has forbidden Israel to mix, and because he has followed their example and sacrificed to their idols, the kingship will be in part taken away from his heirs, and the territory that he had contributed to unifying will be divided. Rehoboam, his son, will only inherit the possessions of Judah and Benjamin, while Jeroboam, his servant, will establish a new, competing dynasty in the north. The gesture of the prophet Ahijah announcing his good fortune to Jeroboam is eloquent: he seizes Jeroboam's new robe and tears it into twelve pieces and returns to him ten pieces, standing for the ten tribes he is called to govern.[62] Two kingdoms now unequally share the land of Israel. This initial tearing apart will occupy a central place in Jewish consciousness that will never be remedied. The disappearance of the kingdom of the north and the deportation of its inhabitants in 722 B.C.E. will only apparently put an end to it. In fact, these events will only aggravate the split, with each Jew feeling nostalgia for these ten lost tribes, exiled in distant lands, beyond the mythical and impassable river Sambation. However, there is much greater nostalgia for the nation's unity than for territorial space. The territorial disparity has only a limited impact on the unity of the national consciousness—basically, because the unity of the people of Israel flows much more from its covenant with God than from its rootedness in a unified territory.

Sedentary People, Nomadic God

The ties by which biblical Israel historically and symbolically binds itself to its land thus appear highly complex. Its attachment to the Law
and its sacerdotal vocation allow it to transcend certain territorial contingencies; it does not dare forget that it has only the usufruct of the
ground it cultivates. This distanced attachment to the land in no way,
however, implies any a priori valorization of nomadism. For Cain,
wandering is a punishment. For Israel in the desert, it is just a spell, a
stage in a journey that leads to the Promised Land, and this destination gives the trip its whole meaning. The prophet Jeremiah does exalt the example of the Rechabites who, obeying the injunction of their
common ancestor, do not drink wine, do not build houses, do not
sow grain or plant vines, and who live in tents. But he does not really
do so to vaunt their mode of existence (which incidentally guarantees
that they will live long days on the land where they are sojourning).
His concern is rather to contrast the Rechabites' sense of the law and
their faithfulness to their earthly father, on the one hand, and the
weakness of which Israel is too often guilty in the practice of the prescriptions transmitted by its celestial Father, on the other.[63]

Biblical liturgical time is based on the agricultural year; the festivals
commemorating the Hebrews' peregrinations in the desert follow the
yearly progress of work on the land. When the land enjoys divine attention and the rains fall regularly, it is a fertile and spacious country, flowing with milk and honey, where bunches of grapes are so big that they
must be carried by two people on a pole, a country that produces wheat,
barley, grapes, figs, pomegranates, olive trees, and honey, where you eat
unstintingly and lack for nothing.[64] Biblical happiness is agricultural
happiness, whose summit is reached in the ideal period of Israel's sovereignty over its soil during Solomon's reign: "Judah and Israel were as
numerous as the sands of the sea; they ate and drank and were content."[65] Inversely, unhappiness is building houses where one will not
live, planting vines whose wine one will not drink. The punishment of
sin is not just exile, it is also the ruin of the land: fertile countryside becomes desert, cities fall under the fire of divine wrath, the whole country

becomes desolate. The hopes of return and restoration are also expressed by the prophets in agricultural terms: the plowman will converge with the harvester, he who presses the grape with him that sows the seed, the mountains will drip with the juice of the vine, the hills will flow with milk, and all the streams of Judah will be full of water.[66]

The testimony about this earthly rootedness and the gratitude that Israel feels to the God who has made it possible is plentiful in biblical literature. It is indeed this gradual and resolute passage from nomadism to sedentary life that primarily characterizes the history of biblical Israel. And soon the urban model will take priority over rural spaces. From this standpoint, the existence of Jerusalem, a Jebusite fortress conquered by David quite late, and its promotion to the rank of capital of the kingdom, profoundly modifies Israel's relationship with its territory, while strengthening and stabilizing it. The territory is now endowed with a center of gravity, a prime site of power, toward which everyone looks. Jerusalem is the first Israelite city in the proper sense of the word: it belongs to no tribe and is inhabited by a population originating in all the tribes. The transfer of the Ark of the Covenant within its walls and then the building of the sanctuary make it the holy city of all Israel.[67] The divine election of Jerusalem extends the election of the people and the land. It is the sign of the fulfillment of the promise and the success of the Covenant: it fully manifests Israel's political autonomy over its land.[68]

But it is no less evident that God Himself follows the example of His people only after a delay, as though reticent about passing, in His turn, from a nomadic way of life to a sedentary one, abandoning His rural existence for an urban one.[69] David quickly transfers the Ark of the Covenant to Jerusalem. But, curiously, the Ark continues to reside under a tent, while the king himself lives in a stone palace. When David contemplates remedying this asymmetry, God does not seem enchanted with the prospect and protests vigorously: "Are you the one to build a house for Me to dwell in? From the day that I brought the people of Israel out of Egypt to this day, I have not dwelt in a house, but have moved about in tent and tabernacle."[70] It is much more difficult for God than for His people to be shut up in a place, still less a fixed place. Solomon, who will have the honor of building the sanctuary, will underline this in his inaugural speech. Does God reside on earth? When all the heavens cannot contain Him, how then could the House that one has built for Him?[71] A single sacred site will always have a hard time being accepted, even after the construction of the Temple; thus the prophet Elijah does not hesitate to build an altar and sacrifice to the Lord on Mount Carmel—not in Jerusalem.[72] The absolute preeminence of the central sanctuary is not, in fact, achieved until after the return of the Judean exiles from Babylon—and, as we shall see, in a radically new historical and territorial context.

God's nomadism thus survives the sedentarization of His people. And the land itself, as the site of the worship of this God, appears to have a nomadic vocation. This comes out in the story of Naaman, a general in the army of the king of Syria, who is stricken with leprosy. When he presents himself to Elisha, the prophet invites him to bathe seven times in the Jordan. The sick man expresses his disappointment at first: he was expecting a laying-on of hands and an invocation of the Lord's name, and he strongly doubts that the waters of Israel are better than those of his own country. Yet he resolves to perform this immersion—and emerges from the river cured. He then returns to Elisha and tells him: "Now I know that there is no God in the whole world except in Israel!" He promises no longer to offer sacrifices to other gods except the Lord and asks to take with him "two muleloads of earth."[73] This whole story is marked with ambiguity. The non-Israelite performs a first displacement by coming to the land of Israel in the hope of finding healing. Having arrived, though, it is firstly in men and in the God they serve that he puts his hopes, much more than in the land itself. However, it is through the earth, or more exactly through the waters that run through it, that he is cured. He does not therefore conclude that it is necessary to remain on the soil that has saved him, and so he returns home. But he takes with him symbolically and concretely a bit of the land he is leaving. The land, so to speak, follows him, and on this delocalized land, he will be able to worship the true God.

What Naaman's story reveals is really the existence of two lands. One is a "human" land, the concrete country that God has given as residence to a concrete people, where a native has a natural vocation to live. For Naaman, this is Syria, which is naturally where he returns. The other is the "divine" land, the atopical site of the meeting between humankind and God. This site is discovered by Naaman in the land of Israel, but he can then take it away with him.

For a Hebrew, the situation is both simpler and more complex. It is more complex because, historically, his natural place is first and foremost the atopical site of the meeting with the Divine, a moveable place that follows him throughout his peregrinations in the desert. It is only subsequently that the land of Israel becomes his natural place of residence, where his rights over it can always be compromised by a breaking of the contract of the Covenant. It is simpler, too, because for an Israelite established in the land of Israel, the "human" land and the "divine" land are henceforth entirely congruent, and because for him, any exile is now both an unnatural disengagement from his place of residence and a sign and cause of an alteration in his relationship with the Divine.

If I Forget Thee, O Jerusalem . . .

The experience of exile therefore gives rise to the frequently poignant expression of a double nostalgia. We shall not here recall the whole of the famous Psalm 137,[74] in which the exiles from Judah sit down on the riverbank at Babylon to weep over the memory of Zion. A single detail demands our attention: when their oppressors ask them to sing "one of the songs of Zion," the sorrowful Judeans protest: "How can we sing the songs of the Lord while in a foreign land?" This is an eloquent shift in vocabulary! For the exiles, a "song of Zion" is nothing other than a "song of the Lord," since Zion is not merely a geographical place; it is the place where the Lord lives. So there is no difference between the "human" land and the "divine" land. Any literature of exile thus spontaneously ascends to a theology of exile, and, as we shall see, into an ethic of exile. Keeping in mind the ruin of the kingdom of Samaria and the dispersal of the ten northern tribes in 722 B.C.E., the Judean exiles of 586 B.C.E. wonder anxiously about the causes and meaning of their exile, and about the legitimacy of their hopes of return.

The different strata of biblical literature furnish various responses to such questions, which despite their apparent diversity are highly coherent. It is because Israel has broken the contract binding it to God that God has broken the tie linking Israel with its land. Israel entered this land to observe the Law there. It is sin that condemns it to exile, at the same time as it condemns the land to desolation. The boundaries of Israel are not guaranteed unless Israel respects the boundaries of the Law. Any confusion, any erasure of the division between the sacred and the profane, between what is permissible and what is forbidden, between good and evil, ineluctably leads to exile. Inversely, any restoration of this division leads to a return.

In order not totally to lose its territory, Israel must, as we have seen, periodically relinquish the hold it has over it, so that it is primarily its relation to time that conditions its relation to space. A confusion in time in effect inexorably induces a confusion of space. Thus some sources insist upon the gravity of infractions of the rules of the sabbatical and jubilee years; because the fallow year was not punctually observed every seven years, the land expelled its inhabitants in order to stand idle for seventy years in a row. Similarly, in Jeremiah and Isaiah, the hope of return is attached to a rigorous respect of the weekly Shabbat rest,[75] and at the time of the restoration, Nehemiah once more puts Judeans on guard against any profanation of this holy day, a profanation for which their fathers were punished with all the disasters that befell them and Jerusalem.[76]

There is another confusion heavy with consequences: the transgression of sexual, ethnic, and religious boundaries. Incest, coitus during menstrual periods, adultery, male homosexuality, and bestiality are among the abominations through which the first occupants of Canaan soiled the country and for which they were extirpated from it. Israel must absolutely abstain from these things: any imitation of the depraved customs of the idolatrous Canaanites irrevocably condemns it to exile.[77] Any alliance with them is prohibited because it is full of danger: "You must not make a covenant with the inhabitants of the land, for they will lust after their gods and sacrifice to their gods and invite you, and you will eat of their sacrifices. And when you take wives from among their daughters for your sons, their daughters will lust after their gods and will cause your sons to lust after their gods."[78] These three major transgressions are in fact closely interconnected and partake of the same negative dynamic: marriage with idolatrous populations leads to practicing idolatry, and the idolatrous cults are themselves associated with reprehensible sexual practices. At the time of the return from Babylon, Esdras and Nehemiah vigorously reassert the prohibition against exogamy and demand that those exiles guilty of such infractions send back their foreign wives and the children born of them.[79]

The great prophets would contribute to breaking the shackles of this strictly legal and cultic causal explanation of exile. Some statements in the Pentateuch had already made sojourn on the land dependent upon respect for more properly ethical norms, such as honor due to parents according to the fifth commandment, or the use of exact and honest weights and measures.[80] But the classical prophets were the ones to carry this ethical conditionality to its full crystallization. It was they who would raise social morality to the rank of a basic condition for the existence of the nation on its land—against the people's idea that God would demand nothing other than the performance of a ritual. Israel must practice above all what is just and right, abstain from oppressing the foreigner, the widow, and the orphan, and avoid spilling innocent blood, if it wants God to let it reside forever on the land that He gave to its ancestors.[81]

Exile is thus a penalty for the indefinitely reiterated transgression of multiple boundaries. But it is also expiation. And it is not destined to last eternally, inasmuch as sincere repentance, the observance of Shabbat, the practice of endogamy, moral uprightness, and a return to the Law and to God will open up the way to gather together and to return to the land. God will have mercy on His people, He will reunite its dispersed members, and tomorrow Israel will repossess the country that its forefathers once possessed. The prophets never tire of announcing the radiant future of the return, the return of all, the definitive return. But if the prophetic visions of its reestablishment eloquently, and in a necessarily particularistic sense, reaffirm the imprescriptibility of the link between Israel and its place, they also ineluctably slide toward utopia and toward the universal, a slide wholly in harmony with the ethical focus we have just mentioned. Firstly, the shift is toward utopia because no partial and fragile return, like that of the Babylonian exiles, can ultimately be taken as a realization, because a relative and precarious sovereignty can never fulfill the hopes of a time when a people will no longer draw a sword against another people, when one will no longer learn the arts of war. Secondly, the shift is toward the universal because the expected restoration does not involve Israel alone, because the fate of humanity as a whole depends on it, because the land of Israel is in a sense called upon to become the land of all nations. The reconstructed sanctuary "shall be called a house of prayer for all peoples" and many peoples will go up to the Mount of the Lord, "for instruction shall come forth from Zion, and word of the Lord from Jerusalem."[82]

The extreme exaltation of the land and of Israel's relation to this land thus winds up as a double paradox. On the one hand, the prophetic literature opens up to the nations a way to universalize the relation with the land. And on the other, it contains, for Israel, the germ of a derealization of the land, as it is being tossed into a meta-history. Of course, the links of Israel with the concrete land are still far from severed. It will take other evolutions, other catastrophes, for this derealization and this transformation to be effective. An edict from the Persian Cyrus, in 538–539 B.C.E. would soon allow certain Judean exiles to resettle on ancestral soil, an autonomous Jewish society to reorganize itself there, and the Temple to be rebuilt. But it remains true that the imperfection of this return and the spirit of prophetic visions will definitely establish a relationship between Israel and its land that is essentially conceived in terms of nostalgia and hope. The land once possessed will never again cease to be a promised land.

Two The Holy Land

New Horizons

The year 70 C.E. is usually regarded as the great caesura in the ancient history of Israel. Many factors have contributed to assigning this year the place it occupies in both Jewish and non-Jewish memory. The destruction of the Second Temple by the Romans was so definitive that it appears to close one epoch and open another. After 70 C.E., except for the last and catastrophic revolt against Rome of 132–35 C.E., the Jewish people ceased to aspire to any political sovereignty, and they would have to wait until the middle of the twentieth century for at least some of them to rebuild an independent nation-state on a portion of the ancestral soil. Christians were long tempted to see the ruin of the Jerusalem sanctuary as the announced punishment for the Jews' rejection of Jesus as Messiah and of his message, and the starting point of a dispersal and humiliation now serving as witness to that rejection—which would only be ended one day by an ultimate conversion. Moreover, in Jewish liturgical practice, the catastrophe of the year 70 C.E. lies at the heart of the annual commemoration of 9 *av*,[1] on which day it is customary solemnly to remind the grieving faithful of how many years have passed since then. And in accordance with Jewish tradition and its cyclical conception of history, 9 *av* is also the date of other serious and painful events in national history: on this day, the Hebrews were condemned not to enter Canaan after the episode of their explorers, and it is also when Bethar, the last fortified site of the revolt of 135 C.E., finally fell, and when the earth of Jerusalem was "plowed up" by the emperor Hadrian.[2] Later and in the same fashion, people would associate 9 *av* with the expulsions of the Jews from England (1290), from France (1394), and from Spain (1492). Above all, and most important,

34

it could not be forgotten that 9 *av* was the date of the destruction of the First Temple, back in 586 B.C.E..

From the standpoint of the Jews' relation to territory, it was this first event that really marked the principal break. Unlike the exiles of the kingdom of Samaria who were deported in 722 B.C.E. to Assyria, of whom the traces were lost, the Judean deportees to Babylon remained self-aware during their exile and persistently aspired to return. They lived in a tension between two places: exile (*Galut*) and the Holy Land. Cyrus's decree, by allowing the physical return of some of these exiles to their lost country and by helping in the re-creation there of a relatively autonomous Jewish homeland, would in no way suppress this bipolarization of the existential Jewish condition, but rather strengthened it. This return was by no means a return to a prior situation. Classical and then medieval rabbinic sources have always been reticent about granting the Second Temple a dignity on a par with the First: a talmudic passage notes, for example, that not having been constructed by a descendant of Shem (as Solomon was), but by a son of Japheth (Cyrus), this second sanctuary could never be home to the Divine Presence—which could only ever reside in the tents of Shem.[3] Moreover, only a small portion of the exiles returned to Palestine, and so the dispersion did not really end; but, by becoming voluntary, at least theoretically, its meaning necessarily changed. Finally, except for the parenthesis of the Hasmonaean period from 140 to 63 B.C.E., marked by the restoration of full political independence and by the reconquest of territories that had been part of the ancient kingdoms of Israel and Judah, Palestine would repeatedly be integrated into geopolitical entities that were extraordinarily vast—the great ancient Persian, Hellenistic, and then Roman empires. These empires, notably the Roman, did not have a national character as far as power structures were concerned: they were ruled by neutral institutional cadres that created an "internationalist" climate propitious to the development of a universalism of civilization. To be a Roman, for example, was not a matter of ancestral origins but of participation in the life of the civilized Roman world, and in 212, Caracalla would grant Roman citizenship to all inhabitants of the empire. This modification of the status of the land of Israel in its relations with the rest of the inhabited world, associated with the geographical dissemination of the Jewish population and the internationalization of the Jewish condition, would constitute one of the major challenges of the new era.[4]

In this respect, the position taken by the historian Flavius Josephus, who, after having fought the Romans in Galilee, later witnessed the destruction of Jerusalem in 70 C.E. from on their side, shows a reversal of perspectives that, albeit by no means general in the Jewish world, is nonetheless revealing. Although born in Jerusalem of a priestly family, and of a mother descended from the Hasmonaean dynasty, Josephus wrote of the ancient history of his people, and of events in which he had participated, as a Jew of the Diaspora. He lived in a world that greatly exceeded the borders of Judea, and his writings no doubt owed much to his personal way of locating himself in that world. So in his eyes, the heart of the promise made to Abraham was, not the gift of the land of Israel, but rather primarily the proliferation of his descendants. And the development of the dispersion was for him much less a punishment than precisely the realization of this promise. Israel had become so numerous that its land could not contain it, and from now on the Jews were called upon to reside and multiply from one end of the world to the other!

Less radical, perhaps, but just as significant is the attitude of the philosopher and commentator Philo, a Hellenistic Jew from Alexandria, who was born a half-century before Josephus and died before the catastrophe of 70 C.E. Although he did make the physical pilgrimage to Jerusalem, as an exegete, Philo had a clear tendency to allegorize the scriptural story of the patriarchs' peregrinations, which he regarded more as a migration of the soul than as a physical migration. He identified the land with the legacy of Wisdom, and also identified its eternal possession with control by the spirit (i.e., Abraham and his descendants) over the body (i.e., Canaan). Merely a stage in the development of the soul, the settlement in Canaan was not the most positive stage—and certainly not the last one. In fact, Philo was not willing to locate the culmination of this voyage anywhere from which Moses was absent. He even invested the legal prescriptions dealing directly with the land with a pedagogic function: the sabbatical year taught a mastery over desire, and the prohibition against selling a plot in perpetuity was a reminder that the world is an alien place in which the sole authentic citizen is God.

Thus, as Josephus did after him, Philo introduced into his vision of Jewish identity a dimension of universalism that might seem scarcely compatible with the explicit particularism of the biblical theology of the land. In effect, his Judaism was a religious or cultural nationality, in which he minimized the link with an ethnic or territorial base. Thus, when he discussed the loyalties owed by a Jew of the Diaspora, he easily distinguished between a Jew's attachment to his *homeland*, that is, to the place outside Palestine where he had been born and grown up, and his attachment to the *metropole* of Israel, that is, to Jerusalem, birthplace of the collectivity to which he belonged.[5]

It would be misleading to take the attitudes of Philo and Josephus as representative of the whole Jewish world in the long period stretching from the reconstruction (538 B.C.E.) to the final destruction of the Second Temple (70 C.E.). But they are no less patent signs, at the close of this period and in Hellenized Jewish milieux, of a change in their relationship to the land of Israel that affected the different strata of ancient Jewry in various ways.

A Partial Reappropriation

The breadth of this gradual enlargement of Jewish horizons of experience offers a striking contrast to the relatively modest restoration that was led in the sixth century B.C.E. by men like Esdras, Nehemiah, and Zorobabel.

Seen as the realization of the prophecies of Jeremiah,[6] the return of the exiles from Babylon is presented by the Bible as the outcome of twin causes: political, since it was Cyrus who decided upon it, and divine, since it was the Lord who inspired him to push His Judean subjects to reconstruct their Temple. Thus the initiative did not come from the Judeans themselves; the return could only occur at the end of the period of exile fixed by God Himself. When they arrived on the soil of their homeland, the handful of men who had resolved to make the trip did not find any of their own kind there, but rather an alien, hostile local population. Scriptural sources mention a "people of the country," or "peoples of the country," who are presented as descending from deportees brought from Assyria by Sargon in the eighth century B.C.E. in order to repopulate a Samaria emptied of its Israelite inhabitants.[7] This initial ethnic heterogeneity would never disappear; it would even have a tendency to become much more marked under the Greek and Roman dominations. The land of Israel does not ever become again the land of the Jews, at least not exclusively. In fact, the spatial criterion and the ethnic criterion would never again coincide: many non-Jews lived on the land, and many Jews continued to live outside it, notably in Egypt and in Babylonia. Moreover, the new colony of Judea did not restore a political and cultural situation comparable with the ancient kingdom of Judah. For one thing, its frontiers were much reduced.[8]

In truth, the enterprise of reconstruction was in no way marked by a preoccupation with reconquering territory. Even much later, in the Hasmonaean era, one did not go to war for land but for the sake of the Law. When in 167 B.C.E., Judas Maccabaeus and his brothers took up arms in reaction to the forced Hellenization policy of Antiochus IV Epiphanes, their goal was clear: "Let us restore the shattered fortunes of our nation; let us fight *for our nation* and *for the holy place*."[9] So the motive for the revolt was primarily religious. The land was only liberated from foreign grasp because this liberation was necessary for a thoroughgoing realization of the Law. The extremism of the Zealots themselves during the first century C.E. cannot be reduced to simple irredentism.[10] It can only be understood in relation to a particular social context and to powerful messianic expectations. It expressed an aspiration to freedom, an affirmation of the exclusive sovereignty of God, and an uncompromising rejection of any pagan tyranny, whether in the form of an outrageous seizure of land or else of unbearable taxation.[11] Similarly, in the following century, the adherence of a sage like Akiva to the revolt of Simeon bar-Kokhba should not be misunderstood. In fact, many—principally talmudic—texts report that Akiva was imprisoned by the Roman authorities, and that he died under torture, but it seems that the principal reason for this fate was his unwavering will to continue to teach the Torah.[12]

Independently of this predominance of the religious over the territorial, the Judaism of the Second Temple period no longer essentially believed that a conquest could by itself legitimize possession. Accordingly, classical rabbinic literature significantly rewrote the biblical history of the initial conquest of the land of Israel. For example, it suggested that the Canaanites were never the legitimate owners of the land, which had from the beginning been granted to Shem, and so Israel had done nothing more than recover something that had been its from the start. It was even intimated that the Hebrews had not seized the land from the Canaanites by force, but that, on the contrary, the latter had spontaneously withdrawn, which praiseworthy action God was supposed to have recompensed by giving them Africa. Finally, notwithstanding the evidence of scriptural narratives and the explicit provisions of the Law, which required the extermination of the first occupants and proscribed any alliance with them, certain traditions evoked the negotiations between Joshua and the Canaanites, who were offered the possibility of a spontaneous withdrawal or a peace agreement. As a general rule, Second Temple thinking tended to substitute a legal, and even pacific, process for the idea of a violent conquest.[13]

These rewritings of biblical history were naturally not unconnected with the historic experience of the Judeans returning from Babylon, who did nothing more than reoccupy a territory that the powerful of this world, like Cyrus, recognized as legally belonging to them. It was not a question of conquest or of reconquest, but of a legal restitution. With respect to the land of Israel, moreover, classical Jewish law clearly distinguished among three types of territories: those that had actually been recolonized by the Jews returning from Babylon, which they possessed by virtue of their right of ownership; then, those territories that had been subjected by Joshua by means of conquest, but were not recolonized at the time of the return; and, finally, those that had been included in the ideal limits of the land according to the Bible but had not really ever been populated by Israelites. The nature of the particular sanctity attached to each of these three zones was a subject of debate. For some, the sanctity of territory conquered by Joshua was temporary and had been annulled by Nebuchadnezzar's invasion—one conquest erasing the other. Inversely, the sanctity of territory recolonized by the returning Babylonian Jews was supposed to be eternal, because no new conquest could possibly annul a right of ownership duly recognized—force could not trump right.[14]

Far from being purely theoretical, these distinctions had practical consequences. The biblical agricultural prescriptions in fact applied in their total rigor only to the zones repopulated at the time of the return. Thus a sage of the second century like Rabbi Meir permits himself the consumption of vegetables from Bet-Shean without raising the tithe. In his eyes, even though it formed part of the land of Israel according to its biblical definition,[15] this locality had lost its initial sacred status because it had not been recolonized in the time of Esdras, so the legal obligation to tithe was no longer required. Talmudic sources would go even farther in implying that the people of the Second Temple era had deliberately decided not to recolonize certain territories in order that the sabbatical year would not have to be observed and charity might always be practiced there. In point of fact, the legal and ritual relationship of Israel to its land seems quite simply to have been outweighed by social and ethical concerns.[16]

In any case, one determining historical fact should be underlined here: the concentration of those who did come back in the area around the rebuilt Temple and in Jerusalem. Henceforth, the focus passed from land to city, and to the city as sanctuary. Whereas Moses had announced a return to the "land" that had been formerly possessed, Nehemiah asked nothing else of God than a return to the place He had chosen as a dwelling for His Name.[17] Hence it was the Temple, first and foremost, that would furnish all of the people, in Judea as in the Diaspora, with the national foundation that they needed. The catastrophe that might still threaten the nation was no longer the loss of its territory or exile, but the destruction of the sanctuary. The land toward which all gazes converged was now a Holy Land—to wit, the place of residence of the Divine Name, the Temple site. The single and unique occasion on which the scriptural corpus uses the name "Holy Land" to refer to Palestine appears, significantly, in Zechariah, the prophet of the return, and strictly in connection with Judea and Jerusalem.[18]

A new spatial configuration now imposed itself, much more marked by an opposition between the center and the periphery than between inside and outside. The nation no longer needed an inside, where it could gather as a whole, sheltered from the impurity of the outside, but rather a center, a place of symbolic convergence. And this center was supplied by the Temple.

The Center and the Periphery

Ezekiel had already placed Jerusalem "in the midst of nations" and presented Israel as living at the "earth's navel." Classical rabbinic literature would repeat this image, declaring that the Sanhedrin was "sitting at the navel of the earth."[19] But, in placing this central point at the heart of a complex system, itself constituted by several concentric circles of increasing sanctity, this literature would manifest a clear evolution of perspective. The center of the earth was no longer a space clearly separated from the rest of the world, where the people of Israel as a whole resided. It was essentially the point in space with which the Jew maintained an exclusive ritual tie, varying according to the place in which he found himself physically, and according to the social group to which he belonged, as well as according to his personal degree of purity. The land of Israel was thus more holy than all other countries because from it alone could be gathered certain agricultural offerings. Jerusalem was more holy than other walled cities in Palestine because within it, and it alone, it was permitted to consume certain consecrated foods. The Temple Mount was holier than the rest of Jerusalem because access to it was forbidden to men with emissions and to menstruating women. Then came, in order, the temple enclosure, the Court of the Women, the Court of the Israelites, the Court of the Priests, the space between the vestibule and the altar, the sanctuary, and finally the Holy of Holies—the most central and most sacred of spaces—where only the High Priest could enter on the day of Yom Kippur.[20] This religious centrality was compounded by a cosmic centrality that confirmed it. The land of Israel was the loftiest of all the countries in the world, and the Temple was the most lofty place in the land of Israel.[21] The sanctuary was both the door of heaven and built directly above the abyss. It was included among the seven things that were conceived before the creation of the world:

the Torah, repentance, the Garden of Eden, Gehinnom, the Throne of Glory, the Temple, and the name of the Messiah, son of David. The creation of the world itself had started there.[22]

The theme of the centrality of Jerusalem and its sanctuary would have a remarkable history in the Middle Ages. But then the *representation* of this centrality would largely overtake its *reality*—it would be substituted for it and function in its place. This was as yet far from the case in the period we are dealing with here, until the catastrophe of 70 C.E., or even later. The land of Israel was not merely central to the historical consciousness of the Jewish people or to its system of symbolic representations. It effectively played the role of center vis-à-vis the Diaspora, perceived as periphery, at a time when the gathering in of exiles remained a major eschatological prospect, even if the dispersal was conceived of more as the result of voluntary emigration or of expansion than as a punishment.

In Hellenistic and Roman times, Judea still exercised an institutional and religious hegemony that endowed this centrality with all the weight of the real. Of course, Jewish cities like Alexandria did enjoy great autonomy; Flavius Josephus did not hesitate to compare the authority of this community's ethnarch with that of the all-powerful head of an independent state. Nevertheless, on the political level, the Jewish leaders of Palestine could directly influence the fate of their coreligionists of the Diaspora. Thus in the first century C.E., the rights granted by the roman emperor Claudius to the Jews of Alexandria were owing in large part to the efforts of Agrippa I, king of Judea.[23]

The Temple of Jerusalem was the only legitimate national sanctuary, although at Leontopolis, in Egypt, there was a regional temple, erected by the priest Onias IV in the second century B.C.E., which continued to function for some time even after the destruction of Jerusalem in 70 C.E. Located in a distant place, however, it would never play a major role, responding merely to the needs of the Jewish military colony of Leontopolis, and even the Jews of Egypt did not regard it as their temple. Similarly, while the scholars of the Holy Land granted it a certain legitimacy, they never saw it as a sanctuary rivaling Jerusalem's. Thus they considered that one who had vowed to offer a sacrifice in Leontopolis ought to do so in Jerusalem, but that if he fulfilled his vow at Leontopolis, he might be considered to have accomplished it. Conversely, one who made the same vow without specifying the place ought absolutely to fulfill it at the central sanctuary in Jerusalem and could in no case be considered to have acquitted himself of his obligation if he offered his sacrifice at Onias's temple.[24]

On the other hand, there were indeed synagogues located everywhere in the Diaspora where one could gather to pray, read, and study the Law. The precise origins of this kind of institution are obscure. They are generally dated back to the Babylonian exile, where they were partly a substitute for the destroyed Temple. But the reconstruction of the sanctuary did not eliminate them. On the contrary, during the whole period of the Second Temple, and notably in the first century, synagogues were numerous, not only in the Diaspora, but also in the Holy Land and even in Jerusalem. However, they were by no means antagonistic to the central sanctuary—although they were spaces belonging to the rising order of scholars as opposed to the space belonging to the priestly aristocracy. Rather, they were the extension, the relaying, even the emanation, of the Temple. The Holy City housed a number of synagogues for Jews from specific countries, sometimes offering lodging for pilgrims and allowing them to develop gradual and mediated contact with the unknown realities of Judea. They played an important role in relations between the center and the different Jewish communities of the Diaspora.

In any case, the Temple of Jerusalem remained the sole site where it was really legitimate—and, according to the Law, obligatory—to offer sacrifices. These sacrifices were practiced on different occasions: for involuntary or deliberate sins, for women's accouchements, as the culmination of conversion to Judaism, and so on. Of course, within the Holy Land itself, the practice of sacrifice was far from systematic, notably in the matter of births, and there is every reason to think that the Jews of the Diaspora themselves developed an attenuated and softened interpretation of this commandment.[25] Similarly, while Scripture stipulated that any male had the obligation to present himself before God three times a year (at Passover, the Festival of Weeks, and Sukkoth), the rite of pilgrimage was certainly not felt to be binding, either in the Holy Land or in the Diaspora.

But the number of pilgrims flowing periodically to Jerusalem from all corners of the empire was nevertheless considerable. The Pax Romana, the reconstruction of the sanctuary by Herod the Great in the first century B.C.E., demographic growth in the Jewish world, and proselytism all contributed to increasing this number greatly toward the end of the Second Temple period. Some historians have estimated that tens of thousands attended each festival. These pilgrims came principally from Jerusalem and from Judea, but also from Galilee, Peraea, and Syria, as well as from the rest of the Diaspora. Moreover, classical rabbinic literature included among the reasons justifying the insertion into the calendar of an additional month a desire to allow some convoys of pilgrims the time to reach Jerusalem before Passover,[26] and granted a status of particular purity to the routes taken by the faithful, including those outside the Holy Land. However, there was no secondary sanctuary on the road that led to Jerusalem. No "theology of the route" developed; notions of penitence or self-sacrifice were not explicitly associated with it; and in any case, the Jewish pilgrim did not follow, in the stages along the way, any particular mythic or historical events. Unlike the Christian pilgrim, who walked in the steps of Jesus, he merely headed, alone or more often in a group, toward the unique holy place of Judaism in order to live alongside his co-religionists from the four corners of the world in a unique communitarian experience.[27]

As important as these cultic and collective manifestations of the attachment to the center were, they were far from being the only ones. The sanctuary did not possess either land or property, and so it depended directly upon the generosity of the faithful for its upkeep. It had to perform public sacrifices on working and festival days and incurred many expenses directly or indirectly linked to worship. A contribution of a half a shekel a year by each adult male was designed precisely to respond to these needs. This obligation, which applied to Jews of the Diaspora as well, is mentioned for the first time in the first century B.C.E. and is alluded to more frequently after the start of the Roman presence in the Holy Land. This was not a voluntary offering; in effect, the half shekel was more akin to a tax, and the non-Jewish authorities regarded it as such. After the catastrophe of 70 C.E., the Romans were naturally led to put in its place a *fiscus judaicus* of two denarii payable by all Jews of the Holy Land and of the Diaspora, henceforth destined for the temple of the Capitoline Jupiter in Rome.

With regard to the arrival in Jerusalem of sums collected from all corners of the Jewish world, the sources reveal three terms corresponding to the three pilgrimage periods. Money from the Holy Land came before Passover; neighboring countries paid before the Festival of Weeks; and money came from Babylon, Media, and more distant countries before the Festival of Sukkoth. This contribution gave those who actually paid it (estimated at a third of those eligible) a sense of direct participation in the worship practiced in Jerusalem, without their having to go there. But the half shekel covered much more than expenses strictly related to worship; it allowed for the payment of those who corrected sacred books and the judges who sat in Jerusalem, it guaranteed provision of water to the city, the repair of walls, and so forth. Thanks to the extension of the sacred space to areas outside the sanctuary, it was to the Holy City as a whole that the contributor concretely manifested his attachment by discharging the annual payment of the half shekel.

In addition, when someone physically went to Judea, it was not only in order to offer a sacrifice at the Temple of Jerusalem or to bring in the levies and tithes reserved for the priests. Some proselytes undertook the trip to round out their conversion, often doing so on the occasion of a pilgrimage, either by choice or else in the absence of a proper rabbinic tribunal in their country of residence. Tombs of Diaspora Jews discovered by archeologists are those of pilgrims who died during their pilgrimage or of people who came to spend their final days there. In fact, Diaspora families regularly established themselves on a permanent basis on the soil of the fatherland, and some even managed to acquire a dominant position there. However, the Holy Land did not owe its power of attraction to the sanctuary alone, because a whole set of institutions and activities had arisen within and around the Temple, which were naturally a focus of attention. The Temple itself was the nerve center of the Jewish world, the stage where anyone who had something to say came to make himself heard, the meeting place of visionaries and charismatic leaders, the theater and the prize of political struggles, and the hearth where the flame of revolt against the occupiers would be lit. It was in the sanctuary that the signal for the first Jewish war against Rome was given, when in the year 66 C.E., Eleazar, son of the high priest, ordered a cessation of the daily sacrifice due to Caesar. But there were other—and longer-lasting—factors. The Holy City was also the headquarters of the Sanhedrin, the high court of justice, whose decisions were communicated to all the Jews of the Diaspora. It was there that the liturgical calendar was fixed, that the new moon was proclaimed, and that the intercalation of the supplementary month was decided. The Holy Land, finally, contained schools where pilgrims stayed (sometimes a long time) to study the Torah under the discipline of famous teachers. Just as much as it was the seat of the Temple, the Holy Land was the seat of authority, the center from which the Law was called upon to radiate.

Living Without the Temple

From this point of view, the destruction of the sanctuary by the Roman armies in 70 C.E. ought not immediately to have upset the balance of forces or the nature of the ties between center and periphery, between the Land and the Diaspora. According to the testimony of Tacitus, Titus had expected that this destruction would completely annihilate the religion of the Jews. It did not achieve anything so radical, but it contributed to accentuating and making irreversible an evolution that had long been under way.

No doubt, the terrible event was very heavily felt in Palestine and in the rest of the Jewish world, and the memory of the ruin, like the hope of reconstruction, would never cease to haunt the consciousness of a people who were tested in their national as well as their religious existence. A great number of commandments that had related to the sanctuary became inapplicable. Sacrifices and offerings could no longer attract divine pardon for the faults of Israel; the great ritual of the day of Kippur was suspended. The land, it was believed, would cease to be a blessing for its inhabitants, and the rains, so necessary to Palestinian agriculture, would no longer fall in season.[28] God's stepping-stone on earth had been removed; the gates of Heaven appeared to be shut.

However, because its own evolution had prepared it to face this new challenge, even before the ruin of the Temple, Pharisee thought succeeded without too much difficulty in disconnecting Jewish faith from the sanctuary.[29] When they were still struggling with the Sadducees for control of the Temple,[30] the Pharisees had fought for increasing participation by the laity in its rituals, as well as for an application of the norms of sacerdotal purity outside the sanctuary and among lay people. They had worked in favor of a reduction in the importance of sacrifice in worship, introduced the notion of intention into sacrifice, and stressed prayer, reading, and study of the Law. "Worship of the heart" could henceforth be substituted for worship in the Temple, at the same time as it made nostalgia for it permanent and called for its reestablishment. Of the three things on which the world rested—the Torah, Temple service, and deeds of loving-kindness,[31] at least the first and third remained. Like "miniature sanctuaries,"[32] the synagogue and the home could take over, or at least ensure a transition. The domestic table became a substitute for the altar, and the father of the family, presiding over the Passover meal commemorating the exodus from Egypt, inherited a little of the dignity of the high priest. Finally, although they no longer physically went to Jerusalem, believers could still turn toward the Holy City when at prayer.

Moreover, as traumatizing as it was, the destruction of the Temple did not result in the immediate eclipse of the Jewish colony of Palestine. At least, it did not so easily diminish its central role in the Jewish world. But it did provoke a migration of its institutions away from Jerusalem. Rabbinic tradition tells a story of this event that is no less eloquent for being legendary. Sensing the imminent destruction of besieged Jerusalem, Yohanan ben Zakai left the Holy City at night hidden in a coffin, which his disciples bore into the presence of the Roman commander, Vespasian. Rising out of it, Yohanan thereupon solicited a favor from the future emperor: "I ask nothing of you except the town of Yavneh, so that I may go there and teach my students and found a house of prayer where I may fulfill all the commandments."[33] Miming death in leaving Jerusalem and then resurrection before Vespasian, Yohanan ben Zakai incarnated the avatars of the religious tradition he represented: a certain form of Judaism, centered on the sanctuary, disappeared and yielded to another, centered on teaching, prayer, and the Law. This displacement of focus was naturally echoed by a displacement in location, though still limited. In effect, if Yavneh (Jamnia) was indeed not very central in relation to Jerusalem, it was nonetheless in the Holy Land, on the coastal plain.

A second transfer accentuating this gradual shift in the center of authority would occur after the repression of the last great Jewish revolt against Rome, led by Bar-Kokhba in 132–35 C.E. While the emperor Hadrian was attempting to found a pagan city, to be called Colonia Aelia Capitolina,[34] amid the ruins of Jerusalem (now forbidden to Jews on pain of death), in the first half of the second century C.E., Simeon ben Gamaliel II imposed himself as patriarch and president of the Sanhedrin at Usha, in upper Galilee, a region previously on the margins of Jewish life and whose inhabitants were not seen to be very rigorous in their practice of the Law. Around 175, his son and successor, Judah the Prince, finally established himself at Bet-Shearim, in lower Galilee, to the southeast of today's port of Haifa, to conduct the work of codifying the oral Law, which took form in the Mishnah around the year 200.

The Jewish authorities of the Holy Land, now relegated to its periphery, still continued to influence Jewish life heavily, both in Palestine and in the Diaspora. Their emissaries supervised the administration of communities, controlled the application of the Law, and levied the taxes destined for the patriarch. Many of their sages made voyages abroad, either to solve political problems with Rome, to teach, or to organize collections. Yavneh scholars were named presidents of rabbinic tribunals outside Palestine. And it was Yavneh, too, that authorized the Greek translation of Scripture undertaken by Aquila in the second century, a translation that soon replaced the Septuagint, held sacred by the Jews of the Diaspora but adopted by the Christian Church. The practice of pilgrimage itself was not completely abolished, but its meaning obviously changed, becoming a commemoration of the fall of the Temple. Jerome (ca. 342–420) mentions that weeping Jews still bribed the Roman guards on the day of 9 *av* to obtain permission to enter Jerusalem and pray a moment on the site of the sanctuary.[35] During Bar-Kokhba's revolt in the second century, a sage of Palestinian origin named Hanania began to proclaim new moons and the insertion of supplementary months in Babylon independently of decisions in the Holy Land. But as soon as the Jewish authorities in Palestine returned to normal functioning, they managed to regain their privilege in this area, and Hanania, Babylon, and the Diaspora had to submit.

The Palestinian sages were no less conscious of the dangers that threatened their country than they were of those who would eventually undermine their authority. While the wars with Rome had practically left Judea a desert and had ruined its economic base, the academies of Babylon came into an ascendance that would result in their domination. In Galilee, Judah the Prince, the compiler of the Mishnah, clearly saw a rival in the Babylonian exilarch. Efforts were made to save the Palestinian economy and to stem the population flight. Much of the legislation drawn up at that time aimed to preserve Jewish rootedness in the land of Israel as much as possible. The transfer of Palestinian lands to non-Jews was prohibited, while their acquisition by Jews was facilitated. The sale of Palestinian slaves outside the Holy Land was forbidden, since serf manpower was one of the pillars of the ancient economy. On the other hand, a slave who had fled from abroad to take refuge in Palestine was set free and could under no circumstances be sent back to his home. Emigration for economic reasons, with the exception of famine, was also severely condemned. The sages tried in particular to limit departures for Syria. Paradoxically, they did so by extending to that country the laws of agricultural legislation that applied to the Holy Land[36]—so that someone who might be tempted to go to Syria to escape the constraints of this legislation no longer had any reason to do so.

Such measures demonstrate the importance the Palestinian scholars attached to demographics. It was this factor that in time would be fatal to the preeminence of the Holy Land as the real—and not simply symbolic—center of the Jewish world. And so it was not unreasonable for a medieval master like Moses Maimonides in the twelfth century, given that for him Jewish history was primarily a history of the Law, to grant only relative importance to the catastrophe of 70 C.E. In effect, many aspects of religious law were not directly affected by the

disappearance of the sanctuary, or even by the collapse of Jewish political autonomy. Some obligations, such as the tithes, were, of course,
applicable only in the Holy Land, but they were so by virtue of a commandment flowing directly from the Bible, whether or not the Temple was standing. For Maimonides, the history of Jewish Law is thus
much more determined by the maintenance or disappearance of a
strong Jewish population in the Holy Land than by the existence or
disappearance of the Temple.[37]

A "Deterritorialized" Judaism?

The numerical weakening of the Jewish colony of Palestine and the
proportional strengthening of the weight of the Diaspora, the corresponding decline of the Holy Land as the center of world Judaism, the
irresistible rise of a rival pole in Babylon, and the indefinite postpone-
ment (after the resounding defeat of the 135 revolt) of any prospect of
restoration and regathering would all contribute to straining the links
between Israel and the land. This quantitative aggravation of the demographic and institutional disequilibrium could not fail to have considerable repercussions of a qualitative kind on the very definition of
Jewish identity and of Judaism as a legal system.

In effect, from the biblical perspective, the Torah is a Law designed
to govern the existence of a free and united people, living on its own
land and drawing its subsistence from it. In this optimal configuration, the territorial ideal and the agricultural ideal are perfectly congruent. Classical rabbinic literature constantly valorized working the
land: in the same way as a people without land is not really a people,
"any man who owns no land is not a man."[38] And just as an Israelite
who leaves the Holy Land is like a child who abandons the maternal
bosom for an alien one, someone who does not produce his own bread
and must go to the market to buy his grain is comparable to an infant
whose mother is dead and who is passed into the hands of wet nurses,
who will never satisfy his hunger.[39]

But there is more. This communion between man and Mother
Earth is, thanks to the Law, a communion of man with God the Father.

In the Temple, man ritually renders thanks to God for the land that was given to him and made fertile for him. The land is recompense for any application of the Law—including the parts of it that are not directly tied to agricultural life. And the land is also, and perhaps foremost, the means by which the Law is fulfilled. Why did Moses suffer so much as a result of not being able to enter Canaan? Was it on account of not being able to enjoy its fruits? Not at all. Rabbinic tradition let it be understood that what the prophet so painfully regretted was not ever having had the chance or the merit to observe all parts of the Law directly related to possession of the land.[40] Now and henceforth, the overwhelming majority of the Jewish people found themselves in the unenviable situation of being frustrated by the lack of the land both as recompense and as condition for a total respect of the Covenant pact.

It is commonly acknowledged that first pharisaic, then rabbinic thought permitted a deterritorialization of Judaism, and that for the lost land, it substituted the Torah, a sort of "portable land" and a mobile center that crystallized national unity independently of conditions in space and time. One text that in its definitive form might be dated to the start of the second century seems to confirm this: "But now the just have been taken away and the prophets have gone to sleep; we too have left our land, Zion has been taken away from us, and we have nothing left but the Almighty and His Law."[41] But while these words affirm the centrality of the Law, they also underline, deeply and inherently, the centrality of the land. In fact, what is the Law without the land? How can a Law that without the land is reduced to a shadow of itself possibly fill the absence of the land?

While it does not clearly resolve it, a traditional exegesis of a passage from Jeremiah is evidence of this essential difficulty.[42] Jer. 31:21 addresses Israel in these terms: "Erect markers, set up signposts!" According to the proposed interpretation, itself based on wordplay, these *signs* are none other than the commandments, by observance of which Israel desires to *signal* itself.[43] And hence the divine message is the following: "Even though I exile you from this land to foreign parts, *signal yourselves* by the practice of the commandments, so that when you come back they will not be new to you." This exegetical development therefore engaged the Jews in exile to continue to respect the Law scrupulously outside the Holy Land—but it also lends itself to different, if not divergent, readings. Some argued that, given that the practice of commandments not tied to the land (such as wearing tefillin or displaying a mezuzah)[44] changed neither in meaning nor intention, whatever the place in which they were observed, this text specifically concerned only *agricultural* commandments—and that it justified, for example, respecting levies and tithes in Babylon, conferring on that observance the value of an exercise, a sort of training, somewhat removed from the meaning it would have had in the Holy Land. For others, on the contrary, this text applied to *all* the commandments, including those in no way related to the land, and it implied a general instrumentalization of *every* religious practice in exile: observing the Law outside the land therefore no longer had intrinsic value, since its only goal was to keep Israel from forgetting the Law and to keep it ready for a return.

Whatever the meaning given it, such a text invites us to recognize the fundamental ambiguity of the enterprise of codifying the oral Law, which would result around the year 200 C.E. in the publication of the Mishnah. The swan song of the Palestinian Jewish center, the Mishnah is the key work around which the two Talmuds would later crystallize. As a summary of the Law, it is simultaneously a sanctuary, a land substituting for the land of Israel, and the aide-mémoire that prevents Israel from forgetting either the Temple or the land. And this is not the least of its paradoxes, since while the Mishnah has every appearance of being a practical guide, defining norms for action, nevertheless its role as an aid to memory prevents it from being exactly in tune with the world its authors faced. In effect, the Mishnah legislates largely for an ideal Jewish world in which the Temple, the priesthood, and the monarchy were still living realities—although around the year 200, they had well and truly ceased to exist.

The Legal Land

No fewer than a third of the rules contained in the Mishnah concern agricultural life and the relation of Israel to its land. Its first concern is to classify, and classification means making a clear division between the pure and the impure, between the permitted and the forbidden, but also between inside and outside, between "us" and "others." But the classificatory dexterity of the masters of the Mishnah was put to a rude test by a real world apparently governed by utter confusion. In effect, biblical agricultural laws presuppose an absolute congruence between ethnic and spatial definitions of Israel: they were designed for an indigenous Israelite society that was homogeneous and wholly united upon its own land. But a radically different situation confronted the Palestinian teachers, such that they never stopped asking *who* should apply the laws they laid out, and also *where* these laws were effectively applicable, now that all categories had been mixed up and all borders confused. Thus they had to distinguish between the Gentile living in the Holy Land, the Jew residing in the Holy Land, and the Jew residing outside the Holy Land. Sometimes the ethnic criterion seemed paramount: therefore, the Gentile of the Holy Land was ordinarily given a dispensation from respecting these laws, since the sanctity of the land and the obligations flowing from it did not extend beyond the framework of an interactive relation between this land and a particular people (Israel). Sometimes the spatial criterion seemed to predominate: therefore, while any commandment not related to the land should be observed in all places, in the Holy Land as in the Diaspora, any commandment related to the land should be observed only on the land.

Any crossing of the boundaries of this space would a priori generate uncertainty. Thus dough produced from grain harvested abroad and introduced into the Holy Land was subject to the *hala* levy.[45] But inversely one could ask whether dough produced from grain harvested in the Holy Land and exported abroad was legally subject to the same levy. Answers to this question varied according to how one envisaged the sanctity of the land. If this sanctity was a contagious quality, physically communicated to the products of Israel's soil, and was not affected by exportation, then the levy should be taken as obligatory. If, on the contrary, the frontiers of the Holy Land defined a sacred space that was clearly circumscribed, and if what left it irremediably lost all sacredness, then no levy should be made on exported dough.[46] Whichever option was finally adopted, the answer to one prior question had been presupposed: the boundaries of the land of Israel. But this question was itself far from easy to settle. And while the Law in its rigor required from the very start that a clear frontier separate the inside from the outside, because what was a legal obligation on this side of the frontier was no longer so, or not in the same way, beyond that frontier, still the disorder of history appeared to have done everything to blur such a necessary demarcation!

This confusion arose in the first moments in biblical history. No attentive reader of Scripture can fail to note a curious gap between the promise made by God to Abraham, which called for the expropriation of ten Canaanite peoples for Israel's benefit, on the one hand, and the effective realization of this promise, which covered only the territory of seven peoples, on the other.[47] One could certainly admit that this deficit of three peoples was called upon to be filled (in the messianic era) and that it became for the land of Israel the warrant for an always possible expansion. Nevertheless, in the intervening period, the levying of the tithe does not apply to the territory of these three peoples, and the masters of the Mishnah were divided over the identification of these regions summoned to be aggregated into the Holy Land. Moreover, territories beyond the Jordan that were indeed part of the land of Israel nevertheless had a separate status; some considered them not part of the initial promise, and that their sanctity was therefore inferior to that of the land proper. So it is asked whether the harvests from this region should occasion the ritual presentation of firstfruits to the sanctuary. Finally, the frontiers prescribed for Israel by Moses were of a kind to arouse many conflicting interpretations.[48] Wasn't the "river of Egypt" that marked the southern border really the Nile (in which case a portion of Egypt should be part of the Holy Land)? What status should be given to the islands off the coast of the land of Israel? What status should be given to the sea itself? To the north, was Lebanon inside or outside the Holy Land? The river Jordan, which was its eastern border, had a worrying propensity to vary in its course; did that mean that the frontier of the land varied along with it? Was this river itself part of the land or exterior to it, or should it be divided into two?

These topographical variables were overlaid with more properly historical variables. We have seen that in the sight of the Law, the territories conquered by Joshua and those recolonized by the Judeans returning from Babylon in the sixth century B.C.E. did not enjoy the same status. But ought one to include among the territories of the return, apart from those actually repopulated in the time of Esdras and Nehemiah immediately after the promulgation of Cyrus's decree, those that had been conquered militarily much later by the Hasmonaeans? In addition, according to Deut. 11:24, any territory conquered by Israel outside the Holy Land properly speaking legitimately belonged to it. Therefore, this expansion was clearly foreseen. But in order to be valid, should it not occur only once the conquest of the land of Israel itself was complete? To what extent, moreover, did the sanctity of the Holy Land extend to these new territories, and did all the commandments tied to the land apply equally there? Finally, far from forming a consistent whole, the Holy Land, in the sight of the Law, was divided into three regions: Judea, Transjordan, and Galilee. And so a husband could not oblige his wife to leave one region for another.

These subtle distinctions concerned more than the application of the agricultural commandments; they mattered for almost the whole of the Law. Many nonagricultural commandments were not observed in the same manner within the Holy Land as outside it. Anyone who rented a house in the land of Israel immediately had to put up a mezuzah; in the Diaspora, a new tenant had a grace period of thirty days. An act of divorce pronounced elsewhere and brought into the Holy Land had to carry the notice: "In my presence it has been written and in my presence it has been signed." This notice was not required, though, of one who delivered a divorce decree in the Holy Land. Here again, the rigorous application of the Law ran up against the crippling imprecision of the boundaries of the land of Israel. Was the town of Acre part of it? For some, the answer was clearly no, and any divorce decreed in Acre should conform to the model used in the Diaspora. For others, on the contrary, Acre was really located within the land of Israel and the notice mentioned above was redundant.[49] Far from being futile, this delicate question of sacred geography merited the most scrupulous examination: didn't the validity of a divorce act, and therefore the status of the persons involved, directly depend upon it?

Holy Land, Holy People

This legal concern about the land, of which the Mishnah is the eloquent illustration, is not only concern for the Law but just as much concern for the land. By focusing on the legal implications of the relation of Israel to its land, rabbinic thought forcefully proclaimed the land's essential character, and it did so precisely in historical circumstances that led ineluctably to a relaxation of its practical dimension. In fact, the very holiness of the land could not be conceived of independently of its link with Israel.

The idea of the land's holiness without doubt aroused many lines of argument.[50] Was this holiness acquired, and thus perhaps transitory and tied to circumstances? Or was it, on the contrary, intrinsic, and thus permanent, even when the appearance of the land's current desolation might seem to invalidate it? In either case, though, the holiness of the land, like the holiness of any other thing, came from God. The land was holy because God had chosen it, because He had chosen to establish Himself there and to concentrate His presence there. Of course, everybody knows that God is Himself called Ha-Makom, "The Place" (par excellence), because He is the place of the world He has created, and that the world cannot be His place (contain Him).[51] This voluntary assignment of residence is perhaps at bottom just a concession to human weakness. It offers a fixed point, a point of anchorage to answer the need of the religious imagination on the part of believers incapable of being satisfied with an absolutely abstract notion of divinity. Constantly placed under the Lord's eye, "from year's beginning to year's end," the land of Israel is "what his soul has that is most precious."[52] It is thanks to God's constant concern for the land that the blessing of abundance comes down to it. A rupture, even temporary, in this privileged link between God and the land abolishes—or at least alters or occults—its holiness. How otherwise could one understand how, according to rabbinic tradition, an idolater like Titus had been able to enter the Holy of Holies, accessible only to the High Priest on one day of the year, and lie there with a prostitute upon the book of the Law and still leave safe and sound?[53]

This holiness conferred by election was something Israel shared with its land, since the election of places and the election of the people were closely linked. God had taken the measure of all the nations, of all the mountains, cities, and lands. And He had not found a nation worthy of receiving the Torah except for the generation of the desert, or a mountain where the Torah might be revealed except for Sinai, or a city where the Temple might be built except for Jerusalem, or a land, finally, that was worthy of being given to Israel except for the Holy Land.[54] Nothing escaped the measuring gaze of the Divine Surveyor. Like Sinai and theophany, like Jerusalem and the Sanctuary, like the generation of the desert and the Torah, the people of Israel and the land of Israel appeared to Him ideally commensurable, and He chose them together, one along with the other, one for the other.

The measurement the Lord used was the Torah itself. The Torah was the measure of all things: of the land, of the people, and of the link between them. Israel sanctified itself by observing the Torah—and in doing so, it sanctified the land. To the initial holiness of the land, which came to it directly from God, which was prior to any conquest and which destruction and exile could not totally abolish, Israel added a second kind of holiness. In effect, when it established itself on its own ground and practiced the Torah there, Israel sanctified an already holy land a second time. The land enjoyed this second sanctification twice: in the time of Joshua's conquest, and in the time of the return from Babylon. However, this sanctification could not be complete in the time of the return, because not *all* of Israel returned to its land. According to the jurists, this simple fact had a direct effect upon the degree and nature of the obligation attached to the observance of certain commandments. Maimonides, for example, considered that the practice of *teruma*, the levy of a minimum of a sixtieth of the crop turned over to the priests, had ceased to be a biblical imperative in the Holy Land. Henceforth, it no longer applied, except as a simple rabbinic prescription, because it implied in principle the presence of all the people on the ancestral soil, which was naturally not the case in

Maimonides' day and had not been the case at the time of the return from Babylon.[55] It was as if Israel itself had become the measure of the holiness of the land and of the measure of the Law.

The ultimate self-affirmation of a Palestinian leadership that was condemned in the long run to irreversible decline, the writing of the Mishnah resisted the weight of history. Undoubtedly, the sanctuary was destroyed, and no one could any longer today bring his firstfruits there. The land was largely emptied of its Jewish inhabitants, and the agricultural commandments retained a concrete meaning for fewer and fewer of them. But the Law was still written as if the Temple were still standing, as if Israel still lived in great numbers on its soil—or as if all that had been lost would one day, and soon, be returned. The legal "realism" of the Jewish teachers of the Holy Land was a wager on memory and the expression of an unshakeable faith in the nation's future.

To a large extent, and while waiting, the study of the Law was a substitute for its practice. And it was through study that Israel erected these "markers," these "signposts" able to guide it in its exile; thanks to study, when the moment came, all the commandments would not appear novel to it. But the remedy had its perverse effects, and if in one way, it made the evil bearable, in another way, it perhaps made it incurable. While it incontestably perpetuated the memory of a lack, it also risked attenuating the pain this lack engendered. By becoming of prime value, study could totally supplant the land. Independent of all spatial and temporal constraints, it would be able to turn any place into a land where Israel could feel at home. Thus the Talmudist Pirkoi ben Baboi in the late eighth and early ninth centuries spared no effort to make the Babylonian legal tradition prevail over that of Palestine throughout the whole Jewish world; he did not hesitate to play on words in saying that any place of study that *signaled* itself by its teaching of the Law and by its piety was called *Zion*![56]

The first confirmed case of a Jew born in exile whose remains were brought to the Holy Land to be interred dates from the end of the second century, in the lifetime of Judah the Prince, compiler of the Mishnah. These remains were those of Huna, the Babylonian exilarch. This practice did not in fact become common until the third century.

It did not become prevalent without difficulty, and it even aroused fierce opposition from certain sages. Until then, the Palestinian teachers had in effect insisted much more on the duty to *live* on the ancestral soil, particularly after the revolt by Bar-Kokhba, when people had begun to fear for the maintenance of a Jewish population in the Holy Land. The two beliefs relating to the benefits of a transfer of the ashes of a man deceased in exile—specifically, that burial in the Holy Land had an expiatory virtue, and that it was in the Holy Land that the resurrection of the dead would begin—appeared only among the teachers of the talmudic era.[57] It was as if at the very moment when the center of gravity of Jewish scholarship was ineluctably shifting from Palestine to Babylonia, the land of Israel was slowly ceasing to be the place where a Jew aspired to live, instead becoming the place where he wanted to die and be resurrected. As if, land of resurrection, the Holy Land was swinging slowly toward the other side of history—to the side of dreams.

Three The Land of Dreams

Other Times: The Land's Middle Ages?

To periodize the history of the Jewish people is not a neutral act, of course. Nor is it an easy task, especially since one must deal with a subject, the Jewish people, whose unity (and therefore, in a sense, whose existence) is far from self-evident. The demographic fading of the Jewish community in the Holy Land and the decline in its stellar position as seat of authority had definitively shifted the heart of Jewish life to the Diaspora. The evolution of Judaism was henceforward marked by a pattern of rise and then subsidence—and, as a general rule, by a multiplication of influential centers (Babylonia, Muslim Spain, the Rhineland, etc.). This diversity of spaces necessarily induced a diversity of relations with time. The rhythm of history and the nature and import of the facts held significant varied from one place to another, even if the Jewish communities scattered across the four corners of the world generally maintained more or less close links with one another. A comparative study of the history of Jewish populations in the West, in eastern Europe, and in Islamic lands consequently underlines at least as many disparities as synergies.

From a certain standpoint, however, what complicates the task of the historian can become, from another standpoint, what facilitates it. In effect, if the history of the Jewish people is the history of a dispersal, one is tempted to model the rhythm of the former on that of the latter. Any notable alteration in the relation of the Jews to place would open 60 a new phase in their history; any expansion or geographic reconfiguration of their dispersal could be used as a chronological marker, could be interpreted as a historical break. Of course, there is nothing completely illegitimate about that approach. There is no doubt that the series of great expulsions at the end of the Middle Ages, culminating in the Jews' being expelled from Spain in 1492, did indeed profoundly modify the destiny of the populations that were the victims of it, shifting the center of gravity of the Jewish world from western to eastern Europe and to the Levant. But it remains to be shown whether these fractures are the only ones to be taken into account, or to what extent they were indeed fractures, and with what lag they might have transformed the cultural profile and the self-awareness of the displaced populations and their descendants.

Far from being the sole prerogative of modern specialists, this type of historiographic approach has illustrious precedents. For medieval scholars, the history of the Jews was essentially a history of the Law and the oral tradition. It was clear to Maimonides that any legal innovation arose from an upheaval in Jewish relations to space. The compilation of the Mishnah and then of the Babylonian Talmud, to his mind, were the direct result of an awareness of the expansion of the Jews' dispersal throughout the world. And it was to the same spatial causality that Maimonides attributed the proliferation and growing diversity of local customs—and the decline of knowledge of Hebrew among the people. Why had Esdras, the chief of the Babylonian exiles who came back to the Holy Land in the sixth century B.C.E., established fixed formulas for prayers and blessings, when the liturgical ideal of heartfelt worship would for preference, according to Maimonides, have been total spontaneity? The philosopher's answer was that the sole reason was to palliate this erosion in mastery of the Hebraic language and to counter the effects of a linguistic assimilation that was aggravated by the scattering of Israel among the nations.[1]

However, can the purely quantitative modification of geographical balances, the displacement of a given group from one area to another, or the overall extension of the dispersal, taken as a whole, really furnish the medieval historiographer or the philosopher of history with sufficient criteria for a periodization? By no means. If the history of the Jews does have a meaning, should we not also give it (or recognize in it) a spatial orientation? Perhaps we ought to conceive of dispersal in relation to a fixed center that is easily found on a world map, or else on a map of the collective imagination. At the end of the fifteenth century, the commentator Isaac Abravanel offered an eloquent illustration of this slide into the qualitative. For him, the expulsion of the Spanish Jews did not launch a simple displacement in locale, a shift of the Iberian Jewish populations from the west to the east of the Mediterranean basin. He thought it had induced a rapprochement between those who were expelled and the central place, the fixed point around which all Jewish history turned: the Holy Land. And it was for this reason that he interpreted the expulsion, not as a simple exile, but as an exodus, announcing for Abravanel the imminence of ultimate deliverance.[2]

This teleological perspective, in which the telos is just as much a place as an ultimate purpose, is found once again, glossed otherwise and secularized, among the master thinkers of contemporary Zionist historiography. In their case, the history of the Jews is understood as the history of a relationship, real or ideal, of Jews to their land. The dispersal is distancing from the land; the Diaspora (*tefutsa*) is understood primarily as exile and as deportation (*gola*). The land of Israel never ceases to be one of the pivots of the history of the Jewish people and of the history of its national consciousness, which are both periodized and judged on the basis of the relationship of the people to their land: there are periods when Israel is gathered together on its land and periods when it is physically distanced from it, moments when its attachment to the land is intact and moments when it is loosened. It is this attachment that, according to Zionist historians, has given rise to the "centripetal forces" liable to encourage the Jewish nation to keep its historical, psychological, and cultural specificity and to manifest its existence in a collective way. By contrast, rupture with the Holy Land "corresponds to the loss of one's historical identity and expresses the desire, conscious or not, to become lost among other nations."[3] Such a criterion of periodization and evaluation draws most of its power less from objective facts observed by the historian over the centuries than from the creation of the state of Israel and the centrality of this event in contemporary Jewish experience—the "end" of the history of the Jews seeming to authorize a retroactive appreciation of its overall course. Only a hundred years ago, it would have appeared to most of the integrated Jews of western Europe at the very least strange and more likely scandalous to make attachment to the land of Israel one of the principles, even *the* principle, of continuity in Jewish history. All the evident contemporary interest in the place of the land of Israel in Jewish history and consciousness can be explained only in the light of the Zionist enterprise.

Even when the approach seeks to be critical, or when, as in these pages, it takes doubt and prudence as its guides, the risk remains of a problematic distortion of perspectives. We should remind ourselves that turning the relation of the Jews to the land of Israel into the exclusive subject of a study does not imply that one takes it as guaranteed that this relation is effectively the axis around which the *whole* history of the Jews turns. It is the major and objective upheavals in this history that have induced a transformation of the Jews' relationship to the Holy Land; this history should not be judged by the standard of that single factor. The Jewish Middle Ages—supposing that this term has meaning—were not simply that moment in the history of the Jews when the land of Israel became a land of dreams. Rather, they were that period in history when their objective conditions of existence apparently had the effect, among many others, of profoundly and durably modifying their relationship with the Holy Land.

Politically condemned to powerlessness, simultaneously exiled and dispersed, the medieval Jews in fact occupied an ex-centric position in the world in which they lived. They could no longer concretely advance their rights over a land that had concurrently become the stakes in a military struggle of prime importance between Christian and Muslim powers. The epic of the Crusades, which placed the Holy Land at the heart of the spiritual aspirations and imperial ambitions of the two great religions born from Israel, simultaneously underlined the dethronement of its first owners. This alienation of the land, which passed from one power's domination to another without either one appearing to have staying power or being able to engender a true renaissance there, also evoked the alienation of the people who had not only been hounded from it but also humiliated and abandoned to the whims of variable and inconstant masters. The situation of Israel and of its land, marked by exile and expropriation, seemed moreover to bring a historical confirmation of the theological pretensions of both Christianity and Islam. Hence how could one dare, against all appearances, to assert the continuity of Israel's mission and the exclusive character of the tie it maintained with its land?

To organize an effective spiritual resistance to the brute facts of history was revealed to be particularly arduous in the cultural universe created by the encounters with Islam and with the philosophical and scientific heritage of ancient Greece. First in Muslim lands and soon in Christian ones, Jewish and non-Jewish thinkers focused their attention on abstract and perfectly atopical themes: God, His essence and existence, creation, prophecy, good and evil, retribution and punishment, and so on. Medieval thinking of a philosophical bent was essentially a quest for absolute truths fundamentally indifferent to the limitations of space and time.[4] Moreover, the conceptions of Divinity and of divine relations with the world adopted by philosophers (impersonal relations governed by a system of natural, universal, and immutable laws) posed problems for the traditional Jewish theme of God's election of a particular people and land. It is remarkable, in this respect, that Maimonides almost completely evacuated the territorial problematic from his philosophical exposition of the truths of Judaism in the *Guide for the Perplexed*, even though the land of Israel was very present in its legal code, the Mishnah Torah.

The struggle was organized on two fronts. The loss of physical contact with the land was compensated for by idealization of it. Old biblical, homiletic, and talmudic sources were put piously to this use. The land of which the Jews still obstinately dreamed was not really this desolate land ravaged by war, fought over by the powerful. It was a land of milk and honey, a land of miracle and abundance, which was less a place than a moment in the history of Israel. In fact, it was a double moment: that of a bygone past of the lost glory and sovereignty of David and Solomon; and also that of a future that people persisted in believing to be at hand, blessed with recovered glory and sovereignty under the leadership of the Messiah. As a land of the ingathering to come, a land of redemption, the Holy Land, and even more so Jerusalem and its Temple, appeared all the more present in the liturgy, poetry, and legends with fewer Jews effectively present on the actual soil of the land. However, some great teachers of Jewish thought, philosophers, and Kabbalists, far from being content with the accumulated treasures of traditional Jewish culture (even though they were constantly meditating on them), would try to elaborate a theology of the land capable of rebutting the attacks of their Christian and Muslim colleagues. This included drawing on the scientific knowledge or beliefs that had become common currency in the medieval world. The stakes were huge. In effect, to think Israel's land was to think Israel itself. Any discourse on the specificity of the land was an indirect discourse about the specificity of the people. What made the land unique was nothing other than what made the people unique.

Stars and Climates

Luckily, medieval man did not live in a homogeneous space. For him, the surface of the earth was not everywhere endowed with the same potential. It was divided into distinct climates that were more or less favorable to humankind, where humans and civilizations developed differently. The excellence of one people, the quality of their language and culture, as well as their capacity to receive prophecy, all depended on the place where they settled, the climatic conditions that prevailed there, and the astral influences to which it was subject. And even if one admitted that divine activity was identical in every place, not every place was identically predisposed to receive it.

Starting with such principles, it was not too hard to establish the pretensions of the Jewish people to their own superiority and that of their land "scientifically."[5] Nor was this inevitable. In effect, the adoption of what is called climate theory did not necessarily lead to an assertion of the preeminence of the factor of locale. Thus, although he adopted this theory, the medieval poet Moses ibn Ezra preferred the Arab version of it: for him, it was Arabia that enjoyed the optimum climatic condition. He even went so far as to use it to explain the beneficial effects of exile upon the Jews who settled in Arab lands and who, thanks to this transplantation, enjoyed a remarkable cultural flowering. For Maimonides, who did not go that far, the land of Israel was actually well situated climatically, but it was not the only such country: Egypt, where he lived and where Moses had been born, was equally blessed. Similarly, Hebrew in his eyes was just one of the languages that developed in a balanced and favorable climatic environment. Nor for Maimonides was the climate of their land what made the Jewish people unique. That climate was good, one of the best—but perhaps not the very best. And in any case, it was not because they had left it that the Jews in exile found themselves deprived of the gift of prophecy. The objective conditions of Jewish life in exile—subjection to other nations, humiliation, fear, and persecution—were much more responsible. And in the messianic era, it was less the return to the ancestral soil than the restoration of an autonomous Jewish power in a liberated, peaceful world that would allow the Jews to develop their intellectual faculties and to rediscover the paths of prophetic inspiration.

Therefore the principle of a heterogeneity of space and an inequality among regions did not necessarily result in asserting the absolute primacy of Israel's land nor the preeminence of the role it played in the history of the people who had once lived there. And once this step was effectively taken, the question of the *nature* of this advantage of the Holy Land had still to be resolved. For thinkers like Abraham ibn Daud in the twelfth century and Hasdai Crescas at the turn of the fifteenth, there was scarcely any doubt that providence could privilege a particular nation in particular times—and thus also in particular places. The difference, in this case, was more quantitative than qualitative: the Holy Land enjoyed a surplus of providence rather than a different type of providence.[6] By contrast, for the poet and philosopher Judah Halevi (ca. 1075–1141?), who placed the land of Israel at the heart of the fourth climate, that is, at the center of the most balanced climate, the privilege was clearly qualitative, and the distinction was in kind as much as in degree: "Adonai is, therefore, called rightly the God of Israel because this view of God is not found among other nations. He is also called 'God of the land' because this [land] possesses a special power in its air, soil, and sky, which enables the approach to the vision of God."[7]

The dominant view in medieval Jewish thought came down from Halevi, with different variations and attenuations. Thus, for some, Israel's exile was precisely a punishment, in the sense that it was chased from a climatically ideal land into hostile territory. For others, the Torah could only be given to a people residing on this land—while the laws of

Noah, less perfect, came naturally to people who were less perfect and residing in regions with less perfect climates. The Italian exegete Ovadia Sforno, who lived in the fifteenth and sixteenth centuries, considered that it was the Flood that had put an end to the eternal spring the whole earth had enjoyed until then, and that had introduced climatic diversity among regions and the cycle of seasons; the land of Israel alone escaped this upheaval and safeguarded for its inhabitants the possibility of intellectual perfection and access to prophecy.

The privileged climate of the Holy Land was often associated with an astrological privilege. It was supposed to enjoy an absolute advantage on this plane, and worship in it and the effectiveness thereof were often conceived of in terms of this advantage. Thanks to its astral position, the Holy Land was the most suitable site for conferring maximum efficacy on the Jewish cult. Inversely, this cult was of a kind to preserve the astral configuration favorable to the land, and even influence the stars to strengthen this beneficial influx. Among the Jewish Neoplatonists of the fourteenth century, the theory of places and the primacy of astrology would even lead to a veritable legal relativism— if not to antinomianism. In effect, they thought man ought to govern his conduct according to what was required by the particular place in which he found himself and by the astral configuration that dominated it. Thus the bans on idols and on certain sexual relations were valid especially, if not uniquely, for the land of Israel. It was there that such actions were noxious, meaning not in line with what the stars demanded in order to exercise their beneficent influence. This was not the case elsewhere. Thus it was only upon entering the Holy Land that Jacob demanded that his kin give up their idols.[8] Saturn, which was Israel's planet, did not need particular intermediaries like idols to diffuse its influence; it did so directly. Similarly, this cold and humid planet did not tolerate an excess of sexual activity, which was of the hot and dry order, upon the territory that it governed. And anyone who gave himself up to such excess could not profit from the particular virtues of this land when it came to science and prophecy.[9]

In such a system, the Torah seemed essentially designed to enable people to escape certain astral influences or else to draw benefits from them, and its observance inevitably lost a good part of its meaning beyond Israel's frontiers. Of course, not all of those who recognized the astrological or mystical advantage of the Holy Land were ready to go so far. And many preferred to relativize its implications. According to a conception already present in ancient homiletic literature, but taken up and developed by Moses Nahmanides (1194–1270) and by kabbalistic thought, while God had chosen the land of Israel for Himself, He had divided all other countries among the tutelary angels of the nations.[10] The Holy Land alone was not subject to the authority of any angelic and astral intermediary. The true gate of Heaven, it received the divine influx directly. And it was through it that all communications between above and below passed. Wherever they were pronounced, the prayers of Israel passed through this gate before reaching their ultimate destination; it was through there, too, that souls ascended after death. Inversely, the tutelary angels appointed to the lands of nations only drew their power from what God gave to them through this channel.

In such a system of representations, the land of Israel was the land by nature and par excellence of prophetic revelation—in the same way as Israel was the people by nature and par excellence of prophetic inspiration. Here one is very far from the relativism and intellectualism of Maimonides. For Halevi, prophecy, as mankind's ultimate perfection, required three prerequisites: first, a particular complexion, which the Jewish people had; then, ethical perfection and good works, which observance of the Torah guaranteed; finally, a favorable climate, effectively furnished by the Holy Land and it alone. Any Jew who was ethically irreproachable and living on its soil was capable, therefore, of attaining prophetic inspiration. Inversely, any prophet of the past or the future could only prophesy in the land of Israel. Of course, Abraham had prophesied in Chaldea, and Ezekiel and Daniel in Babylonia, and Jeremiah in Egypt, but although they had not done so *within* the Holy Land, at least they had done so *for the sake of* the Holy Land.[11] Reaffirming in his turn the principle that "prophecy only resides in the land of Israel," Crescas would go so far as to sustain its talmudic origin. But it must be stressed that this formulation is certainly not present in the treatise Crescas cited, or anywhere else in classical rabbinic literature, either. The Talmud says nothing more than this: "the Divine Presence resides only in the tents of Shem."[12] Not content with substituting "prophecy" for the "divine Presence," Crescas furthermore shifts the accent from the ethnic factor (Shem) to the locale (Israel's land).

The Heart of the World

This oft-developed theme of the climatic and astrological (and thereby mystical) privilege of the land of Israel drew its "scientific" rationale from the commonplaces of medieval scholarship. However, a growing recognition that the earth was round, the great voyages of exploration, and the discovery of human civilizations in climates judged by the old theory to be uninhabitable would all gradually undermine the credibility of these justifications. But the theme itself, which had deep roots, would manage to survive this evolution; we should not be surprised by this. In effect, this kind of thinking about the land had no need of support from a reality that was ultimately without consequence and was, in any case, physically very distant for most premodern Jews. The "scientific" argumentation developed by medieval thinkers was just the circumstantial and ephemeral face of a persistent discourse, one capable of many metamorphoses. Even today, the motif of the centrality of Israel's land has lost none of its vigor in the Jewish imagination, even though modern people, including modern Jews, live in a fundamentally decentered world. Thus a contemporary Jewish writer has stressed that if the Holy Land is situated at the junction of three continents, this is so that the just society to be founded there can more easily become "a light unto the nations."[13] Here as elsewhere, the supposed geographical centrality of the Holy Land is merely the sign or a metaphor for a more profound centrality that goes to the heart of being and history.

Already in the classical era, and even more so in the medieval one, this theme had been variously elaborated. The first analogy was vertical: an axis directly linked the land of Israel to the most external circle of the world; of the seven lands below, maintained the *Zohar*, the major work in the Jewish mystical tradition, Israel was indeed the most lofty. Then came the horizontal realm; many particularly eloquent images were offered: that of the walnut, for example, in which the Holy

Land was the nutmeat, whereas the impure lands of nations were just the shell. And then there was the metaphor of the eye: the white was the Gentiles' territory, and the iris the land of Israel, with Jerusalem as the pupil.[14] Beyond their literary flavor, such metaphors aspired to speak of the profound essence of things. They underlined both the vital function that devolved upon the center and the absolute qualitative preeminence conferred upon it by this position. This function and preeminence were obviously shared by the people who were the legitimate owners of this central land, "which is one level below that of paradise."[15] To inherit this country, the "*heart* of the world,"[16] meant to manifest that one was really "the elect and the *heart* of humanity," and someone who did not inherit it could scarcely pretend to more than the lowly status of "shell."[17] Meat of the nut, apple of the eye, heart of the great universal organism, Israel and its land alone preserved direct communication with the Divine. While the world as a whole found itself encased in the slough of evil, impurity, and chaos, a single breach had survived, a single portal had remained open: in the Holy Land.[18]

Another image, also very ancient, was that of the "navel," which opened still vaster perspectives, because it allowed a combination of spatial centrality and temporal anteriority. According to a late homiletic source, God had, in effect, begun the creation of the world with the land of Israel, just as He began the creation of the embryo with the navel.[19] The navel of the world is thus both the beginning and the foundation of this world: the Mishnah speaks of a "foundation stone" "dating from the days of the first prophets" upon which, in the sanctuary, the Ark of the Covenant, was placed.[20] It was from there that the world had been created and from the dust of this place that the first man was fashioned. The various accounts offered by rabbinic literature—often taken up and endlessly reinterpreted—did not entirely jibe with one another, and the land of Israel could stand in dynamic relation to the rest of the world, although it always retained a central role. According to certain traditions, it was Adam's head alone that came from the Holy Land; his body came from Babylon, and his limbs were from the other countries of the world. According to others, in order to create Adam, God had taken dust from the site of the Temple and from the four cardinal points and then mixed it with a little of all the waters of the world.[21]

The foundation of the world and the original site of humanity, Jerusalem and its Temple were also the center of human history and Israel's history, as if all crucial moments ineluctably returned to this crucial and unique place, as if space furnished the unifying principle of a chronological succession that was perhaps too profuse. It was there that Adam, newly created, had supposedly offered his first sacrifice; there that Cain and Abel had brought their offerings, there that they had fought, and that the first murder in history had been committed—their dispute having been precisely over the ownership of this site where the Temple would one day be erected. Again, it was there that Noah, leaving the Ark, had raised his altar, that Abraham had set about sacrificing his son Isaac, that Jacob had dreamed his ladder. It was there, too, that after having been miraculously transported from Egypt, and for one night only, the people of Israel had proceeded to their first Pascal sacrifice. And it was this site that David had bought from the Jebusite and where Solomon had finally ordered the sanctuary to be built.[22] Thus, this same place, where the offerings of Cain the peasant had been rejected, and from where, guilty of having spilled his brother's blood, he had been driven and condemned to wandering, would become the place where Israel would gather three times a year, expiate its faults in the blood of sacrifices, and give thanks to God for the subsistence it drew from the land that He had given to it. A singular reversal—and a remarkable continuity!

It was therefore clearly in the Holy Land, and still more precisely in Jerusalem and on the site of the sanctuary, that at least three axes met and crossed: spatial, temporal, and mystical. There beat the heart of the world, there was gathered its history, and there its meaning was revealed.

Divine Land

A true territorial exception, the land of Israel was infinitely more than a territory. It was the sign and image of the Jewish exception. The intimacy of the link that united the land to God referred back to the intimacy of the link that united God to Israel. Any alteration in the relationship between Israel and its land was merely the visible sign of an alteration of its relationship with God. No such alteration had an irrevocable and definitive character, however. And none was as profound as appearances might lead one to believe. Few people would concede that the land of Israel ceased being the land of God, and therefore being holy, at the moment when Israel ceased to reside there. Maimonides himself was quite free of the temptation to essentialize and little inclined to confer on the Holy Land a particular metaphysical status, but he could not help reasserting the absolute sanctity of Jerusalem. The city's sanctity was eternal because the Divine Presence had elected to reside there, and it was not about to disappear. The election of Jerusalem was eternal, as was the election of the Jewish people. Also eternal was the link between Israel and its land. God, the people, and their land formed a chain of which no link could be weakened without the danger of compromising the solidity of the whole.

On the model of the Jewish people, the land of Israel was constantly in God's sight. Like them, it enjoyed Divine providence in an immediate way. Unlike the great regions that bordered it, Egypt or Mesopotamia, whose prosperity depended on rivers with regular courses, the Holy Land was exclusively dependent for its fertility upon unpredictable seasonal rains, of which God alone was the master. Any abundance, like any famine, came directly from Heaven, in both senses of the term. Like Israel's exile, the present ruin of the land of Israel was the work of providence—itself the patent sign of a particular providence. Beneath the appearance of exile and desolation, nothing had really changed. If one admits the land of Israel's inherent sanctity, then nothing could change this. The absence of Israel and the presence of new masters could not lessen it in the least. It was not the practice of the commandments on its soil that made the land holy—just the reverse, for by reason of its intrinsic sanctity, the commandments had been instituted. It had already exercised a powerful attraction on the patriarchs even when it was still occupied by idolatrous peoples and soiled by their abominable practices. The land possessed something divine that nothing could alter.

The land was a person, endowed with a will; it could be harmful or favorable, sometimes accepted and sometimes rejected its inhabitants. Those who resided on its soil breathed pure air, and its dust had an expiatory virtue comparable to the sacrificial altar for those who were buried in it. And while "there cannot be found in the inhabited world any land that had been good and vast and populated and that is now desolate like this land," says Nahmanides, this is precisely "because since we have left it, it has not welcomed any other people or nation, and even when efforts are redoubled to colonize it, they do not manage to do so."[23] This incapacity of successive conquerors to put down roots in the Holy Land manifests the positive resistance it offered to any illegitimate takeover. The land of Israel can only be affected by whatever it wishes to be affected by. Pure in its very essence, it cannot really be soiled by anything. The earth of the Gentiles and the bread it produces are both unclean.[24] But the Gentiles do not have the power to soil the earth of the Holy Land. Destruction and subjection to a foreign yoke have only a limited impact: the divine influx perhaps no longer descends upon it with the same intensity as before, but the rind of evil cannot dominate it, and the land has the power to reject impurity. In the same way as the souls of Jews who have died outside the Holy Land must return there, so also the souls of non-Jews deceased on its soil must leave it and return to their proper domain. There is no place in the land of Israel for rebels and sinners, and they will be chased away from it after their deaths like dogs. "And at the end of time, the Blessed One will seize the corners of the land and shake out every impurity from it."[25]

If the effects of impious acts committed in the Holy Land over the centuries are held to be null, ancillary, or fundamentally inessential, then this amounts to assuming that history flows over it like water off a duck's back. Escaping in fact from any nonlegitimate ascendancy over it, the land of Israel is already no longer situated within history, but well outside it. Underneath the rags of despoliation and ruin is hidden an essential land, divine and invariable, that the present tribulations in no way affect, which will one day be once more called upon to reveal itself in all its untarnished glory. Indefinitely idealized, the land of which the medieval Jews dreamed was truly that land toward which they very concretely directed their prayers three times a day. But it was also much more than that, and in a way something quite different. The more it was perceived as holy, the more it was experienced as other—and dangerous. Firstly, as other: the Hasidic master Nahman of Bratslav (1772–1811)[26] tells of having met people who admitted to him how surprised they were, upon arrival in the Holy Land, to discover that it really belonged to this world and that the dust found there was like the dust of other countries. Then, as dangerous: inspiring the fear and provoking the recoil that the sacred by nature arouses, so the Holy Land became strictly speaking uninhabitable, forbidden to common mortals, requiring of whoever dared tread its soil an exceptional degree of spirituality.

Modern Jewish apologetics has had a tendency—all the more so as Zionist pressure became stronger—to maintain that after the destruction and dispersal, nothing had basically compromised the relationship of the Jews to the Holy Land, which had never been weakened, even by a symbolization of sacred space (such as the pure and simple replacement of the terrestrial Jerusalem by a heavenly Jerusalem); nor had it been weakened by the transfer of this sacredness to some other space or institution. A simple reading of the texts, though, casts doubt upon this axiom as overly simplistic.[27] As soon as the link of Jews to their land lost any concrete basis, and the land of Israel historically ceased to be the territory of the assembled nation or even its nerve center, then even if Israel had definitively renounced the idea of a political reconquest of its site, it could not have renounced other types of reconquest. The desire for place, as nostalgia, as awareness of lack, could not simply feed on itself. This desire, in fact, never remained totally unquenched. The power of dreams and the artifices of allegory could render Zion present at any time and anywhere. Herein precisely lay the paradox: the more one thought of the land, the more it was forgotten. Or even more drastically: constantly thinking of it, ceaselessly naming it, was perhaps the best means of forgetting it.

The Land as Metaphor

The spiritualization of Zion observable in the medieval Jewish world did not necessarily result—as was the case in the Christian world—in a devaluation (or even an eclipse) of the Jerusalem here below. Jewish thinkers, notably the Kabbalists, often endeavored to associate these two levels of reality. This is notably what the theosophical Kabbalah attempted and succeeded at.[28] Any meditation on the land of Israel in the world below was by the same token an elucidation of the mysteries of the Land of Israel in the world above.

For the Kabbalists, in fact, the land of Israel symbolized a feminine celestial entity. It was associated with Kingship (*Malkhut*), the last of the ten cosmic forces emanating from God (the *sefirot*) that constitute the higher world. Kingship itself was identified with the Divine Presence (the *Shekhinah*), or feminine in God. The land of Israel thus became one of the key elements in a fundamental sexual symbolism. It was directly related to two other entities of the celestial world: Beauty (*Tiferet*), identified with the Torah, which was the virile force, and Foundation (*Yesod*), identified with the Just (*tsadik*), which was the virile member through which passed the divine influx directed from on high to below. Most of the commandments, notably regarding legal coupling, were perceived by the Kabbalah as contributing to restoring an original harmony and to fostering the union in God of masculine and feminine principles. In the same way, worship practiced by Israel in the Holy Land was considered vital because it had the value of *imitatio Dei* and permitted the worshiper to influence the internal life of the divine world. The righteous ones who resided in earthly Israel, by the simple fact of this residence, imitated and incited the relationship of possession established, in the higher world, between divine masculinity and the land of Israel above. Thus the *Zohar* asserted that "when the children of Israel were in the Holy land, everything was as it should be."[29]

In a similar spirit, the theosophical Kabbalah tended to distinguish between Jerusalem and Zion, to identify each with a particular cosmic force—Jerusalem symbolizing a feminine force in God and Zion a masculine one—and to think of their mutual relations in equally sexual terms. Thus Zion, the geographical center of the earthly world, referred back to Foundation, the center of the higher world. Zion-Foundation was the masculine member containing blessings (semen) and feminine Jerusalem received this beneficent influx, which was then transmitted to the people of Israel. Arguments for this sexual symbolism could be found in the real world: Zion was a tower, and Jerusalem was a city. The link with the earthly Jerusalem was maintained: the influx descending from Zion (Foundation) toward the heavenly Jerusalem (Kingship) conceived an embryo that was the earthly Jerusalem, which was tied to her celestial mother by the navel. Even in ruins, the earthly Jerusalem remained attached to her heavenly counterpart and was truly in this sense still Heaven's gate—a door opened upon the celestial world.[30]

This escape upward, this way of associating the land of Israel with a higher reality, what we might call its "overrealization," though, still carried the seeds of its "derealization." As soon as it becomes a divine reality, the Holy Land on high is necessarily much more "real" than this trivial world where flesh-and-blood creatures live. Inversely, because it takes its essential being from the higher world with which it enjoys privileged contact, the Holy Land here below risks losing to the same degree any "reality" in the earthly sense. It is just a step to move from idealization to allegorization, from the metaphysical temptation to the seductions of metaphor. This step was easily taken, thanks to which the land was less and less itself, as it became more and more something other. The words traditionally used to name it (land, Jerusalem, Zion) came *primarily* to designate mystical or philosophical realities perfectly independent of it. The land became just a signifier with multiple signifieds, which might or might not maintain a direct or indirect relation with the primary signified—the land in the earthly sense. Thus Canaan was no longer simply the name of a people and the country over which this people had once held supremacy. It was, first of all, a word that had autonomous semantic relations with other words. It could be connected to a Hebraic root (*kn*ᶜ) meaning "to bend," and, independently of any territorial connotation, evoke the humiliation and annihilation of self before the divine will on the part of someone who observes the commandments.

The prophetic Kabbalah would take full advantage of such word manipulations. Therein, Jerusalem was principally a term composed of letters, themselves invested with their own significance, and maintaining a particular link with the names of the Divinity. According to the way in which "Jerusalem" was spelled in Hebrew,[31] this word referred either to the absence or presence of the Divine within the soul—two levels of consciousness that were a direct function of ignorance or knowledge of the ineffable Name of God. For Abraham Abulafia in the thirteenth century, the word *Jerusalem* thus referred *firstly* to a state of consciousness. The true Jerusalem was the human intellect; the true Holy Land was the body of man as receptacle of prophecy. While the earthly Jerusalem as the ideal place of worship for all Israel still played an essential role in the theosophical Kabbalah, in the prophetic one, it disappeared in favor of a purely spiritual world, interior and individual. From this point of view, the allegorizing philosophers of the Middle Ages were scarcely distinguishable from the prophetic Kabbalists when they suggested, for example, identifying Jerusalem-on-high with the Agent Intellect and Jerusalem-here-below with the soul of man.[32] In the eighteenth century, Dov Baer of Mezeritch proclaimed simply: "The man who is not honest is called Babylon. . . . And the man who is righteous is called land of Israel."[33]

Given the symbolic and altogether atopical meaning that could be associated with them, then, the presence (even frequency) in a document of terms like *Zion, Jerusalem*, or *land of Israel* cannot be taken a priori either as signifying the author's attachment to the places these words designated or as revealing the profound nature of that attachment. And sometimes one can legitimately ask to what extent the mention of the Holy Land in a given kabbalistic or philosophical context still has anything to do with the ineradicable nostalgia for Zion that a certain kind of historiography thinks it is able to discern in the heart of each medieval Jew.

From this point of view, the case of medieval poetry is particularly instructive. Sacred poetry is naturally saturated with references to Zion.

The richness of an age-old tradition, the influence of liturgical models and commonplace thoughts, and the integration of this type of writing into synagogue worship all suffice to explain this phenomenon. Sometimes expressing the suffering of destruction and exile and sometimes the hope of restoration and redemption, the elegies recited on 9 *av*, as well as the poems inserted into daily prayers and into the Shabbat service and festivals, incontestably transmitted profound nostalgia. But what kind of nostalgia? It was much more a nostalgia for the Holy City, for Jerusalem, and more precisely for its Temple, than for the land itself. And what had been lost and what one aspired to retrieve was perhaps less a place than an innocence. The sanctuary had been the site of an innocence that was periodically regained: it was there that the sacrifices and the solemn rites of Yom Kippur earned the people expiation for their sins. It is noticeable that medieval elegies insist much less on the material sufferings of exile than on the absence of Jerusalem and the blessings it had spread over Israel. Tranquility, a peace of mind, the marvelous feeling of pardon from sin—all that was now lacking. But prayer was there, precisely, to try to fill this lack. People hoped, believed, knew that prayer could effectively replace sacrifice and assure pardon.[34]

As soon as one leaves the terrain of religious poetry for that of secular poetry as it developed in medieval Spain, the observed ambivalence is all the more flagrant. Even if it had to obey very strict conventions on the formal level, even if it was often the fruit of actual commissions from patrons, Spanish secular poetry certainly gave more place than liturgy to the subjectivity of its authors—which makes it all the more precious. What can be observed from reading some of the most eminent representatives of this prestigious school? In these secular poems, the land of Israel is really often an image more than anything else. For Salomon ibn Gabirol in the eleventh century, for example, exile is more a spiritual condition than a political reality. He feels free to use Zion as the symbol of the lost wisdom of ancient times, or as a metaphor applied to Hai, the head of a Babylonian academy whose death he is mourning. The great men he is eulogizing are similarly compared to the sacred utensils and other holy objects of the Temple, and their deaths are a new destruction of the sanctuary. Nor should we be sur-

prised that Moses ibn Ezra, the most Arabophile poet of his generation, resorts to the imagery of exile to evoke, not the exile of his people, but his own departure from Andalusia for Castile! And when he
takes up the celebrated phrase from the Psalms "If I forget thee
[Jerusalem]," it is not to express his indestructible attachment to the
ancestral land but rather to stress his faithful memory of Granada and
of the friends he has left there.[35] From this point of view, by making
Zion into a privileged theme of his profane poetry, Judah Halevi would
make a real break. But if for him this shift was accompanied by an actual emigration to the real Holy Land, many of his successors would
be content to evoke in their verses a mythical and ideal land, linked to
the motifs of exile and redemption. In the eighteenth and nineteenth
centuries, even the Hebrew poetry of the Jews of North Africa, which
is the direct heir of the Spanish medieval tradition, offers, it seems,
only rare examples of a direct and concrete relationship to the actual
land of Israel below.[36]

A Taste of Paradise

While many medieval literary works betray a clear tendency toward
the spiritualization and/or the metaphorization of the land of Israel,
the intensity and depth of this idealization vary from one text to another, from one author to another, but also from one era or cultural
area to another. Moreover, the link between attitudes and the concrete
living conditions of Jewish populations is not easy to determine. Were
the sublimation and "overrealization" of the Holy Land a means of escaping through the dream from the hard realities of an exile that could
not otherwise be suspended? Were metaphor and "derealization," on
the other hand, the result of an accommodation to exile when its yoke
was less heavily felt and when more harmonious relations were established with non-Jewish populations? It seems difficult to subscribe a
priori to such a mechanistic schema, particularly since, as we have seen,
"overrealization" and "derealization" are by no means fundamentally
antithetical processes. Moreover, the overwhelming majority of sources
traditionally examined are scholarly sources, kabbalistic meditations,

philosophical commentaries, and poetic elaborations, which are often
very sophisticated; it is a delicate matter to measure their representa-
tiveness at the level of Jewish society as a whole. It is doubtful whether
ordinary Jews had much idea of the subtlety that some of these cultural
productions could attain. What means do we have today to appreciate
the real impact of a sermon, spoken by a scholar, upon an audience of
simple believers? How can we judge to what extent the contents of the
liturgy to which they had access were in fact internalized? Insofar as the
very words could be actually understood (since Hebrew had always
been a scholarly language that was very unevenly mastered), did these
words do any more than fashion a collective unconscious that was generally inactive, than maintain a vague expectation, than offset the difficulties of daily life with the more or less effective counterweight of a
stereotyped hope? Of course, all these elements might be capable some
day of crystallizing and of furnishing, when the circumstances were
right, the ingredients of an emotional energy able to justify and nourish positive political action.

Whatever the case, it is clear that the choice for medieval Jews was
never only between dream and abstraction, on the one hand, and the
concrete land, on the other—between, on the one hand, constructions
of the intellect or imagination, and, on the other, emigration. Nor was
the choice simply between a strictly local attachment to the Holy Land
or a delocalized representation of it. Delocalization could itself be
understood in many ways; for example, one could believe that a dilution of the unique place was foreseen for the end of time. So Abraham
bar Hiya (twelfth century) announced that at the resurrection of the
dead, all the deceased from Israel who had died in the Diaspora would
awaken to inherit the countries of their exile, "such that all the countries of the world will be called land of Israel, unless the land of Israel
considerably grows—to the point of filling the entire world."[37] Another possibility was that this dilution had already been realized; for
example, the Kabbalist Isaac of Acre (end of the thirteenth century to
middle of the fourteenth) thought that Israel's posterity, in whom the
Divine Presence permanently resided, in whatever geographical places
they found themselves, themselves represented the true land of Israel.

Few authentic religious aspirations could easily accommodate the excesses of mystical, geographical, or temporal proximity—as well as excessive distance from the object of desire. The land of Israel exhaled a perfume of paradise. It was paradise itself. To be visible *from* this world without being totally *of* this world, to maintain hope while providing some consolation in advance, paradise had to be neither too close nor too distant, neither too easily accessible nor absolutely out of reach. The land of Israel was also the heart of the world. It was the seat on which it rested, the axis around which it turned, the orient of sacred space. So in order to be visible *from* here without being really *of* here, and to furnish the believer with the point of reference he needed, this orient should be neither too near nor too far, neither too easily accessible nor absolutely out of reach. In both cases, some mediation was always possible—and even necessary.

In certain contexts, this mediation will be supplied by the righteous one (*tsadik*). Ancient rabbinic sources conserved the trace of beliefs that made the survival of the world dependent on one or more righteous people. In the thirteenth-century Kabbalah, the association between the righteous one and "the pillar of the cosmos" almost always meant God Himself as the Just. But Simeon bar Yohai, the second-century master to whom the *Zohar* is attributed, was equally presented as the just person thanks to whom the world was not destroyed. He himself was the "pillar of the world." The person who saw him was compared to Abraham seeing the Holy Land. He contained the whole universe in exactly the same way as the rock on which Jacob laid his head in Bethel contained the whole land of Israel.[38] The Just stands at the center of the cosmos; he is the earthly extension of what in God is called the Just (meaning the ninth of the emanating cosmic forces, Foundation). Particularly after the sixteenth century, Jewish mysticism would take up and develop a conception of the Just as *axis mundi*. Hasidism, especially, would give a whole new dimension to the figure of the *tsadik*, the charismatic head of the community, the actual Jacob's ladder by which the faithful person could start his ascension toward God. It would hesitate between the idea of a plural leadership, with each *tsadik* being the center of his own believers' world, and the idea

of a single leader for each generation. It was in the writings of Nahman of Bratslav that the "righteous one of the generation" became a
major theme: he was the Holy of Holies, the cornerstone, the mythic
rock from which Creation originated and upon which the Temple had
been built, as well as the channel through which Israel had access to
the true interpretation of the Torah.

By his presence alone, the righteous one transformed the place where
he lived into a veritable land of Israel—a land of Israel sufficiently surrounded with prestige and mystery to remain wholly other, but also
a land of Israel that was accessible, toward which it was physically and
mystically possible to go. It was a near/distant land, at the very heart
of exile. When Nahman decided to move to Bratslav in the Ukraine
in 1802, his disciples cried: "Rejoice and exult, thou who dwellest in
Bratslav!"—borrowing a phrase from Isa. 12:6, but replacing Zion
with Bratslav. At the end of the nineteenth century, Uri of Strelisk, a
disciple of Jacob Isaac of Lublin, was supposed to have said: "One
who comes here is to *imagine* that Lublin is the land of Israel, that the
master's court is Jerusalem, his room is the Holy of Holies, and that
the Shekhinah speaks through his mouth."[39]

Nearby Lands, Distant Lands

So could *imagine* once more be the key word here? If physically going
to Lublin was basically an artifice to let you "imagine" you were going
to Jerusalem, then the mediation and substitution offered by the
tsadik and his place of residence, despite their belonging to what was
immediate and concrete, seem no less a work of the imagination than
are idealization and metaphorization. Moreover, seeing Lublin in order to dream Jerusalem—does that not amount to dreaming Lublin,
too? However, this double dream and the phantasmagoric confusion
of "here and there" are precisely what enabled Jewish communities of
the Diaspora, right up to our day, to nourish with a little more than a
dream—and therefore to appease—a nostalgia for Zion that was both
fragile and essential to their self-awareness.

In reality, any Jewish center of any importance could pretend to the provisional and enhancing status of an interim Jerusalem. Innumerable cities claimed this title: Kairouan, the Jerusalem of Africa; Toledo, the Jerusalem of Spain; Salonika, the Jerusalem of Greece; Frankfurt am Main, the Jerusalem of Germany; Medzibezh, the Jerusalem of Podolia (the place of residence of Hasidism's founder, also called the "Little Land of Israel" by his disciples); Prague, the Jerusalem of Bohemia; Vilna, the Jerusalem of Lithuania, and so on. Some traditions even allowed one to superimpose a kind of Palestinian mythic geography upon local historical geography. Thus the Jews of medieval Spain were assured that the names of certain towns in their country of settlement had been given them by the first Jewish colonists in memory of localities in the Holy Land. Lucena, for example, was supposed to have been baptized with the name of the biblical city of Luz because its pure air was propitious for the development of Jewish science, just as its Palestinian model's air had been for prophecy. And Maqueda and Escalona in Castile became Makkeda and Ascalon in the Holy Land.

Until our own era, the Ashkenazi world, too, would consecrate a similar type of equivalences: in its literary mythology, the *shtetl*[40] was a "Jewish kingdom" (*yidishe melukhe* in Yiddish), and an extension and continuation of, or substitute for, the original Holy Land. The founding tales as relayed by Yiddish and Hebrew novelists traditionally tell of a divine intervention: it was God who pointed out to exiled Jews the provisional place in which to settle. It was He who directed them miraculously toward Poland when they were fleeing suffering and persecution. And when they approached Lublin, nature brought its own approval to their itinerary, by permitting them discover a strange forest in which a treatise from the Talmud was engraved on each tree! The very name of the country authorized this appropriation and gave meaning to the migration and its momentary suspension: Poland in Hebrew was called Polin, which could be broken down as "Po lin" or "Spend the night here!"—while awaiting the dawn when all Israel would at last assemble on its land. The temporary domicile of Jerusalem exiles, the Jewish village of eastern Europe was a Jerusalem-in-exile. Even its destruction in flames was interpreted by the novelists who described it as one more link in the long chain of major Jewish disasters, a kind of duplication of the ruin of the Temple—unless it augured (in a typical ambivalence) less an exile than a new and liberating exodus.[41]

We know that Babylonia was the first to claim the eminent status of Holy-Land-in-exile and that it did so to the detriment of the land of Israel, against its academies and rabbis. And Babylon always retained a central place in the Jewish imagination. But the fact that it was the place where, of the two Talmuds, the one whose authority would come to be recognized by the Jewish world as a whole was written did not suffice to explain this exceptional favor. Babylon was in fact an ambiguous land. It was the place of exile and oppression, the land of idolatry and impurity. But it was also the nation's place of origin, the homeland of Abraham, of some of the prophets, and of venerated scholars. The explanations advanced for a rabbinic prohibition on the consumption of earth in Babylon express this ambiguity very well: for some, to eat its soil amounted in effect to eating impure creatures (since, according to legend, it was there that all the cadavers of people and animals killed by the Flood had been precipitated), whereas for others, it would be like eating the flesh of their fathers.[42] It is also significant that pilgrims to the Holy Land traditionally passed through Babylonia. This was already the case in the twelfth century for Benjamin of Tudela and for Petahia of Regensburg, whose account lingers especially on this stage of the voyage. But what counted for Petahia was, not only the tombs of prophets that he could visit, but also the spectacle of the flourishing life of Jewish communities, the political autonomy they enjoyed, and the personality of the head of the academy whom he met.[43]

The reality or fantasy of a Jewish autonomy considerably enhanced the prestige of a place that sheltered it or was reputed to do so. A little of the glory of the land of Israel, the prime site of national independence both yesterday and tomorrow, redounded throughout the Middle Ages upon two eminently emblematic places. One was purely imaginary: the mysterious country, situated beyond an impassable river, the Sambation, where the ten lost tribes from the kingdom of Israel were supposed to have gathered when it was destroyed by the

Assyrians in 722 B.C.E. Many legendary tales evoke this independent Israelite state, and periodically there appeared people who presented themselves as coming from these lost tribes, such as the traveler Eldad the Danite in the ninth century and David Reuveni, an adventurer with messianic pretensions, in the sixteenth century.[44] A second symbol of political autonomy, this one more anchored in the real but promptly turned into myth, was the celebrated Khazar kingdom, which became Jewish thanks to the conversion of its sovereign around 740, if we are to believe the tenth-century correspondence in Hebrew between Hasdai ibn Shaprut, a famous Jewish statesman from Muslim Spain, and the Khazar king Joseph.

All these interim lands of Israel must have fulfilled a rather ambivalent function. They could both reinforce and weaken the memory of the eternal land of Israel. They could serve it—but also substitute for it. They could fill a lack—but also make it deeper. Thus Hasdai ibn Shaprut saw the Khazar kingdom as a sign (but only a sign) of the coming rebuilding of Jerusalem, while declaring himself ready to renounce all his present privileges to gain any place of exile where Israel was sovereign. But the fall into the imaginary world seemed inevitable, sometimes because in the real world, the Holy Land no longer offered any support for the dream of Jewish autonomy, and so one imagined a place distinct from the Holy Land where this autonomy was a reality, and sometimes because people simply transfigured the immediate environment in order to turn it into a Holy Land that was half-experienced and half-dreamed.

In fact, throughout the land's Middle Ages, lasting from the confirmation of exile and dispersal as the objective and apparently definitive conditions of the Jews' existence right up to the first efforts toward a return to the ancestral soil, Jews seemed fated to resolve in a fantastical way a persistent tension between their inability to be really where they were (and where quite often their right to be was not recognized) and their inability to renounce being where they were not, were no longer, or were not yet. The place where they aspired to be, the natural site where all their nostalgia was focused, and where they thought they had some chance of feeling at home, the place by which they really wanted to be defined, was spontaneously called by medieval Jews either Jerusalem, Zion, or the land of Israel. Sometimes these were the actual Jerusalem, Zion, and land of Israel, but purified, magnified, glorified, suspended in time, visible images of their own hidden glory, the dreamed-of signs of a privilege that reality denied them. But sometimes they were also homelands of another kind, and in a sense more accessible: the cosmic force on which the fate of this lower world depended, or the level of consciousness of people freed from the shackles of their earthly condition, or else the resident town of a rabbi who spoke the Law and let the Word of God be heard.

The nostalgia of the medieval Jew was dual: historical and existential, Jewish and human. It was both the nostalgia of the exiled from Judea and the nostalgia of those who are fundamentally alien in this world. The historian can only take note of this ambiguity, which is not the only one. In effect, it would be just as reductive to see the theology of the land as proof (and only as proof) of the ineradicable attachment of medieval Jews to the land of Israel as it is, on the contrary, to see idealization, metaphorization, or substitution as proof (and only proof) of their detachment from it. When he uses the imagery of exile to describe his trip from Andalusia to Castile, Moses ibn Ezra is not only showing that Andalusia has become his homeland or his new Holy Land; at the same time, he is presenting his exile in Castile as the reactivation in his own life of a collective experience that is both fundamental and paradigmatic: the exile of Israel outside its land. In the hearts as well as in the writings of the medieval Jews, Jerusalem is never either as present or as absent as we are sometimes inclined to believe. We should not be surprised, because while the reality of exile indefinitely lengthened the distance, for its part, the consciousness of exile indefinitely deepened the nostalgia.

Four The Exiled Land

As strong as the seductions of the dream might be, the consciousness of the medieval Jew was not governed by them alone. In fact, Judaism was not a theology cut off from the real world; it was also a practical observance. It certainly did not have the single ambition of speaking of what was; first and foremost, it spoke the Law. And as eloquent as the speculations of philosophers and Kabbalists and the images of poets may appear when we take them as self-contained, their meaning and effective influence still remain relative. Or, to put it another way, their meaning and real influence are not fully manifest to the observer unless they are placed in relation to another major preoccupation of the medieval Jew: to know the deeds approved by God in order to perform them. On this level, Jerusalem and the land of Israel were not just objects or bearers of representations. The medieval Jew could not forget that the destruction of the sanctuary and his own physical estrangement from the ancestral soil prevented him from performing a considerable number of the essential stipulations of the Torah. Faced with the theologies and the triumphant power of Christianity and Islam, Judaism could only feel doubly weakened by exile: subjected to a foreign yoke that imposed its rules in many domains, had it not moreover become a shadow of itself, deprived as it now was of an essential aspect of its Law?

Theologians and legal scholars devoted the major part of their efforts to answering this challenge, maintaining an awareness of exile, and hence of the lack that was the condition sine qua non of the group's survival, but also making this exile and this lack bearable—even conferring on them, while waiting, a positive quality. This meant that hope, for both reconstruction and return, had to enable the believer to project himself into the future. Yet this hope should not obscure the present or minimize its worth. If that were the case, then the temptation of a legal relativism, even a real antinomianism, would always be possible, in which the faithful were brought to believe that observance of the Law was not really applicable to everyone until the time of hope had come, once the gathering of Israel on its land had been realized—when the Law would be applicable in all respects. Like hope, the awareness of mourning had to be sustained. But it also had to be contained within limits, so that it did not prevent the enjoyment of today or the hope for tomorrow. As a Palestinian master of the time of the catastrophe of 70 C.E. put it: "Not to mourn at all is impossible, because the blow has fallen. To mourn overmuch is also impossible, because one can only ask of the community what it is capable of enduring."[1] Many practices of Judaism in exile—its management of time, of worship, and space—were marked by this basic ambivalence.

Land and Liturgy

Take the management of time to start with. Curiously, in fact, destruction and dispersal did not fundamentally modify the liturgical calendar. Even when pilgrimage became impossible, or at the very least difficult, and, in any case, of problematic liturgical efficacy, since the Temple had been destroyed and therefore no worship could take place there, the three high points in the Jewish year were still the great festivals, meant to be occasions of pilgrimage: the feasts of Sukkoth, Passover, and Weeks. These three solemn occasions, which were also agricultural festivals, regulated the seasonal rhythm of the liturgy throughout the Diaspora in the same manner as in the Holy Land. At Passover and Sukkoth, therefore, people continued to say prayers for the dew and the rain, which more answered the needs of the land of Israel than the particular climates of the believers' actual places of residence. At the Festival of Weeks, one still ritually shook the not-yet-opened date palms (the *lulav*) and the citron, "imported from the South and the East at great expense."[2] Each year, in January or February, at the semi-

festival of Tu bi-shevat, people continued ritually to eat fruits, since
this celebration corresponded in the Holy Land to the end of winter
and the beginning of a new year for the levying of tithes. By rejecting
the automatic periodic intercalation of a supplementary month to enable the shorter lunar year to catch up with the solar cycle, stipulated
by the precalculated calendar used by the Jewish majority, and continuing to decide when to add a month based upon actual observation of
the ripeness of the barley in the springtime Holy Land, the Karaites
went even further in this direction.[3]

Certain gestures and certain readings thus allowed the prolongation
of the memory of a vanished form of worship and of the place associated with it. Although sacrifices were no longer offered in the Temple,
in liturgy, people remembered their nature and how they unfolded.
And if, on the day of Yom Kippur, the High Priest no longer went
into the Holy of Holies to obtain pardon for Israel, the synagogue
service was organized around the detailed account of this holy day
as it had taken place in the sanctuary when it was still standing. The
continuity of liturgical time thus stood against the vicissitudes of history and guaranteed a relative fidelity to that place, despite the fact of
being torn away from it. Still, ambiguity was not totally removed. The
three festivals of pilgrimage, which by definition recall Jerusalem, simultaneously commemorate the three founding moments of Israel's
identity before the Hebrew conquest of Canaan—the departure from
Egypt, the theophany in the Sinai, and the wandering in the desert.
As festivals of pilgrimage, they evoked ownership of the land, but as
historical festivals, they merely expressed a hope of ownership. Nor
should we forget that Purim, the most popular holiday in the Jewish
calendar, which occasions the most lively and colorful celebrations, recalling the miraculous salvation of the Jews of Persia thanks to the intervention of Queen Esther, is the festival of exile par excellence. Nor
should the national and political dimensions of the events commemorated by Hanukah—the victory of Judas Maccabaeus over Antiochus IV
Epiphanes in the second century B.C.E.—be overestimated. The rabbis
preferred to see it as the exaltation of spiritual resistance to paganism
and to the temptations of idolatry. The text inserted on this day into

the daily prayer does not refer to the liberation of the national territory; the military high points are only surreptitiously mentioned; the
main, and only real, fighter has been God Himself; and the benefit
procured by this campaign was mainly the removal from the Temple
of all alien presence, its purification, and the lighting of lamps within
its walls.

As a general rule, the fact that synagogue worship often appeared so
clearly centered on Jerusalem by no means implied a priori that a preoccupation with territory or even an attachment to place was of primordial importance in it. Jerusalem was not the land of Israel. Jerusalem was primarily the seat of the Temple, the ideal site of an ideal
worship. And it was that loss, much more than loss of land, that believers mourned during the fasts that punctuated the Jewish year: 10
tevet (December–January), which commemorated the start of the siege
of Jerusalem by Nebuchadnezzar; 17 *tamuz* (June–July), which recalled
the first breaches made in the walls of the city by Nebuchadnezzar and
by Titus; and 9 *av*, finally, the anniversary of the destruction of the First
and then the Second Temple—also the date, tradition said, of the birth
of the awaited Messiah.

The land as such is not absent from worship, of course. It is even
quite present at various moments of the day, when the believer recites
thanksgiving graces after meals.[4] When he simply drinks wine or eats a
cake or one of the fruits for which Israel's land is famous (grapes, figs,
pomegranates, olives, dates), he pronounces a blessing on the land.
And if the fruits that he eats have been harvested in the Holy Land itself, he not simply thanks God "for the land and for *these* fruits," but
"for the land and for *its* fruits." When the meal includes the consumption of bread, the recited words are much more elaborate, and the second of the three core blessings is "the blessing of the land." However,
mention of the land that God had the goodness to give to the fathers
of Israel is immediately associated, within that same blessing, with the
gift of circumcision and of the Torah, as well as with the exodus from
Egypt and liberation from slavery. Still more significantly, the third
and final blessing in this set relates specifically to Jerusalem as the site
where the sanctuary was built and whose coming reconstruction it
heralds.

A similar slide can be seen in the Passover evening ritual: while the reading of the Hagada, the liturgical recitation of the exodus from Egypt, opens with the phrase "This year here, next year in the land of Israel," it ends with the following words: "Next year in rebuilt Jerusalem." The structure of the Amida, whose nineteen blessings form the heart of each of the three daily religious services, is no less revealing of this hesitation between evocation of a land grasped in its concreteness and the affirmation of the eschatological and messianic theme of liberation and restoration. In this long prayer, first recited individually in a low voice by each believer and then taken up in a loud voice by the officiating minister, only three blessings can be said to be topocentric, and only in a very particular sense. The tenth blessing mentions "our land" as the future gathering place of Israel's exiles, but the accent is much more on the fact of the awaited gathering than on its locale. The fourteenth blessing calls specifically for the reconstruction of Jerusalem, residence of the Lord and seat of David's throne. The sixteenth mentions only the sanctuary, expressing the hope of a restoration of sacrificial worship and of a return of the Holy Presence to Zion.

In such contexts, the site in itself is ultimately much less important than the associated expectations, which are essentially atopical and principally cultic and religious. The Hagada ritually read on Passover evening is both an evocation of the exodus and a solemn reaffirmation of the hope for a liberation to come, as is clearly illustrated by one of its key passages. It is a restatement of and commentary on the phrase in Deuteronomy 26 that biblical legislation requires the peasant to say on the day he presents the firstfruits of his crop at the Temple. But the Hagada offers only a truncated version of this quotation. First recalling Israel's origins, the Egyptian experience, and the exodus (Deut. 26:5–8), the biblical text is followed by two verses (Deut. 26:9–10) that the Hagada seems deliberately to omit: 9 "He [God] brought us to this place and gave us this land, a land flowing with milk and honey. 10 Wherefore I now bring the firstfruits of the soil which You, O Lord, have given me." The omission of verse 10 is natural because it is directly tied to the ceremony of presenting firstfruits and has no place in the ritual context of the Passover evening. But what can we make of the absence of verse 9? Does it simply indicate that in the eyes of the

Hagada's compilers, it is the exodus from Egypt that matters much more than the destination, the liberation much more than inheriting the land?

In reality, focusing on messianic expectations and focusing on Jerusalem and the Temple do share the same dynamic. It is quite remarkable that from the end of the thirteenth to the fifteenth centuries, Spanish manuscripts of the Hebrew Bible often devote two pages, if not more, to representing the sacred utensils of the tabernacle erected in the desert. These illustrations are placed at the front of the book and not where they would correspond to the text. One often finds the Mount of Olives represented in them, too. This custom betrays a very powerful hope of messianic restoration: the Mount of Olives is in fact called on to open up to let the resurrected pass through on their way to the rebuilt sanctuary, and one tradition has it that the utensils of the Temple of Solomon had been hidden in grottoes before its destruction and are destined to reappear at the end of time.[5]

Such practices really testify much more to nostalgia for a time (the end of history) than for a place (the Temple). Moreover, as a unique and properly local reality, the place has a tendency to disappear. From this point of view, it is symptomatic that the same Spanish Jews in the fourteenth century had the habit of calling their Bibles "God's sanctuary" (*mikdashya*)—with the tripartite structure of Scripture (Pentateuch, Prophets, and Writings) evoking the three rooms of the sanctuary (vestibule, Holy, and Holy of Holies). Thus the book that recounts the Temple of yesterday and announces the restoration of the Temple of tomorrow is itself, here and now, a kind of temple. The synagogue is the best testimony to this basic ambiguity and to this confusion in time and place.

The synagogue is in effect the multiple place where the Jew expresses his nostalgia for a unique place. Between the walls of this multiple place, physically turning toward Jerusalem, he prays for the restoration of the unique place. The prayer substitutes for sacrifice at the same time as it calls for its restoration. The synagogue replaces and yet does not replace the Temple. It does not carry its name, but is akin to it as a segmented sacred space in which men and women are separated. Like the Temple, it is a hierarchical space: the ark that contains the scrolls of the Law is more holy than the rostrum where the Law is read, which is more holy than the oratory taken as a whole, which is more holy than the adjoining rooms and outbuildings. Again, like the Temple, it is a space oriented upward: the believer "ascends" to the Torah to proceed to the reading of it.[6] In the Middle Ages, in the Ashkenazi world, particularly in central Europe, one observes a tendency to endow synagogues with attributes evoking the sanctuary: the recess containing the scrolls of the Law is called the Holy Ark (like the Ark containing the tablets of the Law in the Temple), and it is covered with a veil called the *parokhet* (like the veil that separated the Holy from the Holy of Holies); a great candelabra with nine branches for Hanukah is placed south of the Ark (recalling the candelabra with seven branches in the Temple.)

Moreover, an ancient tradition grants extraterritorial status to synagogues. Whereas, according to some, Jerusalem is called upon to become so great as to touch the Throne of Glory and so large as to reach the gates of Damascus, according to others, the synagogues of the Diaspora are miniature temples, which at the end of time will be carried away, with the exiles, to Jerusalem.[7] From this would come the custom of not paving synagogues, which would seal their link with the land of exile and risk hindering their future flight toward Zion. Some legends about the Altneuschul synagogue in Prague are even more eloquent on this score: they maintain that one of the stones of the Temple of Jerusalem was integrated into its foundations, and that at the coming of the Messiah, when the synagogue goes to Jerusalem, this stone will quite naturally find its place again in the Third Temple.[8] In such a system of representations, the time factor clearly triumphs over the spatial dimension. At the end of time, the multiple places that are the synagogues of exile will merge with the unique locus of recovered Jerusalem. And the Jew who today treads the ground of his synagogue treads, by anticipation, the ground of the Holy Land. Exile is no longer simply exile; the land is no longer simply the land.

The Land and the Law: Rabbinic Hermeneutical Exercises

The ambiguity that marks worship in its relations with time and space allows both the land and exile to be saved, not forgetting "there" even when one lives "here," and not ceasing to live "here" when one dreams of "there." The man who whitewashes his house will refrain from covering a section of wall in memory of Jerusalem. Someone who organizes a banquet will set aside one or two dishes in memory of Jerusalem.[9] In both cases, the memory of Jerusalem and its ruin is intact. But the house can be whitewashed, and the banquet offered. As for the Jew who cannot have himself buried in the Holy Land, it suffices to put a little dust brought from there in his tomb. A concern for Zion thus symbolically colors many aspects of daily life and many moments in liturgical practice. But it never does so in an absolutely exclusive or oppressive manner.

While such ambivalence is possible, and even the rule, with respect to all the Law's stipulations that are applicable at any time and in any place, both in the Diaspora and in the Holy Land, it is not at all acceptable as regards those stipulations that only a Jew residing in the Holy Land can and should put into practice. In this domain, one has to decide and either renounce them or leave. But such a renunciation is not an easy thing. Is a Jew in exile who observes all the commandments not tied to the land of Israel without fail really a spotless Jew, a Jew in the full sense of the term? Or is this an interim solution, a stopgap, a compromise that is ultimately unsatisfactory? The observance of commandments that only the coming of the Messiah and the rebuilding of the sanctuary will make possible do not, of course, depend on him. But will he not, in order to accomplish there at least the commandments tied to the land, which, conversely, henceforth depend only upon himself, be spontaneously tempted to go halfway down that road and move to the Holy Land?

Exile has never been able to make the land of Israel disappear from the normative legal horizon. As in the Mishnah, a third of the codified regulations in Maimonides' legal code continue to concern agricultural life and the relationship of Israel to its land. The great medieval jurist had never wanted, in fact, to establish a formal distinction between the commandments applicable in exile and those only so in the Holy Land or that required the existence of a sanctuary. Far from setting the latter aside, he set them forth in the same way as the others. Like his Messiah, Maimonides' land of Israel thus relates to a juridical actuality of the most immediate kind; it is in no sense a matter of a distant eschatology.[10] However, the question remains of whether the commandments linked to the land, or reinforcing Israel's ties to its land, do not finally, forthwith—that is to say, prior to ultimate deliverance—constitute a real obligation.

Contemporary religious Zionism greatly insisted on the importance of certain legal regulations, if not of certain homiletic developments that were decisive in its eyes.[11] For example, there is the formal prohibition against a Jew leaving the land of Israel. Maimonides clearly notes this prohibition.[12] But he does not neglect to hedge it with qualifications: in fact, a Jew is justified in leaving the Holy Land in order to save himself from idolators, to marry, or to study Torah, and only upon condition of his coming back. He can also make a trip for business purposes. On the other hand, he is forbidden to take up long-term residence outside the Holy Land unless there is a severe famine raging there. Of course, even when these particular circumstances legally allow it, leaving does not conform to the norms of strict piety. This value judgment and the restrictions on the duration of the absence should not allow us to overlook the essential point, which is that the obligation to reside in the Holy Land always enters into tension with other imperatives that are just as essential: to assure one's subsistence, to found a family and have descendants, to preserve oneself from the dangers of paganism, and to study the Law. Moreover, the land of Israel is not the only place that one ought not to leave: "In the same way as it is forbidden to leave the land to go abroad, it is forbidden to leave Babylonia for other countries, as it is written [Jer. 27:22] 'They shall be brought to Babylon, and there they shall remain [until I take note of them—declares the Lord of Hosts—and bring them up and restore them to this place].'"[13] It is as if alongside the obligation to reside in the Holy Land, there were another obligation: not to flee an exile decreed by God and to which God alone will put an end. In fact, it is precisely in this sense that a talmudic scholar had already used the same verse from Jeremiah (and much less equivocally than Maimonides) to establish that anyone who left Babylonia for the land of Israel transgressed a positive commandment.[14]

Another rule often invoked is the right of a husband who desires to live in the Holy Land to force his wife to emigrate or to repudiate her without penalty if she opposes this.[15] It is as if, at least in this case, attachment to the land of Israel overrode an institution (marriage and family) that was nonetheless fundamental to the survival of Judaism. As clear as the principle formulated for this case may appear, we have to recognize that medieval rabbis generally hesitated to apply it. It became apparent that emigration to the Holy Land was sometimes merely a pretext used by a husband to get rid cheaply of a spouse who had become troublesome. Anxious to assure the protection of the legitimate rights of the latter, some jurists refused to apply the talmudic rule when the purity of the husband's intentions was in doubt. Others obliged the woman to follow her husband only if moving did not imply too long a voyage and if there were no pirates to be feared along the way. As a general rule, the jurists judged it completely legitimate that concern for the wife, her children, and their subsistence should ultimately be more important than the desire to emigrate. They also recalled that it was permitted to quit the land of Israel to study Torah abroad, and that, if one could adequately study it in exile, there was no obligation to go to the Holy Land. A medieval Talmudist would go so far as to overturn the initial principle by maintaining that to live in the land of Israel could under no circumstances be held to be a religious duty as long as it proved difficult, if not impossible, to apply many of the land-related precepts of the Law there.

Here, as in the previous case, the jurists were in fact led to take actual circumstances into account—the dangers of the voyage, economic necessities, and various interests other than that of the land, such as intellectual aspirations, family unity, and so forth.[16] Inversely, when the circumstances changed, the rabbis' position could also change. Thus we observe a reversal of attitude in the Maghreb beginning in the second half of the eighteenth century. Until then, it was customary to allow a Jew who had decided to go to the Holy Land but who had eventually given up the idea to disengage himself from business commitments undertaken in preparation for the trip. It was also customary to grant to wives who refused to emigrate the total sum stipulated in their marriage contract in case of divorce. Then a new approach appeared, refusing a priori to limit the talmudic principle's scope. It no longer systematically accepted the pretext invoked by recalcitrant spouses, and it took into account the newfound safety and ease of transportation; it distinguished between certain dangers and those that were only potential; and in certain cases it pointed out that, objectively, it might be more dangerous to remain in an unstable Maghreb than to leave it.[17]

A third rabbinic dictum, to the effect that a person who lives outside the land of Israel is like someone who has no God, or even like someone who worships idols, is also enlisted by contemporary exegetes with a Zionist tendency.[18] Such an assertion has major consequences: it seems to threaten the principle of the universality of the Divine Presence and a priori to deprive Jewish life in the Diaspora of any legitimacy whatsoever. No doubt it was for this reason that Rashi limited this dictum's scope to the era when the Temple still existed, as well as to the Jew who *left* the Holy Land—as distinct from one who had been born in exile and who should not be reproached for continuing to live there.[19] Other medieval thinkers saw this precept as nothing more than the affirmation of God's particular providential relationship with the land of Israel, while certain Hasidic masters went so far as to subvert its meaning altogether. For them, where one lived mattered little: what counted was the place one thought about. Thus someone who was in the Holy Land but thought about his business in the Diaspora was *like* a man who has a God; in reality, he does not. Inversely, someone who was in the Diaspora but sincerely thought about the Holy Land was *like* a person without a God, but in reality he was the one who had a God. Basically, the believer living in the Diaspora was not required to emigrate but only to pray *imagining* that he prayed in the land of Israel, in the shadow of the rebuilt Temple. Does the "land" the famous precept spoke of in the end have anything to do with the Holy Land? Perhaps it should be understood only as this: to be "in the land" is to be stuck in the terrestrial and corporeal, and thus to imagine one has a God and yet not have one; inversely, to be "outside the land," meaning detached from corporeality, is to condemn oneself to be perpetually dissatisfied with oneself, to imagine oneself not having a God, whereas one is precisely the only one who really has a God. The reversal is now complete: the land has lost any properly local sense and has become a pure symbol of negativity!

Such examples fully demonstrate the vanity of efforts made by certain apologists. No anthology of dicta from the Mishnah or Talmud can ever, by itself, substantiate the idea that the Judaism of exile always asserted the absolute primacy of the obligation to reside in the Holy Land. It is sufficient to reinsert these dicta into the particular context of their appearance and to follow the exegeses to which they were subjected over the centuries in order to discover that medieval rabbinic hermeneutics was able to bring out the hidden complexity of apparently simple rules, and that it was prepared to take some liberties with the principle of noncontradiction.

The Duty of Aliyah *or the Duty of Exile?*

One author more than any other is regularly invoked to uphold the principle of a positive duty to reside in the land of Israel that is valid at any time, including during exile: Moses Nahmanides.[20] Nahmanides, who would himself make the voyage to the Holy Land and die in Acre in 1270, in effect relied on Num. 33:53 to establish the obligation of every Jew to live in the Holy Land, including under non-Jewish domination ("and you shall . . . settle in it"). It is not only in order to obey the commandments tied to the land that one ought to go; this departure is in itself a fundamental religious duty inscribed in the Torah. In a certain way, for Nahmanides, *all* commandments relate to the land— because it is only on its soil that their accomplishment acquires its whole theurgic value, and only there that Kabbalah, as he understood it, could be wholly realized. Of course, the risk of such a position is that it may empty religious life in exile of any substance. In fact, for Nahmanides, the observance of the Law in the Diaspora does have its own theurgic value; it manifests the constant authority of the Torah and symbolically expresses the universality of the divine Kingship.[21]

But it is still no less an interim solution, the condition for maintaining Jewish specificity, a kind of training with a view to a future realization that will be infinitely more complete in the Holy Land.

It is also true that in his Book of Commandments, Maimonides (to the great scandal of Nahmanides) did *not* include the obligation to reside in the land of Israel in his list of 613 basic prescriptions of Jewish law. According to one of his sixteenth-century commentators, this silence arose from the fact that for Maimonides, this obligation of residence, like that of conquering the Holy Land, did not have constraining value except in a given era, that of Moses, Joshua, and David, which it had since lost and would not recover until the messianic era. It is also possible that this absence resulted simply from the organizing principle chosen by Maimonides in his reckoning of commandments, where he distinguishes between principal ones (chapter headings) and derived ones (found under the chapter headings). In his legal code, the Mishneh Torah, Maimonides has the habit of starting with a basic commandment and then passing on to other provisions of biblical origin, as well as to rabbinic prescriptions that he thought were associated with it. Thus it was only after developing the prohibition against residing in Egypt, which is included among the 613 commandments, that Maimonides mentions, as a corollary, the obligation to reside in the Holy Land, the ban on leaving it, the love of the sages for its dust and stones, the expiatory virtues of its soil, and so on.[22] It is the Egyptian ban that is kept as chapter heading—a ban that Maimonides explains by the particularly deviant customs of that country's population, and that is only valid for the individual and when Egypt is in the hands of idolaters.[23]

Such a way of proceeding clearly reveals the major preoccupation of this great medieval jurist: the environment into which the Jew is going to be plunged really counts far more than the place. For Maimonides, we recall, it is not the simple fact of living outside the Holy Land that deprives the Jew in exile of the gift of prophecy, but actually the objective conditions of his existence, the oppression and fear of a foreign yoke weighing down on him. Were these objective conditions of existence so fundamentally different in a Holy Land then under Muslim jurisdiction, where Jews were clearly in the minority? Other jurists, especially in the Ashkenazi world, would usually insist on the limits that should circumscribe the desire of an individual to emigrate to the land of Israel. If it would be impossible for him to meet his needs reasonably, if the search for subsistence might oblige him to relinquish his study of the Torah, if the Holy Land did not possess places of study that were at least comparable with those of the Diaspora, and so on, then it would be better for him to remain in exile. In this instance, it was clearly study of the Torah that counted most. Love of the land only came afterward. A contemporary orthodox master like Moshe Feinstein would stress that if residence in the land of Israel really is an exalted act on the religious plane, it is not because it is obligatory but because it is meritorious—meaning that one who does so acquires merit, but one who does not has not committed a sin. In fact, how could rabbis have decreed a commandment that they knew perfectly well was impracticable in the circumstances?

In reality, any position taken on the nature of the link Israel preserved with its land throughout exile implied taking a position on the nature and purpose of exile itself. So if exile was an evil, it was not only that, and it was perhaps even also a good. Judaism could scarcely see it only as punishment for infidelity to the Law—unless it risked strangely echoing the Christian discourse. With its idea of a "City of God," the community of hidden elect, pilgrims wandering the world, Christianity had effectively appropriated the positive significance of exile in its dual aspect as religious propaganda and as suffering accepted for the salvation of humanity. At the same time, the real exile of the Jews themselves lost its sense of sacred history and became an object of mockery and contempt, a testimony to Christ's truth, the sign of the Covenant turning into the mark of Cain, that is to say, of the wandering of the penitent pilgrim.[24] Some Jewish commentators would therefore insist on the fact that it was more the nature of the land itself than Israel's sin that explained the exile: this land vomited out its inhabitants even if their sin was relatively minor. For others, exile and any aggravation of it corresponded to the birthpangs of the Messiah: any new expulsion was interpreted as exodus or as the beginning of exodus. According to Halevi and Maimonides, Christianity and Islam, born of Judaism, were a sort of divine ruse to bring the nations closer to authentic monotheism. In the sixteenth century, Israel was thought to have a beneficent influence on the beliefs of peoples among whom it resided. The simple fact that it had survived the eminently negative conditions of exile proved to the Gentiles, whose maneuvers were ultimately always confounded, the existence of God and the favor He continued to grant His people. In kabbalistic thought, finally, the scattering of Israel and the events of history became a means of assuring the reparation (*tikkun*) of cosmic catastrophes that had taken place before the beginning of history. It was not redemption (*geulah*) that brings reparation, but reparation that brings redemption. The Divine Presence had not abandoned Israel at all, but rather followed it in its exile.[25] Therefore, exile became a mission. Israel was charged with raising the sparks of sanctity that were dispersed around any place, or in the phrase of the Kabbalist Isaac Luria Ashkenazi in the sixteenth century, "gathering the lilies of holy souls scattered among the thorns."[26]

The theology of exile is thus susceptible to all kinds of inversion. For some a punishment for sin, for others, exile is sin itself. In some cases, to go into the Holy Land may take on the allure of a rebellion against divine sanction and in others, it is, on the contrary, the accomplishment of a positive commandment. Between these two extremes, when it is neither sanction nor sin but rather a mission, exile maintains an eminently dialectical relationship with the land of Israel. This relationship can tend, over time, to a blurring of frontiers, as when Naftali Bacharach asserted in the seventeenth century that the people of Israel dispersed and studying the Torah purified the air of the countries in which they resided, such that the whole world was called upon to become as pure as the land of Israel. This relationship could also be conceived of in terms of complementarity, with the Holy Land and the Diaspora each playing a specific and essential role in the dynamic of *tikkun*. But it was a relationship that in any case never made *aliyah*, "ascent" into the land of Israel, a trivial matter. It was, in fact, rarely encouraged and was most often restricted to a few, if not simply prohibited.

The Forbidden Land

The continuity of a migratory movement toward the Holy Land has often been invoked to attest to the force and concrete dimension of the attachment of Jews to their land. But nobody can deny that this migratory movement only ever involved an extremely small fraction of Jews, and that these displacements were sporadic. Why should we take this conduct, quite marginal on a demographic level, as more significant than the massive and undeniable fact that the overwhelming majority of the Jewish people perfectly well accommodated themselves to exile? We have to realize, to give but one example, that all the time that Palestine was under Arab Muslim domination (634 to 1099 C.E.), "ascent" toward the Holy Land remained a rare phenomenon. Although the Karaites called resolutely for departure, and while this appeal was sufficiently heard for Karaite colonies to appear in Jerusalem and Ramleh, one observes nothing of the kind in the normative Jewish world, where even cases of *yeridah* were viewed with relative indifference.[27] As for the few cases of "ascent" that were actually observed, they accompanied larger migratory movements, linked to economic distress or to the anarchy reigning in the Abbasid Caliphate in the tenth century.[28]

Moreover, the simple fact of a given individual's departure for the Holy Land does not in itself furnish any information about the exact nature of his attachment to the country where he has chosen to go. Thus the emigration of a man like Halevi, although it is traditionally appealed to by Zionist historiographers, has given rise to the most diverse interpretations. The impact of the Crusades, placing the Holy Land at the heart of the great confrontation between Islam and Christianity and resulting in the conquest of Jerusalem, has been evoked; so, too, have the degradation of the Jewish condition in Muslim Spain, with the pogrom in Granada in 1066, the Almoravid and then Almohad domination, and the fall of Toledo into Christian hands in 1085; Halevi's desire to expiate the sins of his youth, whether relating to doubts arising during his philosophical studies or to sexual promiscuity or even deviancy; his rejection of Jewish court life in Muslim Andalusia, which was skeptical, hedonistic, sure of itself, and yet fragile; and so forth. Ben-Zion Dinur (Dinaburg), a master of Zionist historiography, has even maintained that Halevi wanted to set an example and get the Jews to follow him, which seems very unlikely. Today, one thinks rather of the general context of messianic effervescence tied to advances in the Reconquista.[29] In any case, this need to grasp the motives for Halevi's decision only underlines its exceptional character; to remain was in any case much more natural.

As for specific collective migrations into the Holy Land, and if one excepts the development of a large community coming from Spain and Portugal to Galilee in the sixteenth century, historians agree on recognizing that it is finally not possible to discern a continuous wave before the 1740s. Then came immigration clusters, first of Sephardim, principally from other regions of the Ottoman Empire; next, the Hasidim of the 1760s and 1770s;[30] then the Perushim after 1808; and finally oriental Jewish immigrants, notably from Morocco, after the 1830s.[31] Here again, though, it is only too easy to misunderstand the causes and significance of these displacements. One cannot simply maintain that an amelioration in means of transport, the greater security of means of communication, and the political stability in the Holy Land were sufficient to liberate a secular aspiration and to allow its realization. In fact, in many cases, to leave was also to flee: with respect to the Ashkenazis, there was the pressure for Russification and the considerable growth of the Jewish population in the Pale of Settlement in Russia; while with respect to the oriental Jews, there was the poverty and instability of the Maghreb. Finally, one should beware of the illusions of perspective. Any collective migration is not the sign of collective adherence to a precise ideological project. Thus in 1777, three disciples of Dov Baer of Mezeritch arrived in the Holy Land accompanied by a group of about three hundred people. But that was certainly not a mass Hasidic immigration: the fact was that only a small handful of Hasidim left for the land of Israel, to whom a few hundred miserable travelers attached themselves en route, though having no ideological affinity with them; they were "parasites," in some sense, about whom the Hasidim complained bitterly and who upon arrival went on to join the ranks of the anti-Hasidic Ashkenazi party in the Holy Land.[32]

Observed behaviors, even when they appear identical, may denote radically divergent positions. There were not simply, on one side, those who considered the sanctity of the land of Israel to be intact and *aliyah* to be required of everybody, and, on the other, those, like the Kabbalist Ezra ben Solomon of Gerona in the thirteenth century, who instead urged their contemporaries to endure the sufferings of exile as a necessary expiation and who judged that whoever left for the Holy Land in fact abandoned the Divine Presence, which now resided where Israel had been scattered. The split was not always along neat lines. And just as love of the land and affirmation of its sanctity were by no means sufficient reasons for leaving, the very fact of leaving did not necessarily presuppose a repudiation of exile.

In fact, some people, far from denying the difference there might be between inhabiting the land of Israel and living in exile, still adopted a resolutely elitist point of view (as did the Kabbalist Yehuda Leib Pohowitzer at the end of the seventeenth century), judging that *aliyah* was a mission only for a minority of the righteous who were capable, by their actions in the Holy Land, of protecting all Israel and hastening deliverance. The Hasidim who came to live in the Holy Land saw themselves as an avant-garde, as emissaries and representatives of the Diaspora, and they preached a resolutely selective immigration.[33] The strongly asserted sanctity of the land of Israel was at least as frightening as it was attractive. This clearly appears from the writings of the 1777 immigrants. They knew that because of the exile of the Divine Presence, the land of Israel was the place in the world were the Divine was most humiliated—and that for this reason, it was in fact more difficult to realize oneself spiritually there than in Diaspora. But this lowest of descents was in their eyes at the same time, in accordance with an essential Hasidic principle, the means of the highest ascent. This is precisely why the leaders did not push their flocks to imitate them. The trip was only for exceptional people who would not be distracted from God's worship by these spiritual and material difficulties. The Hasidic leaders who settled in the Holy Land thus entered into a contract with the communities they had left in exile: they would endeavor to turn the divine influence they would be able to raise in the land of Israel to the benefit of the Diaspora, which for its part would only have to provide for their material needs.

The land of Israel required too much of its inhabitants for them to tread its soil with impunity. The extreme affirmation of its sanctity could have a highly dissuading impact. One of the great figures of German pietism in the thirteenth century, Eleazar ben Moses of Würzburg, would rely on this principle in one of the strongest warnings in Jewish literature against *aliyah*, comparing the Holy Land to the Mount Sinai of theophany: whoever approached it risked death.[34] Similarly, his contemporary Meir ben Baruch of Rothenburg warned candidates upon departure that sins committed in the land of Israel were much more heavily punished than those committed in exile; therein lay the meaning of Num. 13:32: "a country that devours its settlers."[35] Contemporary thinkers of religious and radical anti-Zionism would push this idea to its ultimate expression by making the Holy Land an arena of a cosmogonic conflict, played out between Ein-Sof and Satan,[36] a place where any immigrant should know that by his coming he was declaring war on evil and simultaneously risked exposing himself to its destructive influence; it was a place both divine and demonic, where only the best-armed combatants could survive without injury.

Like *aliyah* and the exaltation of the land of Israel, *aliyah* and messianism were equally related to each other in an ambivalent manner. There could be messianism without the pull of *aliyah*. The strong current of messianic expectations that appeared in the seventeenth century around the figure of Sabbatai Tsevi, it seems, had never conceived of emigration to the Holy Land as a priority, and the preoccupations of its ideologues were fundamentally more religious than political or territorial.[37] Inversely, there could be *aliyah* without messianic fervor. Thus, when emigration became common among scholars, particularly in the West, in the thirteenth century, and groups of Jews, French rabbis to the fore, settled in Jerusalem and in the Holy Land, their motivation was religious: they wanted to be able to perform the commandments linked to the land and thereby attain a degree of spiritual perfection. Their concern was concrete, practical, and legal: behind it lay no messianic effervescence, no mystical aspiration toward the sacred.

Moreover, for many, *aliyah* was only an acceptable step when it was not connected with a messianic fever; consequently, the mass movement toward the Holy Land observed in Castile in the second half of the fifteenth century was vigorously condemned as an attempt to hasten deliverance. Even when *aliyah* and messianic expectations went hand in hand, this did not necessarily mean that emigration was thought of as a way of precipitating the end—it could be merely a desire to "be there" and to prepare oneself to welcome redemption by performing positive acts. As a general rule, rabbinic Judaism appears to have been periodically divided between a desire to anticipate salvation, sometimes perceived as imminent, and fear of forcing it prematurely. Thus we can understand why each time a collective movement arose that was associated with strong messianic expectations, voices were heard warning against the risks of deviation and recalling the three "oaths" that, according to several classical rabbinic sources, forbade Israel to rebel against nations, to hasten the end, and to leave exile "like a wall" (i.e., collectively), while nations for their part were committed to "not subjugate Israel more than was reasonable."[38]

These oaths clearly expressed the principle of maintaining the status quo until God Himself decided to deliver Israel. Contrary to a common opinion, the insistence upon these oaths is not of recent origin. Ultra-Orthodox anti-Zionists and Orthodox Jews who favored emancipation in exile were not the first to have recourse to them to justify their positions. Far from being simply perceived as a homiletic elaboration without legal bearing, these oaths have in fact been regularly used since the Middle Ages to establish the principle of a dissociation from the Holy Land and to put a brake on the impulse to leave exile en masse. This was used by thinkers who attributed a deep theological, symbolic, and mystical significance to Jewish life in the Diaspora.

However, the prohibition in the "oaths" raised at least two kinds of questions. The first was whether it applied only to the group, precluding only mass departure and thus leaving the individual free to go to the Holy Land. In fact, this was the generally accepted option: thus, a distinction was made between emigration by an individual, whose meritorious act attracted a blessing on himself, and a collective break with exile, which was clearly reprehensible. While it was thought that, until redemption, the Holy Land could aid in the sanctification of righteous individuals, on the other hand, it was exile that purified the nation as a whole. The second question was whether the ban on leaving was linked to the principle of not rebelling against the nations, and whether it was sufficient to obtain permission from the nations for this ban on mass *aliyah* to lapse. The answers to this question varied, too, of course. But for many people, this ban was valid in all circumstances, and still today some sectors of ultra-Orthodox opinion will not admit that the 1947 UN resolution concerning the creation of a Jewish state sufficed to make these oaths null and void.

Encounters with Palestine

This being so, whether emigration was individual or collective, indifferently encouraged or expressly reserved for an elite, it was never the only way for Diaspora Jews to concretely express their attachment to the real Holy Land; nor was emigration the sole means, in the Diaspora, to keep in effective contact with the Jewish Palestinian communities. The importance, if not the necessity, of maintaining such contact was variously felt in different periods and places. The factors largely contributing to it were messianic excitement, a numerical strengthening of the Jewish colony in the Holy Land, and a rise in the influence of its scholars and academies.

Such was the case in the sixteenth century when the settlement of a large number of Jews who had been chased out of Spain and Portugal and an influx of remarkable jurists and Kabbalists once again gave life and prestige to a Palestinian community that again became, thanks to them, if not *the* center, then at least one of the major centers of the Jewish world. This Jewish resurrection of the Holy Land in the sixteenth century has been much studied, and sometimes has been seen as laying the foundation for a reconstruction that would not be fully realized until the contemporary era. People have been tempted to interpret the efforts of Rabbi Jacob Berab, who settled in Safed, to restore the institution of the Sanhedrin in Palestine, as the expression of a desire to establish the Holy Land as the legal and political center of the Jewish world as a whole. Similarly, the reconstruction of a Jewish Tiberias (with the backing of the Ottoman authorities and under the auspices of two powerful Sephardic benefactors, Doña Gracia Mendes and her nephew Don Joseph Nassi) has often been understood as resulting from "a grand design that was part of a general current of Jewish Renaissance."[39] But Jacob Berab's initiative failed, and no Sanhedrin saw the light of day, notably because of the ferocious opposition of the rabbinic authorities of Jerusalem. Likewise, a grave economic crisis at the end of the century ruined the new city of Tiberias and emptied it of its Jewish inhabitants.

If the Holy Land did not succeed in regaining an indisputable centrality comparable to the one it had enjoyed, for example, in the time of the Mishnah, its influence was nevertheless assured thanks to the polymorphous activity of its scholars. Here was where Isaac Luria and his disciples developed a form of the Kabbalah that would radiate well beyond its borders, and where lived Joseph Caro, the author of the *Shulhan 'Arukh* (Prepared Table), a legal code that became authoritative in the whole Jewish world—although it had to be completed by the commentaries of an Ashkenazi scholar of the Diaspora, his contemporary Moses Isserles. It was then, too, that the center of gravity of the Holy Land itself, in fact as well as in imagination, passed from Jerusalem to Safed, a Galilean city. Several factors combined to return primacy to this region. An economic boom and political stability fused with the memory of the status that Galilee had formerly acquired at the end of the ancient period, when Palestinian Judaism retreated after the catastrophes of 70 and 135 C.E. Simeon bar Yohai, the second-century Palestinian master whom the Kabbalists held to be the author of the Zohar, was buried in Meron, and Luria and Caro were buried in Safed. The route that led from Safed to Meron was punctuated with the tombs of venerated scholars.[40] According to an ancient tradition revived by immigrants to Safed, it was in the north of the Holy Land, that is, in Galilee, that the Messiah would reveal himself and that the resurrection of the dead would begin. This conjunction of objective facts and mythic glory explains why, beginning in the second half of the eighteenth century, other immigrants, this time from the northern lands of the Ashkenazi world, converged in their turn on Galilee, around Safed or around Tiberias, the Hasidim's preferred destination.

The strengthening of Palestinian Jewish communities, and the prestige that they enjoyed in the Diaspora as outposts of the Jewish world, but also their economic dependence upon the exile communities, largely account for the concrete ties that developed between the Jews of the Holy Land and the Jews of the Diaspora. Paradoxically, the very intensity of these ties contributed a good deal to preventing the Jewish population of the Holy Land from establishing itself as a specifically Palestinian colony. Once there, Ashkenazim, Sephardim, and oriental Jews of all backgrounds never ceased to be conscious of their own identities. All of them lived, and were conscious of living, in the Holy Land itself, in an eminently exilic situation, where they depended upon the goodwill of non-Jewish authorities. These communities did not fuse but instead formed a sort of microcosm of the Diaspora. In some respects, they even had much closer ties with their communities of origin than with one another.[41] And whereas some Jewish cities in the Diaspora called themselves "Jerusalem in exile," Tiberias readily became a "little Meknes" in common parlance, owing to the large number of its residents who came from that Moroccan city.

Living with their backs turned to the land and their gaze directed toward exile, the Palestinian Jewish populations, for whom study and prayer were the principal activity, depended materially on the aid poured out by the Diaspora. There, charity toward scholars and the poor of the Holy Land was perceived as an essential religious duty. There was even regular agitation around the question of whether it was more urgent to rescue distant brothers than to alleviate the hardships of the community at hand, while regulations were issued banning the use of the funds gathered for the land of Israel for any other purpose. It was this imperative that a few swindlers periodically sought to exploit by passing themselves off as Palestinian emissaries or by fraudulently using outdated accreditations.[42] In the Holy Land itself, the management of gifts from the Diaspora was entirely in the hands of the Sephardim, who alone were responsible to the Ottomans for paying the tax owed by the Palestinian Jewish collectivity—until the Hasidim succeeded in emancipating themselves from this tutelage.[43] In the Diaspora, the collection, concentration, and conveying of the sums gathered was often assured and controlled by centralized organizations, with various ramifications. The local or regional notables who assumed this responsibility might carry titles as prestigious and ambiguous as "master" or "prince of the land of Israel."[44] By necessitating contacts and collaboration at the international level, the centralization of the system of aid to the Holy Land had the effect of strengthening the ties among the exile communities themselves.

From the sixteenth to the twentieth centuries, a similar yet different role was played by the emissaries regularly sent into the Diaspora by Jewish institutions and communities in the Holy Land in quest of funds. These emissaries were scholars, and they often intervened in the internal life of the communities they visited with the authority conferred on them by their erudition and especially by their place of origin. They were, in some ways, the Holy Land coming to meet the Diaspora. Their physical presence incarnated a dream and offered Jews in exile the opportunity to touch something from the real land of Israel. But they were also the sole means for these communities to enter into contact with *other kinds* of Jews, as when a Sephardic envoy crisscrossed Lithuania or when an Ashkenazi visited Yemen.[45] The long peregrinations of emissaries, their incontestable prestige, and the needs for which they made themselves the spokesmen all manifested the ties of dependence that united the land of Israel and the Diaspora, while simultaneously consecrating the centrality of the Holy Land—essentially as a place of study and prayer, however. Their activities made the land, land of dreams and of actual neediness, play a dual and ambiguous role—between the affirmation of the unity of the Jewish world and the revelation, in estrangement, of its irreducible diversity.

Voyagers and "Geographers"

To receive a letter from a relative or friend who had settled for good in the Holy Land or to hear the tales of a passing emissary was still just an indirect way for a Jew in exile to apprehend the realities of Palestine.

The best way to discover them without going so far as emigration properly speaking was a pilgrimage.[46] As a medieval phenomenon, pilgrimage to the land of Israel, however, had little to do with its ancient model, which the Temple's destruction had rendered useless. It was by no means a religious obligation, and no prescription concerning it can be found in the great codes of Jewish Law. Traveling to Jerusalem was not presented as a normative act, and even the ethical literature does not recommend it as an act of penitence. But pilgrimage to the Holy Land was still valued by communities, and pilgrims enjoyed an undeniable aura, even if they had to deal with the understandable hostility of abandoned wives and families. Thus, Crimean Karaites who left in the seventeenth and eighteenth centuries were honored on their return with the title of "Yerushalmi" (Hierosolymite), which they kept until their deaths and had engraved on their tombs. Many set off as a result of a vow made in a difficult time, for example, during an epidemic, or as thanksgiving for some happy event. Departure was preceded by psychological preparation: one tried to obtain pardon from all those one had offended, one promised to change one's life upon one's return, and so on. But people knew that they were taking grave risks, and the expenses of the trip had to be covered. Some left with their savings; others tried to get from one community the wherewithal to get to the next one; scholars taught or sold a book printed along the way.

The accounts that many of these pilgrims, some famous and others less so, have left of their voyages are a good means of grasping the significance they gave to the venture and the way they perceived the places and peoples met en route. Many of these accounts are veritable guidebooks—religious, touristic, commercial, and financial—practical manuals of a sort intended for travelers. But they are usually much more than that. The Holy Land as a Near Eastern reality was not the only, or sometimes even the principal, subject of these narratives. Thus in the twelfth and thirteenth centuries there was a great difference in attitude between Sephardic and Ashkenazi pilgrims: while the latter focused on holy sites and the tales of miracles associated with them, the former were at pains to evoke everything they encountered, whether Jewish or not, and sprinkled their tales with economic, political, and ethnographic jottings. Italian Jewish travelers of the fifteenth and sixteenth centuries, for their part, manifested a universal curiosity, an acuity of observation, and a desire for comparison that are totally remarkable—since to go to Israel was for them also a way of discovering the world in its splendid diversity. Moreover, the frontiers of pilgrimage's geography were not at all to be confused with those of the Holy Land in the strict sense; in fact, some nearby countries in which there was an ancient and prestigious Jewish presence, like Syria and Iraq, enjoyed an equivalent status.

In addition, going to the land of Israel did not imply that one visited it in its entirety or that one studied all its aspects. The Karaites went only to Jerusalem, because the only Karaite community was there. Many a traveler scarcely explored more than Galilee. On top of that, any new visit always had a taste of déjà vu. Highly sought by the pilgrim, sites and landscapes never offered themselves innocently to his gaze. The surprise they could arouse in him was born more of a sentiment of strange familiarity than an awareness of confrontation with the unknown. In the twelfth century, the traveler Petahia of Regensburg recounted that after having visited the tomb of Judah the Prince, the editor of the Mishnah, he met a living descendent of his, a certain Nehorai, himself the son of a certain Judah and possessing a family tree proving his noble ancestry. There was no estrangement here! Geographical displacement above all allowed him to weave together written testimonies (the Mishnah, genealogies) in a reassuring temporal continuity, less historical than cyclical (the circular renewal of generations). At the site of his pilgrimage, the pilgrim obtained confirmation of a filiation and a unity that defied the unfolding of time and the breakup of space. At the end of the fifteenth century, the Italian commentator Obadiah of Bertinoro, in his *Letter from Jerusalem*, was stupefied to find the Jewish past to be present and incarnated in the land; he marveled to find that places had kept their biblical names and that the grapes of a certain valley were still exceptionally large.[47] The land was merely a palpable and living reflection of the Book. The letter triumphed over any historical—or geographical—considerations. Sometimes a tradition about the presence of the sepulcher of a saint in a given place arose solely because of the resemblance between the names of saint and site. Two common letters, or even one, sufficed. At Kfar Nahum, one honored the tombs of the Prophet Nahum and Rabbi Tanhuma, a Palestinian sage of the fourth century; at Hukuk, one found the tomb of Habakkuk.[48]

Imaginary tales and stereotyped descriptions were easily mixed with the traveler's immediate observations and personal impressions, erecting a screen between the reader and the real. Moreover, with the exception of the Western Wall, the Temple Mount, and the cavern of the prophet Elijah at Carmel, all the holy sites visited were tombs. The vestiges of ancient sanctuaries, disused synagogues, and even places where sacred history relates that miracles occurred in Israel's favor did not become sites of pilgrimage.[49] The tombs visited, of which more than five hundred have been counted, attracted most especially Oriental and Hasidic pilgrims. Sometimes one has the feeling that for these voyagers, the Holy Land was, in fact, just an immense necropolis. It is certain that these sepulchers projected onto the explored space a certain number of temporal vantage points. They were the geographical and earthly inscription of founding moments in Israel's history on its soil—but also elsewhere than on its soil. But since it was essentially a matter of the tombs of saints, prophets, and scholars, ancient or more modern, this geography bore the traces of a history that had no intrinsic tie with the site, since it is a history of Jewish science that is independent of space and time data. It was the person buried there who conferred on the site its status as holy—and who gratified its visitors with endlessly retold miracles. Worship was rendered as much to the teaching that the sage incarnated as to his person or the ground into which he had been received. Because of him, in hope of a cure, a sick or painful limb was coated with the oil of lamps burning on his tomb or a plaster was made with dust from the site. The saint was not dead; his soul was always living and active on the site of his burial. In the visits made by the Kabbalists of the Safed School, a junction was created between the soul of the believer and that of the deceased, which then came back to life and the light and could be made to speak; one learned things from it, secrets of the Torah—and the same life and light entered into the visitor's soul. The visit itself was called separation, or divorce (*gerushin*), because the pilgrim separated himself from ties to this world and sanctified himself in honor of the Divine Presence residing there. The tomb was a place to escape from place.

"Heaven's Gate," the Holy Land of pilgrims, was an essentially subterranean reality. The sepulchers visited were often situated in grottoes—and often grottoes that had been emptied of their contents! The revered body was generally reputed to have been placed in a *second* grotto, buried and sealed up, situated underneath the open and accessible grotto. A tree planted nearby, plunging its roots into the soil, was sometimes a sacred tree that it was forbidden to cut down and whose fruits could not be picked. Similarly, a spring that flowed nearby was generally credited with a particular therapeutic virtue, which was not the case with the "surface" waters of Lake Tiberias (the Sea of Galilee), the Jordan, or even the Red Sea. Benjamin of Tudela, a great traveler of the twelfth century, evokes the existence under Mount Zion of a fabulous cavern containing the remains of the kings of Israel, a scepter, and a crown—a cavern inadvertently discovered one day, but since then totally inaccessible.

What preoccupied the pilgrim, what he sought and could never really find on the ground he trod, was the essence of the land of Israel, a symbolic land, vector of meaning, buried deep in the earth's entrails, nested in the highest firmament. This essence evoked both death (under the earth) and survival (in Heaven)—never the simple life here below, *on* earth and *under* the sky. Punctuated by visits to tombs and grottoes, the earthly itinerary of the voyager strangely anticipated the subterranean itinerary that, according to ancient tradition, the body of a Jew buried in the Diaspora would follow in the time of the resurrection, when the Lord would make him migrate from cavern to cavern right to the Holy Land and there give him life again.[50] More a spiritual itinerary than a change of locale, the voyage to the land of Israel had a virtue in itself that far outstripped its earthly destination: it was probably for this reason that a Hasidic master like Nahman of Bratslav thought he had accomplished his mission as soon as he had set foot on the sacred soil and so decided to leave again without delay.[51]

In these circumstances, we should not be surprised that questions of pure geography rarely preoccupied Jewish scholars.[52] Medieval commentators were reduced to making conjectures to interpret the passages from the Bible and the Talmud that related to the geography of the Holy Land; rare were those who, having settled there, could rely on their own observations. These questions did not take on a pressing quality until they had precise legal implications, which could only be the case in the Holy Land itself. We see Galilean rabbis of the sixteenth-century revival ask gravely and expertly where the border between the land of Israel and Syria (where the rules of the sabbatical year did not apply with the same rigor) lay exactly, and what status to grant certain frontier zones of the Holy Land, in view of the obligation to observe a second feast day in the Diaspora.[53] But that kind of thing remained exceptional. And in the middle of the eighteenth century, Moshe Yerushalmi, an Ashkenazi, probably of Polish origin, who had settled in Galilee, wrote a description of the Holy Land for pilgrims, which he pretended was entirely based on his own voyages, whereas careful study of his text shows that he had manifestly never set foot in Hebron or Jerusalem and that, with respect to everything but eastern Galilee, his information is uncertain and secondhand—to the point where his surname "Hierosolymite" appears to have been usurped.[54]

The first book of general and Palestinian geography to appear in Yiddish was the work of a proselyte, Moshe bar Abraham, at the beginning of the eighteenth century.[55] The author relies on two sources, one Jewish and Hebraic, the *Epistle of the World's Routes* (Iggeret Orhot Olam) by Abraham Farissol, written in Ferrara in 1525, and the other Christian, the German translation of a Latin work by Petrus Bertius published for the first time in 1600. Moshe bar Abraham's text itself contains two parts: one is devoted to diverse legendary Jewish elements, like the theme of the ten lost tribes, which he borrowed from Farissol; the other is a general geography, including a particularly elaborate description of the land of Israel. This inhomogeneous mixture of authentic scientific culture of Christian origin, on the one hand, and of mythological curiosity of Jewish origin, on the other, is highly significant. The legendary geography is Jewish; the positive geography is Christian. And the evocation of the Holy Land as it was, as an objective geographical reality, is entirely drawn from Bertius, only appearing precisely in the "Christian" part of the book. It is as if, deprived of its mythic dimension, Palestine was no longer, or not yet, fully part of the Jewish mental universe.

Nostalgia

There is a fascinating ambiguity about the ties that exiled Israel knitted over the centuries with its land, and that even the pilgrim's observations or the geographer's descriptive concern could not manage to resolve. A short tale by the Nobel Prize-winning Israeli author Shmuel Yosef Agnon, a fable drawing on traditional Jewish material, perhaps expresses the nature of this ambiguity better than any analysis:

> A sick old man was advised by his doctors to drink goat's milk. But the goat he bought kept disappearing and the searches for her hiding-place were fruitless. She would come back by herself, her udder full of milk "that was sweeter than honey and whose taste was the taste of Eden." To elucidate this mystery, the son of the old man devised a stratagem: he attached a cord to the goat's tail and as soon as she looked about to leave, he grabbed it and followed her. The goat led him to the entry of a cave where a long subterranean journey began, lasting "for an hour or two, or maybe even a day or two." At the other end of the tunnel, the young man discovered a marvelous country that was soon identified for him as the land of Israel. He understood that it was because the goat fed there, very near Safed, on plump and sweet carobs and because she drank from the fountains of the Holy Land that this goat gave such good milk. Seeing men "like angels" greeting the Sabbath Queen, the young man decided not to leave for home. With the special ink that scribes use to write Torah scrolls, he penned a note to his father and slipped it into the goat's ear, in the hope that his father, upon seeing her come back, would caress her so she would flick her ears and the note would fall out. The goat did indeed go back, but she did not flick her ears and the desperate old man was convinced that his son was dead, that some savage beast had devoured him en route. In anger, he had the goat slaughtered— and only then did the note fall out. Upon reading it, the old man discovered new and more serious reasons to lament: he could have

gone "in one bound" to the Holy Land, but with the goat dead and his guide gone, he was condemned to "suffer out his days in this exile"! Since that time, the mouth of the cave has remained hidden and there is no longer a shortcut to the land of Israel. And the youth, "if he has not died, shall bear fruit in his old age . . . calm and peaceful in the Land of the Living."[56]

Perhaps the sick old man is Israel and the milk that keeps him from perishing is the dream, both carnal and ethereal, of a distant land. But this land, although it exists, is a dreamland, exiled at the other end of time and space, in a time that is not of time and a space that is not of space. The people who live there are already angels; only a humble goat has retained the instinct, both natural and mysterious, to find its way there. The underground voyage that alone leads to it has something to do with death and resurrection. And if, meanwhile, access is practically forbidden, this must have something to do with sin. In the old man's hands—in Israel's hands—there remains only this note written in the ink of the sacred scrolls: the Book that speaks of the land and promises it.

In the modern era, a small part of the Jewish people, as if suddenly rejuvenated, would no longer be satisfied with the promise. They would try to make a reality of the dream, and make of political and pioneering activity a "shortcut" leading back at last to the rerootedness so ardently desired. But far from being an abrupt reversal, this newfound modernity of the land would continually be nourished by the revitalized images of its ancient and medieval eras. Galvanized by invigorating contact with the ideologies and nationalisms of a seething Europe, could the Jewish militants of the new era ever totally exorcise the seductions of the Book, and without it open up for themselves the improbable route to an improbable land?

Part Two   Metamorphoses

Five The Rediscovered Land

As we have seen, during the centuries of dispersal, the meanings of the words *Zion* and *exile* varied astonishingly, although the two concepts remained organically linked. If exile existed, it was in fact because there had been a Zion; exile could only be thought of in reference to a lost land. Still, both exile and the land of which people spoke had been spiritualized; they had largely moved beyond their corresponding political and historical realities. Zion appeared to be a metaphysical homeland that people carried with them wherever they went. Along this journey, religion had served as the glue holding together the dispersed Jewish populations. Within this religion, the land of Israel was a kind of founding myth, while Jews for many generations had been profoundly cut off from the Palestinian geopolitical entity. Having become so abstract, the land could only function as a symbol and so it could not help but lose a large part of its emotional charge, at least in the hearts of those who began to turn their attention outside the Jewish world.

"Here" and "There"

In any case, the complexity of the Jews' relationship to the land was not attenuated with their entry into modernity, the most striking consequences of which would eventually be emancipation—and its corollary, integration. Rather, that relationship took on new meanings in addition to the existing ones.

For the seventeenth-century philosopher Baruch Spinoza, who was of Marrano origin, and then for Moses Mendelssohn, the eighteenth-century father in Berlin of the Jewish Enlightenment known as the Haskalah, both of whom are hailed as founders of modern Jewish thought, the land of Israel played a peripheral role.[1] For Spinoza, Israel's election had disappeared when it stopped exercising sovereignty over its territory. The land of Israel was not the object of particular care on the part of the Creator, and no specific holiness was attached to it. This being so, and understanding the mutability of things human and supposing that their religious principles might cease to soften their hearts, Spinoza admitted readily that an opportunity could arise for Jews to reestablish their empire.[2] Spinoza, and after him Mendelssohn, who advocated that the Jews leave the ghetto, transformed them into a nation among others. Among the latter's disciples, the idea of a symbolic Jerusalem, image of redemption, soon led to the notion of Israel's mission among the Gentiles. This tendency took shape in eighteenth-century Jewish thought, and it would prevail for almost two centuries—at least in the West. The French Revolution, which made Jews citizens in 1790–91, and then the Napoleonic Wars, which extended Jewish emancipation to other European countries, gave this idea a new legitimacy.

The intellectual and cultural movements born in the wake of this dynamic advanced the universalism of Israel's mission. Such was the case among Reform Jews in nineteenth-century Germany, who strove to give the Jewish religion as acceptable an image as possible to the non-Jews around them, a "civilized" image, adapted to the modernity that Judaism was adopting in its desire to obtain the legal emancipation that was still beyond its reach—despite the integration that was occurring. The prayer books of Berlin services at the beginning of the century modified or omitted passages that called upon God to gather together the people of Israel and to restore them to their own soil.[3] The Reform Jews neither hoped nor wished for a return to Jerusalem to reconstruct the Temple. The beginning of the Reform movement in the United States, inspired by the German model, was equally marked by this tendency to suppress references to a return to Zion. But it would be the German Reform Jews who would go farthest in this direction, investing all their hopes in an emancipation within their adopted countries. Even for German neo-Orthodoxy, a current generally opposed to Jewish Reform, aiming to reconcile rigorous observance of the laws and customs of rabbinic Judaism with the requirements of modern society, the independence of Israel on its land in the ancient period did not play a prime role. This was a fundamental shift away from the traditional vision that associated the abstract symbol with an earthly locale that was always present, if distant.

These thinkers and movements finally detached the present and future of Jews from any tie with the land of Israel and eliminated any dream of a future restoration of a Jewish state: they effectively deterritorialized the symbol. The messianic hopes were transferred to European soil, and therein lay the principal novelty. The Judaism of central Europe played an important role in the conceptualization of this unprecedented phase in the history of the Jews' relationship to Zion. Perhaps it was because integration had preceded legal emancipation there, leading its proponents to demonstrate a certain zeal for universalism. In any case, the price of successful integration demanded a detachment from the land of Israel: the country of adoption had to be established to be a New Jerusalem. In certain non-Jewish milieux, the attachment of Jews to the land of Israel was perceived as in contradiction with the rising tendency for them to fuse with the surrounding society. This was true also in France, but in central Europe, Jews still had to *merit* the full citizenship to which they aspired.

While nineteenth-century Reform thinkers like Abraham Geiger, the neo-Orthodox Samson Raphael Hirsch, and Nahman Krochmal, the master of the eastern European Jewish Enlightenment, each in his own way made himself a spokesman of this break with tradition, other and more subtle voices continued to make themselves heard in that region. Among these was that of the historian Heinrich Graetz, an eminent representative of the "science of Judaism" developed in German-speaking countries.[4] While the Jewish reformers in Mendelssohn's sphere of influence did their utmost to deny the political nature of Judaism in order not to be accused of constituting a state within a state, Graetz clearly affirmed the contrary and insisted on Judaism's political and geographical dimensions. In his eyes, "the Torah, the Israelite nation and the Holy Land are interconnected by an almost magical relation, they are indissolubly united by an indestructible link."[5] The Jewish people had developed their identity in the desert before their entry into the land of Israel, and they had to do the same after their dispersal, to preserve their integrity outside the mother country through faith in a messianic future. Between the historic past and the future redemption on ancestral soil, there was exile, during which Israel experienced an intense life that filled the territorial void. For Graetz, Judaism was indeed inseparable from the land of Israel, even though he sought to legitimize Jewish life within the European political and social order. On this point, he situated himself somewhere between Orthodox and Reform Jews, and by making political sovereignty the essence of Judaism, he undeniably opened the way to Jewish nationalist considerations, which borrowed a great deal from the various European nationalisms being deployed at that time.

Like the German Jews, the French Jews, including the most conservative of them, did not consider themselves to be in exile and felt little nostalgia for Jerusalem. They saw themselves as a religion, not a people, and Zion was for them no more than a fragment of historical memory. They, too, believed in Israel's mission in the Diaspora. The loss of Alsace and Lorraine to Germany in 1871, the rise of anti-Semitism (of which the anti-republican extreme right became the champion), and finally French Jews' attachment to the values of liberty, equality, and fraternity all disposed them to adhere to the republican regime. For them, the French Revolution had realized Judaism's grand ideals of justice and progress, and the French Republic was pursuing its work by constructing a society founded upon these same ideals. Thus between republican France and the Jews, there was not only a common interest but also a common identity. The Jewish Orientalist James Darmesteter theorized this synthesis of Jewish, progressive, and French values. Beginning with emancipation's first generation, a few voices like those of Alexandre Weill and Joseph Salvador had already expressed themselves in favor of a more or less similar combination. This Franco-Judaism presided over a shift from the term *Juif* to *israélite*, leading to the (at least apparent) abandonment of the notion of a Jewish people—specifically, of a collective culture and identity going beyond the framework of religious rites and beliefs.

In America, Simon Wolf, the leader of B'nai Brith,[6] declared in 1888 that the United States was "our Home, our Palestine" and added that "we have no other ambition than to prosper in this land of our adoption to whose growth—material, social, and intellectual—we have contributed our share."[7] Hence religion was what defined the Jew, to such an extent that Wolf preferred that people call him a Jew rather than a Hebrew or Israelite, two terms that seemed for him to have a tribal connotation. As we have just seen, *israélite* was the term favored by Wolf's French counterparts because it was perceived as having no pejorative connotation or national significance. The diversity of preferred terminologies does not, however, detract from the unity of inspiration that presided over their development. When the religious dimension did prevail, other Jews of a liberal tendency had no difficulty stressing the universal character of Judaism's message as valid for all of humanity and not just as reserved for a separatist sect. Therefore, within this framework there was no conflict whatsoever between confessional membership and acculturation. Even after the foundation of French political Zionism, Gustave Kahn, writing in the columns of the *Soir* newspaper in Brussels, offered a socialist and universalist echo of Wolf's declarations: "the new Jerusalem will be the whole realm, the whole socialist realm."[8] For a thinker like Hermann Cohen, the "Promised Land" was the moral world as it was deployed through history; in the eyes of Franz Rosenzweig, any reterritorialization of the Jewish people—who were a "people of the world"—would be a regression. The land of Israel, in being disconnected from reality, melded into something universal.

Consequently, these personalities thought the Jewish question must be resolved in the Diaspora and neither in Palestine nor in any country reserved for Jews alone. As between "here" and "there," certain circles clearly preferred "here." Yiddish had a word to name this choice—*doikeyt* or "being here," in contrast to the "being there" of the Zionists and Jewish territorial nationalists. "Being here" expressed a solid attachment to the lands where Jews actually lived and a ferocious opposition to their being transferred to a specifically Jewish territory; on the other hand, *doikeyt* did not imply any basic hostility to emigration. At this same period, Jews were eager to proclaim the depth and antiquity of their roots in their adopted countries. Liberal Jews and their associations advocating the Russification or Polonization of their co-religionists had confidence in the present and the future of the Diaspora. However, they did not demand total fusion with the surrounding society, meaning a renunciation of any Jewish identity; rather, their credo was integration. The heroes they hailed when they looked back over the Jewish past were neither kings nor warriors but the prophets, whose universalist message might permit the linking of historic Judaism and Christianity. Such liberals tried at all costs to find spiritual and historical affinities with the host populations that would be sufficiently strong; this was compounded by a patriotic fervor that did not tire of proclaiming the names of Jews who had died on the field of honor for the greater glory of their adopted countries.

While these patriots sought the solution to the Jewish question in integration, the diasporic nationalists turned their hopes in a different direction. Whereas for the former, being Jewish amounted to simple confessional membership, the latter put the nation to the fore. These two currents of modern times developed within quite different contexts. Diasporic nationalism was born within the eastern European context, while Jewish patriotism took root in societies where Jews were already emancipated, or at least integrated. Diasporic nationalists or autonomists believed in the possibility of the Jewish nation prospering in the Diaspora lands, so it was not necessary to reassemble the nation and transfer it to a specific place. They hoped to get the governments of the host countries to grant civic equality to the Jews as individuals, and simultaneously to recognize them as a national minority, possessing legally defined rights, especially in the cultural realm—which might entail, for example, the financing of Yiddish schools by the state. Their claims exceeded demands for emancipation and integration, and in fact testified to the impossibility of realizing such demands in the countries concerned. The Socialist Bund[9] and the "Folkists," a small nationalist and autonomist party, defended comparable positions on this issue. The Bund called for a cultural autonomy founded on the Yiddish language and demanded that the Jewish community have the right to live as a national minority. The historian Simon Dubnov, considered the founding father of diasporic nationalism, insisted in his writings on the autonomy that the Jews had actually enjoyed in the Diaspora in the postbiblical period; theirs was a legally recognized autonomy, as witnessed by the existence in eastern Europe of institutions like the Council of Four Lands in Poland and the Council of Lithuania. In the sixteenth and seventeenth centuries, this self-government, Dubnov explained, had allowed Polish Jews to create their own national culture. Such arguments led Jewish nationalists to want to collaborate with other European nationalities who were deprived of power in order to create a multinational environment in eastern Europe able to allow all these groups, including the Jews, to develop their specific cultures as they had in the past. This optimistic vision would last into the 1930s among the defenders of a Jewish future in the Diaspora.

Again in eastern Europe, the movement of Jewish Enlightenment that had begun in Germany enjoyed a new upsurge in the nineteenth century. Contrary to the various currents mentioned up to this point, the eastern European Haskalah saw cultural emancipation as a preliminary step toward political emancipation, and its writings gave a larger place to Zion, if only by means of a return to scriptural literary models. But the Zion of these writers was an idea, a legend, and an illusion, still quite removed from the real land of Israel.[10] For them, the land was still—and above all—the Book, an image, nourished by centuries of religious tradition, given weight only by the tirelessly revisited Book itself. For the integrationists, as for the diasporic nationalists, Palestine was essentially a memory—a memory threatened by forgetting, a memory with no return.

This memory without return was also that of Orthodox Jews, even if they appeared to have little in common with all the varieties of "new Jews" who had appeared in western and eastern Europe, born thanks to a political breakthrough or else aspiring to achieve one. Their memory of the Promised Land was inhabited by the continuity between an idealized past and a messianic future, itself understood as the restoration of Jewish sovereignty. For the Orthodox, Jews were a priori a religious nation, God's People, and to quote a phrase that was current in Yiddish, they defined themselves primarily as *toyre traye*—"faithful to the Torah." Their ingathering in the land of Israel was not to be achieved without divine intervention, because it did not depend on human will alone. For the Orthodox, the period in Diaspora was not as a rule an end in itself, as could be the case for the integrationists and diasporic nationalists, but rather a preliminary stage—though of unpredictable duration. It was considered an exile, a punishment for sins committed, and at the same time it was the framework for the realization of the Jews' spiritual mission as the chosen people. Human efforts to put an end to it were futile, if not outrageous. Consequently, we may understand the negative reactions that the Jewish national renaissance would later provoke in these circles. But at that time, Orthodoxy was not monolithic and embraced various positions on both emancipation and Zionism.

During this nineteenth century in full effervescence, in whichever milieu one looks, Jewish understanding of the land always appears engaged with an idealized past, a symbolic present, and a messianic future. The literature produced by the Haskalah in eastern Europe shows all the traits of a mythic land whose seductive power was perhaps all the more irresistible because Jews were cut off, not only from the ancestral land, but also from *any* cultivated land. But perhaps it would be excessive to generalize, for here and there were some exceptions to this uprootedness, which was caused by the restrictions that had long circumscribed Jewish life in Christian lands. In the Muslim world, moreover, the relationship between Jews and the soil of their places of residence was less abstract. However, as a general rule, to possess the land and to belong to it were not what characterized the existential condition of the Diaspora Jew. This alienated relation to the land was even one of the criticisms leveled against the Jew, who was as much alienated from his historic land, now transformed into a "unifying" memory, as he was from a land he could not acquire or cultivate. He suffered a double alienation, of a kind to reinforce a mythic relationship with any land whatsoever.

One of the characteristics of the movement of Jewish Enlightenment as it evolved was its didactic insistence on the development and self-liberation of the Jew as a new man, as a humanist conscious of his emotions, a friend of reason and intelligence, of art and nature, by which he clearly distinguished himself from the Jew of the ghetto.[11] Many representatives of this Enlightenment shared an idealized vision, not only of mankind, but also of nature. The Arcadian literature of sixteenth- and seventeenth-century Europe served as their inspiration.[12] Transferred to Hebrew poetry and drama, with their eternal mountains, dwellings covered with foliage, and flocks and shepherds, this kind of nature, while serving as a literary convention, also to some extent replaced a lost Orthodoxy. It introduced a radical novelty when compared to the religious literature that still dominated the culture of Jewish communities. Nature and landscape insinuated trouble and subversion into a literary tradition that until then had centered on the text, which they now opened up to the outside world—but to an imaginary one.

It was this nature and landscape that Jewish writers of eastern Europe would use to promote an ideal of renewal within the land of Israel, which was itself subversive in the context of that time, dominated as it was by the integrationist credo. This ideal, however, was quite removed from any kind of pragmatism. The authors were not yet in a position to offer their readers realistic natural settings. At the most, they created a historical background for their plots by using their imaginations. The land they described had nothing to do with modern Palestine, with the Zionist philosophy, which was in gestation at the time, or with any kind of religious fervor. Geographic and topographic facts played only a minor role; their vision of the land of Israel depended principally on biblical evocations. But the flora, fauna, and landscapes of Scripture are embarrassingly poor, and so the absence of pictorial description of Palestine was compensated for by a pastoral evocation of nature. These writers told about a land that was born of an encounter between biblical tradition and western European Arcadian literature. This combination was close to the European conception of Judaism at that time. An "acculturated" land was projected onto the land of Israel, an abstract and unseen land that expressed nostalgia for the glories of a national past freed from the chains of oppression and constraint.

These preoccupations found their best expression in Abraham Mapu's lyrical novel *Ahavat Tsiyon* (Love of Zion), which appeared in 1853, a pastoral idyll inspired linguistically and topographically by the Bible and written in a romantic vein. It was the first Hebrew novel in which the author projected himself into a biblical landscape. Mapu was influenced by French writings of the eighteenth century and by the works of his contemporary Eugène Sue. Mapu's land of Israel was the result of this mixture, a land idealized by the Bible and reidealized by the European pastoral tradition. Friedrich von Schiller and others helped Hebrew writers in this transposition; their evocations of the Holy Land drew on the "Hebrew Melodies" of Lord Byron and the works of the French writers Chateaubriand and Lamartine, as well as on Heinrich Heine, Walter Scott, and William Blake. The romantic wave that dominated the literature of the Jewish Enlightenment reached its height in the work of Micah Joseph Lebensohn. In his *Shirei Bat Tsiyon* (Songs of Zion's Daughter [1851]), Jerusalem finds itself located on the banks of the Jordan and combines all the attributes of the Holy Land—cedars, olive groves, fig trees, vineyards, and milk and honey—along with all the elements of the pastoral—trees, flowers, bubbling brooks, and eternal springtime. In *Shelomo ve-Kohelet* (Solomon and Kohelet), a two-part poem that appears in the same collection, everything occurs in the spring as Solomon falls in love with a shepherdess. Place-names are directly taken from the Bible (Lebanon, Gilead, Carmel). But traits of the European environment are projected onto the land of Israel. Lebensohn could thus evoke the snowy landscape of his Lithuania, a rather rare backdrop in Scripture, and describe valleys covered with snow in Lebanon! Later, in the pioneering literature written on the spot in Palestine by ardent Zionists, one finds the same borrowing of elements from the European landscapes of their childhood or youth— as if one could never totally return to the land of Israel, or as if one could only come back there with the ballast of a little of the soil one had left.

In fact, when the Haskalah evoked Judean shepherds, peasants, or soldiers living in close harmony with nature, it was less in order to exalt the land of Israel than to promote a reform of the Jewish man and of the social structure of communities, reforms that it hoped to see accomplished precisely in the Diaspora.[13] A physical return to Palestine had not been on the Jewish agenda for centuries, and the number of Jews who actually lived there was not very large. The occasional immigrants tended to be religious and so headed for the four holy cities of Jerusalem, Hebron, Safed, and Tiberias, seeking to end their days in study and prayer. They formed the core of the old Yishuv,[14] made up mostly of Ashkenazim, when the first pioneers landed in Palestine.

The Christian Rediscovery of Palestine

While such a prospect was still far from the top preoccupation of those involved, the idea of a massive return of the Jews to Palestine did make headway in certain Christian circles. In fact, it had begun to take shape after the sixteenth century among Protestants in England.[15] The Reformation in that country, from which the Jews had been expelled in 1290, fostered a renewal of interest in the Jewish people. The translation of the Scriptures into the vernacular had strongly influenced the minds of English Protestants, including their attitudes toward Jews and their possible return to the Holy Land. The place of the Bible in Elizabethan and Jacobean England lay behind a renewal of Christian eschatological thought, which until then had generally ignored the possibility of a national Jewish restoration. From now on, the idea of the Jews returning to Palestine as a preliminary stage to the Second Coming, and their conversion to Christianity, began to play a dominant role in prophetic interpretations and predictions. Until the 1640s, such a prospect was envisaged only by isolated individuals, but soon a whole millenarian current began that affected English attitudes toward Jews and went so far as to demand the rescinding of the 1290 act of expulsion and their readmission to the country. In the first half of the nineteenth century, the Evangelical renaissance, especially among Protestants, itself took a millenarian turn, advocating a regrouping of the Jews in Palestine—and their conversion. In 1840, the Foreign Secretary, Lord Palmerston, suggested that the establishment of Jews in the Holy Land should be encouraged as a strategy for sustaining the Ottoman Empire. This agitation resulted in the creation of missions like the London Society for Promoting Christianity Among the Jews, founded in 1808 and very active throughout the century.

In the United States, New England was also touched by millenarianism. In the 1820s and 1830s, Joseph Smith, founder of the Church of Jesus Christ of the Latter Day Saints (the Mormons), took a certain interest in the Jews. He sanctified America as the Promised Land of Joseph's descendants, while Palestine was still the land promised to Judah's descendants (meaning the Jews), and announced the latter's forthcoming return to their ancestral land, as well as their conversion to Christianity. In 1840, Orson Hyde, a Mormon who belonged to the church hierarchy, undertook a mission to Jewish communities in western Europe and Palestine.[16] He preached the reunion of the Jews and the reconstruction of Jerusalem, reaffirming Mormon doctrine on these points. But, by upholding the principle of Israel's autonomy and by lending his support to Jewish hopes of an end to exile, he distinguished himself from other missionaries who were little inclined to make room for the political sovereignty of an Israel that had no organic relation with the Church. This example, among others, well manifests the ambivalence and complexity of the attitudes of American millenarians toward the Jews. They did accept, in general, that the restoration of a Jewish state in the Holy Land was a necessary stage in the accomplishment of the final days. But we should not suppose from this that they were automatically concerned, as a consequence, to contribute actively to the advancement of the Zionist cause on a political and economic level.

Except for the activity of William E. Blackstone, any millenarian support for the Zionist movement was generally passive. Any accomplishments by Zionism always had an instrumental value in their eyes, and this position did not vary until recently. The first waves of Jewish immigration into Palestine in the nineteenth century and the creation of the first farm colonies were interpreted as a sign that the Jews were preparing for the role they would play at the end of time, as well as a sign of Jesus' impending Second Coming. Even today, millenarians interpret the birth of the state of Israel and its military victories, as well as its territorial expansion, in this light. They see events in the Middle East as confirmation of the idea that history advances in line with their understanding of God's plans for humanity. But while support for Zionism was formerly passive, in our day, it is quite active; in the 1970s and 1980s, the contemporary heirs of the millenarian tradition did not hesitate to use their influence on American politics to defend the cause of the Jewish state.

In the eyes of American millenarians, the emigration of Jews to Palestine was the realization of biblical prophecies. In certain cases, they went so far as to promote Jewish settlement of the Holy Land. In 1891, a petition signed by 413 eminent Americans demanded that measures be taken for the return of Jews to Palestine. It was William E. Blackstone who took the initiative in what became known as the Blackstone Memorandum. His efforts in favor of the establishment of a Jewish state preceded the appearance of political Zionism: it was five years before the publication of Theodor Herzl's *Der Judenstaat: Versuch einer modernen Lösung der Judenfrage* (The Jewish State: An Attempt at a Modern Solution of the Jewish Question) and six years before Herzl assembled the first Zionist congress. Herzl's and Blackstone's proposals were quite similar. Both envisaged millions of Jews moving to and settling in Palestine and creating a state. And neither of them took into account the presence of Arabs in the country. However, an essential nuance separated them: whereas Herzl thought a return to Palestine was a solution to the Jewish question, Blackstone envisaged it as a step toward the Second Coming. His project had no direct influence on Herzl's, but American Zionists reacted quite positively to it, whereas Jews advocating acculturation in the places where they were actually living showed themselves hostile to it. Blackstone's initiative had no effect. In 1916, he prepared a second memorandum with a view to converting President Woodrow Wilson to the idea of a Jewish homeland in Palestine. This memorandum, which saw Zionism merely as a tool in the realization of Divine plans, was never officially presented to the president, however, because American Zionists were opposed to it.

These millenarian expectations led various groups of Americans, Germans, and Swedes to settle in Palestine, where they hoped to witness the Second Coming. As with Blackstone in the United States, Britons like Lord Shaftsbury, Lawrence Oliphant, and others lent their enthusiastic support to the renaissance of the Holy Land. Reinforced by romanticism, the millenarianism then in vogue among Protestants fostered, in wider circles, renewed interest in and sympathy for, not only the Jewish past, but also Jewish colonization of Palestine. Thus the French novelist Alexandre Dumas *fils*, in *La Femme de Claude* (1873), and the English writer George Eliot, in *Daniel Deronda* (1876), argued for an assembling of Jews in the Holy Land. Eliot's novel, notably, describes the itinerary of a Jewish character, Mordecai, who wants his people freed from oppression by means of a return to the ancestral soil. He leaves his Christian friends and England and heads east.[17] In the Christian as in the Jewish world, though, it was essentially as a symbol invested with the authority conferred on it by the Book, and weighted with a strong emotional charge, that the Holy Land occupied people's minds.

Certain political developments also contributed to bring the Holy Land back concretely into Europe's field of vision. Napoleon Bonaparte's expedition in February 1799, for example, was the first time since the Crusades that a Western army had ventured into this region.[18] The event was of a nature and sufficient scale to stimulate European minds. A manifesto published under the future emperor's name exhorted the Jews to come to Palestine to take possession of their patrimony.[19] This apocryphal document stressed their rights to this heritage, unjustly denied for thousands of years, and evoked the possibility of a renewal of the Jews' political existence as a nation among nations. Even if the authenticity of this manifesto is questionable, the ideas that it contributed to propagating had begun to make headway. It articulated two aspects of the territorial principle that were not always compatible: political sovereignty and historical rights. When the viceroy of Egypt, Mehemet Ali, laid claim to Ottoman Syria in the 1830s, Palestine, which was administratively part of it, was once again in the news, within the framework of the famous (and no less embarrassing) Middle East Question. The digging of the Suez Canal after 1859 also contributed to this. Starting in the 1840s, the Europeans opened consulates in Jerusalem and extended their power by presiding over a set of religious, philanthropic, and scientific institutions and over a network of schools. France, for its part, continued to position itself as protector of Eastern Catholic peoples. This European interventionism created the conditions for a modernization of local Christian colonies, while stimulating the competition among, and aid to, the Jews of Palestine.

In the wake of the Orientalist wave sweeping through thought and culture at the time, romantic Europe was pleased to evoke an impalpable Palestine, a Holy Land situated beyond time and space.[20] But in the same era, the practice of pilgrimage was developing; progress in transportation, by land and sea, encouraged tourism. A whole literature was born in the wake of this fascination. For the nineteenth century, Palestine was a unique land because it was the land of the Bible. And it was as readers of the Bible that European thinkers gradually became familiar with the idea that this region was also a physical entity. Whenever it was actually visited, the Holy Land was still viewed through the prism of the Book. Most of the travelers who went there were familiar with Scripture; they were not only in search of a holy atmosphere, they also sought the sites they had heard of or whose names they knew from their reading. Biblical events, characters, and sites already populated their memories. The nineteenth century also saw a proliferation of studies, dictionaries, atlases, and articles, both popular and scientific, that were devoted to these questions and were widely disseminated in the Western world. The birth and development of biblical criticism contributed greatly to augmenting this interest. Bibles illustrated with drawings, maps, and sketches of ethnic types and architectural styles were published. For travelers, Palestinian Arab society and its way of life evoked the biblical period. Western artists ventured into the region, drawing holy sites and biblical landscapes, thus making them accessible to their compatriots.

In travelers' eyes, Palestine was not only a divine and ethereal reality, but also an ancient historic land, an integral part of the Middle East, even if it played in their imaginations a minor role compared with metropolises like Constantinople, Baghdad, or Cairo. However, it was perceived as a devastated, desolate, and undeveloped land, offering a striking contrast with its glorious past. Until the nineteenth century, there was scarcely even a reliable map of the region, and the exact locations and altitudes of sites were unknown. Many were not even identifiable. As for Palestinian fauna and flora, they were outside the field of knowledge, as some parts of the region had not been visited for centuries by Westerners. From this standpoint, the nineteenth century was indeed one of rediscovery. Thus the first scientific works on Palestine were published by Ulrich Jasper Seetzen and Johann Ludwig Burchardt, for example. The Palestine Exploration Fund was created in London in 1865, and other societies of the same kind were born in the United States, in Germany, and in Russia, while in France, the Orientalist Charles Clermont-Ganneau became famous for this kind of activity. Palestine was also an inseparable element of the exotic

Orient, then in fashion. Painters and photographers were fascinated by it. But paintings were already more realistic that those of the seventeenth century, and the photographs complemented and corrected the current image of the region.

This polymorphous curiosity and the non-Jewish literature it inspired gave rise to the representations of the Holy Land that were current in the nineteenth century.[21] Writers, travelers, and scientists who visited it compiled a great quantity of material. Pilgrims from England, Germany, France, and the United States, as well as researchers, circulated varied and detailed information in Europe.[22] The romantic currents in literature and art, as well as historical and archaeological research, gave these materials quite an exotic charm, and this flow of information also reached Jewish readers, who no longer had to depend on Hebrew or Yiddish literature in order to encounter the realities of Palestine. However, Jewish travelers to Palestine remained few. The rare accounts of voyages written by Jews of European background appeared in the 1840s, as did the *Journal* of Lady Judith Montefiore. Moreover, European literature devoted to the Holy Land was not exempt from preconceived ideas; in England, France, and Germany, literary traditions and Christian ideologies heavily influenced it. Few took account of the real problems of the local communities or were interested in aspects of reality that clashed with their expectations or their beliefs. The primary book, the Bible, was overlaid with other books, writings, and readings that contributed to make the land of Israel both more distant and closer to the Jews. One was still in the realm of myth, but a myth renewed by geographical discovery and enriched by the gaze of the Other.

This gaze was that of a sovereign Europe, increasingly dominant in the Ottoman Empire. Palestine, an integral part of this coveted empire, was no longer just the Holy Land of previous centuries; it had its place in the strategic plans of the world's powers and European political strategy. At the end of the 1830s, it already appeared as a place of convergence for various settlement programs. The millenarian reawakening in certain circles, especially in England, and the hopes for change that agitated the world in the 1840s were combined with political vicissitudes relating to the Middle East Question. Echoes of both the religious revival and those events were heard and absorbed by traditional Jewish society, as well as by Jews who were largely acculturated to the non-Jewish environment. The revival of European interest in the Holy Land could not help but contribute to the renewal of the Jews' attachment to the land of Israel, even when some of them were on their way to blending into non-Jewish societies. Reacting directly to the settlement plans launched by Christian circles in the Holy Land or internalizing the European image of a Jewish Palestine (an image largely dependent on the revival of nationalism from the end of the 1830s to the 1880s), some Western Jews manifested their concern for the fate of this distant country in concrete ways. In the 1840s, the British philanthropist Moses Montefiore was so influenced by millenarian initiatives that he went to meet their promoters.[23] His own project for settlement was not far removed from those of some Christian dreamers. Starting in 1827, he made seven trips to Palestine, the third (in 1849) in the company of the English millenarian George Gawler. In the 1850s and 1870s, his path once again crossed that of millenarians who wanted to create agrarian colonies in the Holy Land.

Palestine Revisited by the Jews

The impact of nationalist effervescence in Europe is clearly felt in the works of the German Jewish socialist Moses Hess, for whom the spiritual renaissance of Judaism could only take place in the land of Israel. Early on, therefore, he advocated agrarian settlement on a large scale and the creation of a socialist state in Palestine. His 1862 book *Rom und Jerusalem: Die letzte Nationalitätsfrage* (Rome and Jerusalem: The Last Nationalist Question) was the first writing by a Jew to treat the Jewish question as a national issue in secular terms. He claimed that to escape persecution, Jews had to put an end to exile. Even if he had the vision of a redeemed and rehabilitated Judaism, the messianic hope of someone like Hess clearly drew its dynamic from the awakening European nationalisms. Of course, he was not the first to see the assembly of Jews on a single territory as a possible solution to the Jewish problem. Projects of this kind date back to the eighteenth century. But the first defenders of the territorial principle did not always grant a very clear place to Palestine within this framework. In giving them a designated homeland, Hess reintroduced into humanity's historical movement a people who had been a priori deprived of national attributes such as a common language or territory. This repoliticization of the Jewish people did not necessarily imply a desymbolization or demythification of the land of Israel. On the contrary, Hess reinserted the land into the general context of nationalist Europe, keeping its symbolic dimension and its emotional charge—both of which the religious pre-Zionists, his contemporaries, would associate with their idea of national unity.

In fact, traditionalist circles were not ignorant of this rise of European nationalisms. Some of them had already interpreted the progress of emancipation as a herald of messianic redemption; for them, this emancipation was making possible, with the consent and help of the more generous world powers, an unexpected tightening of Israel's ties with her land. Thanks to their measures to improve the status of Jews, the Ottoman sultan and the Russian tsar were sometimes perceived as redeemers of Israel. The Damascus Affair of 1840, a blood libel like so many others in the Ottoman Empire in this era, mobilized the European Jewish elite and led to the foundation of institutionalized modern Jewish solidarity. This elite thereby manifested an attachment (more than strictly speaking "confessional") to its Jewish identity, and was in turn itself later credited with a redemptive dimension. In this optimistic climate, certain Orthodox groups, though still a minority, were no longer content to wait passively for divine intervention to accomplish salvation; they accepted the idea of human action in order to hasten it.

In Prussia in 1832, Rabbi Zevi Hirsch Kalisher declared that the redemption of Zion would begin with action by the Jewish people and that the messianic miracle would then follow. And in his publications between 1839 and 1843, the Bosnian Judah Alkalai raised the urgency for the Jews of returning to Palestine, proclaiming that "the final and supernatural redemption to be brought about by the Messiah must be preceded by the physical return of the Jews to Zion."[24] Kalisher, Alkalai, Elijah Guttmacher (a partisan of the same solution), and others who are less well known were all imbued with traditional messianic values, but they considered the emancipation of the Jews to be an initial phase in a process of redemption that was already under way.[25] They drew on the sources of Jewish tradition but took into account the political experiences, both Jewish and non-Jewish, of their time. The settlement of Jews in Palestine was to them indispensable to the unfolding of the messianic project, and any human initiative like that of philanthropists such as the Rothschilds or of organizations such as the Alliance israélite universelle was liable to hasten the outcome.[26] In 1836, Kalisher handed the Rothschilds a proposal to buy land in Palestine, and in 1862, he wrote to them about the necessity of Jewish agrarian colonization of the Holy Land. In 1840, Alkalai suggested the creation of a fund to finance the acquisition of land in Palestine to settle the Jews, which would call upon gifts from Jewish philanthropists like the Rothschilds, the Montefiores, and others. Some years later, in 1857, he defended the idea of the establishment of a Jewish state.

However, the national Jewish consciousness that developed in certain milieux, both religious and secular, was far from a dominant tendency in the Jewish world. It was situated on the margins of the general dynamic that prevailed in the West at the time. And it was not an accident that most of the Orthodox apostles of the return came from regions that were geographically peripheral to western Europe, between East and West, between tradition and modernity. Like Moses Hess, a secular pre-Zionist, these rabbis would only be rediscovered by the Zionists as their "precursors" much later.

Within the same traditionalist circles, leaving for Palestine could also be seen as the best way of fleeing a European Jewish society tainted by modernity and reform. In the 1860s and 1870s, some groups saw the rural settlement of Palestine as an important element in the process of messianic redemption. This idea spread in central and eastern Europe as much as in Palestine itself. The first attempt at settlement was undertaken by an Orthodox group in 1878–79 on land purchased northeast of Jaffa, a place to which they gave the name Petah Tikvah (Gateway of Hope). This attempt failed, but it inspired other efforts. Societies for the colonization of Palestine arose. A desire for a return to the old order, such as was promoted in Hungary by the Hatam Sofer (Moses Sofer),[27] and a resistance to the eruption of modernity within the communities favored the establishment of a Jewish society in the Holy Land, which would function as a sort of alternative to the option of acculturation to the non-Jewish environment that was dominant among European Jews. So in the 1870s, some traditionalist circles, students imbued with nationalist sentiments, and Jewish philanthropists were all simultaneously proposing the rural colonization of Palestine. If traditionalist circles were interested in agriculture, it was for purely pragmatic reasons, since they were anxious to combine work on the land with study of the Torah, and to provide sustenance for urban communities in the Holy Land.

In parallel with this set of initiatives, there were projects for "regeneration" developed by integrationist Jewish elites in Europe who wanted to help their coreligionists in the Middle East. The objective was to allow oriental Jews to accede to a level of emancipation comparable with what Western Jews had acquired, by working to help them merit it through education and "productivization." Palestine naturally found a place within such preoccupations. It is in this light that we should understand the foundation in 1870 in Jaffa of the agricultural school of Mikveh Israel by the Alliance israélite universelle.[28] The same concern inspired the support lent by Baron Edmond de Rothschild to the colonies in Palestine starting in 1882. These "regenerative" aims had been those of non-Jewish promoters of emancipation back in the eighteenth century. Now it was the turn of the emancipated Jewish elites to be concerned with the fate of their oriental fellows who were less fortunate in this respect. Palestine was not the privileged target of the Alliance's educational activities, of course, for it opened schools, apprenticeships, and agricultural schools elsewhere in the Middle East and in North Africa. It was just one of the facets of global activity aimed mainly at helping Jews in Muslim lands. While the enterprises of the Alliance and by Baron de Rothschild finally took quite different directions than those their founders had dreamed of, the initial intentions were in line with ideas current among western European Jews at the time.

These Jewish philanthropists wanted to combine their activity with the political action of the European powers. There was no discontinuity between them, and the philanthropists had total confidence in Europe. Protections granted by Western governments and aid from consulates on the ground were considered able to guarantee the existence of the Palestinian Jewish populations of European origin and to foster the establishment of new institutions and the success of new Jewish initiatives. Moreover, European settlements like the Germans' stood as examples showing the agrarian potential of the Holy Land, to be studied and imitated by Jews. Jewish philanthropy, still animated by Enlightenment principles, wanted to ameliorate traditional Jewish society through education and training in new skills, including agricultural skills. Charles Netter, founder of Mikveh Israel, did not move beyond this initial project. Later, he opposed emigration to Palestine and encouraged Baron Maurice de Hirsch, his contemporary, to create Jewish colonies in Argentina. Although Baron Edmond de Rothschild's efforts took place after the Russian pogroms of 1881–82, which led many Jews to lose confidence in Enlightenment principles of integration, they were still in accord with the ideas then dominant in the Jewish world. For Edmond de Rothschild, the mission of the colonies was not only to absorb Russian immigrants fleeing the pogroms; they were also to demonstrate the aptitude of the Jews for agriculture and by the same token respond to the recurrent criticism that they lent themselves exclusively to commercial occupations and money dealings.[29] And this really worked, to the great satisfaction among many parties. Rothschild had envisaged the creation of these colonies for Jews from eastern Europe even before the pogroms, along with Charles Netter, but the project had failed with the death of the latter. From the beginning, and even if Rothschild reigned as master over his colonies, he preferred not to have his name associated with Palestine and chose anonymity, resulting in the pseudonym given to him: "the Well-Known Benefactor." Promptly destroying any document relating to his actions in the Holy Land, Rothschild would not let himself be identified with the political objectives of Zionism until after the Balfour Declaration in 1917. In his management of his colonies, he did not take local facts into consideration, and nor did the Alliance, which in its schools applied a French teaching program supplemented with Jewish subjects. Rothschild involved the colonists in viticulture without concerning himself with the sales prospects of the wine produced. This wine-producing policy mainly resulted from Rothschild's familiarity with vineyards, thanks to the property owned by his family in the southwest of France. Like most of the philanthropists, Rothschild was content to export his model and impose it on the local people without worrying about their real needs. This attitude clearly belonged to a cultural and economic colonialism founded on the ideology of Europe's superiority. However, starting from different points, both philanthropists and Orthodox groups were united in their desire to change the local society through agrarian settlements, and all observers agreed in attributing the "degeneration" of the Jews of Palestine to their estrangement from agriculture.

Ancient Land, New Land(s)

In these same final decades of the nineteenth century, some people in eastern Europe turned toward a synthesis of the modern nationalism of a Moses Hess and the messianic aspirations of a Kalisher or Alkalai, with everything resting upon the gains brought by emancipation. From this perspective, the great supracommunal institutions of integrated Jewry appeared able to help realize the national hopes of all the Jewish people. This is how the Jewish Board of Deputies in Great Britain, for example, was perceived. Born in the 1760s, it was considered to be the recognized organ of communication between the Jewish community and the British government. The same can be said of the Alliance israélite universelle in France. In the 1870s, however, the hostility of which the Jews of eastern Europe were victims steadily increased, and it was more and more difficult to believe that Enlightenment ideals would suffice to resolve the Jewish question in Russia. The Jewish intelligentsia became more radical and turned toward either socialism, which stressed a universalist foundation, or a nationalism centered on Jewish particularism. The pogroms of the 1880s united the partisans of the Enlightenment and their adversaries around the Jewish nationalist Hibbat Tsion (Love of Zion) movement,[30] from whom the first Palestinian pioneers were recruited. These dramatic events changed minds not only among those who had believed in the possibility of the Jews' being integrated into their environment, but also among those who had hoped that the enlightened nations of Europe would support the Jewish national awakening, as they had done in the case of Greece and with Italian unification. The disillusionment born of the pogroms encouraged the Jews to take charge of their own destiny without counting on the goodwill of the West.

In the same era, moreover, the success of emancipation in Europe did not prevent some from raising the problem of the future of Jewish identity again. The Jew was nowhere perfectly accepted, not just in Russia. We know that this fact influenced Theodor Herzl at the time of the Dreyfus Affair in France.[31] Of course, the Affair was not what revealed anti-Semitism to him; in Vienna, he had long been familiar with the phenomenon. It is equally reductive to attribute the birth of political Zionism to anti-Semitism; this interpretation, drawing its justification from the Shoah, is really no more than a projection. But for Herzl, it was difficult to be more French and more patriotic than Captain Dreyfus; so when the suspicion of treason hung over him, it was his Frenchness that was being called into question, bringing his Jewishness to the fore again. Herzl and others were therefore led to ask themselves about the limits of the benefits of acculturation. The return to the Jewish people carried out by some of those who had lost confidence in the benefits of emancipation was for them a return to an organic society from which they had not yet been totally cut off. The example of other nations, like Bulgaria, that had fought for their independence and had achieved sovereignty over their own territory would also contribute in the 1870s to the crystallization of a national Jewish consciousness among the younger generation. The Bulgarian case was particularly telling in this respect: from the start, stimulated by the recent experience of non-Jewish Bulgarians, Zionism enjoyed a remarkable upsurge in this Sephardic land.[32] In this era, however—and we should make no mistake about it—this type of growing awareness was by no means general, and nationhood was not the dominant aspiration among Jews in Europe or elsewhere.

When Zionism was beginning to gestate, the Jewish presence in Palestine was still too small to justify a claim to local self-determination. For the Jews, the situation was very different from that of other movements for national liberation in Europe.[33] Thus it was by recalling the continuity of the Jewish presence in the land of Israel that some activists tried to legitimize their claim to historic rights over this land. As a general rule, the principle of historic rights weighed much more heavily in the Jewish case than did self-determination, a fact directly linked to the existential condition of a dispersed people living outside the land-symbol on which some of its members had set their sights. Zionism was born of an awakening of Jewish consciousness and not from the reality of physical existence in Palestine. It thus found itself loaded with a whole host of associations of ideas and emotions that had accumulated in the collective memory and were capable of inspiring sentiments and aspirations that crystallized around the notion of national renaissance. Zion and Zionism as a national movement thus maintained equivocal relations with each other. It is clear in any case that it was not the attachment to the land of Israel, and still less a perpetual religious tie to this land, that first gave birth to Zionism; on the contrary, it was born of the urgency of finding a solution to the Jewish question at the time, in the general context of the rise of nationalisms in Europe. It was a matter of radically changing the image that the Jew had of himself, as well as of his way of life, by erecting a new society and new culture and by restoring Jewish political sovereignty. From the start, the question of the relations between Zionism and territoriality proved complex, a subject soon debated in the writings of the founding fathers of the movement and in the ideological controversies that agitated circles sympathetic to Zionism, as far back as the Hibbat Zion and during Herzl's lifetime.

In Russia, in *Auto-Emancipation* (1882), the basic text of the Hibbat Zion movement, Leon Pinsker expressly rejected the land of Israel. To him, it was not the Holy Land per se that should be the goal of efforts, but simply a "land for us." In Lithuania, Moshe Lilienblum, also linked with Hibbat Zion, similarly thought the Jews' problems flowed from the fact that they were a nation without any sovereignty over territory. The solution resided in emigration away from Europe and in the restoration of Jewish sovereignty elsewhere. Pinsker thought for a while of the United States, and he rallied only later to arguments in favor of Palestine. Lilienblum, on the other hand, early on leaned toward the

Holy Land, and from 1881 on, he stressed the necessity of agrarian settlements and the purchase of land in this region. In 1883, he proposed sending out collection boxes for family donations, heralding the future blue boxes of the National Jewish Fund, created later by the Zionist movement.

In the wake of Hibbat Zion, societies for colonization multiplied in Russia. The first organization of this type had been founded in 1860 in Frankfurt an der Oder in eastern Germany on the Polish frontier, but it only really took off after 1863. The following year, another colonization society was born in Berlin, but the main impetus for this type of activity occurred in the 1880s. The statutes of these societies mentioned a triple obligation: *aliyah* (emigration to Palestine), nationalist propaganda, and agricultural work.[34] They gathered together religious and secular Jews whose agenda was colonization. The movement extended to the rest of Europe, especially in the east and the Balkans, and in the 1890s, it enjoyed a veritable explosion with popular settlement societies. Some put together up to a thousand small investors; others numbering fifty or a hundred wealthier members concentrated on buying land. In France, the Jishoub Eretz Israel society was founded,[35] and there was even a plan to create a society for the encouragement of agriculture and industry in Palestine.

The glorification of the tiller of the soil, of someone who finds the whole meaning of his life in his work and in love of the land, profoundly marked educated Russian youth, as witnessed, for example, by the foundation in 1882 of the Bilu movement,[36] and the departure of a certain number of its members for Palestine, where they were among the first pioneers of the "new" Yishuv (in contrast to the "old" Yishuv, the Palestinian Jewish community already in place). These young idealists were neither the first nor the only ones to put their hopes in the establishment of a reformed society and in the creation of a new type of colony in a country of immigration. French socialists had themselves tried to found their "Icarie." In the same period, Russian radicals were trying out their own models of colonies in the United States. As for the Jewish group Am Olam ("Eternal People"), also born in the wake of pogroms, it also turned to North America with the idea of creating rural settlements there.

Shaken by the dramatic events of the 1880s, Jewish philanthropy, too, sought solutions to a Jewish question that had become sharper than ever. As we know, the bulk of the emigrants from Russia and Romania ended up in the United States, and only a tiny portion headed for Palestine; few were animated by a real national consciousness. During the period of mass emigration to the United States, Baron Maurice de Hirsch, who was of German origin, established a significant aid program to resettle eastern European Jews who had left, not only to escape the pogroms and anti-Jewish measures, but also in search of better economic opportunities.[37] At the time, priority was given to the Americanization of these new immigrants. In order to avoid great concentrations of them in urban zones, between 1901 and 1933, Hirsch's fund partly subsidized the Jewish Agricultural Society by guaranteeing loans to Jewish farmers. Hirsch, who wanted to orient Jews to working the land, looked for countries likely to welcome his projects for colonization. It was Argentina—and not Palestine—that he finally seized upon. In 1890, the first rural settlement was founded in the province of Santa Fe and was baptized Moisesville; the second dates from 1891 and bore the name Mauricio. The same year, Hirsch decided to form the Jewish Colonization Association (ICA) to manage his colonization projects. In time, twenty colonies were created in Argentina, composed of some 3,500 families. The ICA also developed some settlements in Brazil and Canada. However, the Hibbat Zion, which was trying to channel the emigration of Russian Jews to Palestine, was opposed to Hirsch's program. On the other hand, aid associations on the Russian border and in the cities welcomed it, because he supported them in their task. In short, the land of Israel was still far from being the sole solution that was envisaged to improve the lot of the Jews of eastern Europe.

In *Der Judenstaat* (1896), Herzl himself was still indifferent to the land of Israel, but at the Second Zionist Congress, in 1898, he spoke of the historic right of the Jews to Palestine. Later for a time he accommodated himself to the "Ugandan" solution, envisaging the settlement of Jews in Africa in what is today Kenya, at a time when colonization was already under way in Palestine. He was not the only one. Israel Zangwill, the great British Jewish writer, who was to become the exalter of territorialism, adhered to the idea current in large sectors of Western Judaism that the projected Jewish homeland should serve as a refuge for Jews who were politically and physically oppressed, and that it should become in time a cultural center for all Jews and all of humanity.[38] Between 1903 and 1905, he led the fight for the Uganda project, recalling the difficulties inherent in the choice of Palestine by reason of the Arab presence and the theological and political problems that would not fail to arise there. In 1905, after Herzl's death, however, the World Zionist Organization rejected the African option, and Zangwill provoked a schism and created the Jewish Territorial Organization (ITO). The aim of this new organization was to procure an autonomous territory for those Jews who could not or would not remain in their countries of origin. The existence of this autonomous territory by no means implied the disappearance of the Diaspora. Initially founded to respond to the British offer in East Africa, the ITO negotiated with the British government for Cyrenaica in North Africa in 1907; the following year, for Mesopotamia; and then, in 1912, for the Benguela plateau in Angola. These attempts failed because either of local conditions or the opposition of the holders of these territories to their being given to the Jews. In 1906, Jacob Schiff, an American Jewish financier and philanthropist, suggested to Zangwill that Jews settle in the United States. In 1907, the first immigrants under this plan arrived in Galveston, Texas, but they quickly dispersed throughout the country. Thanks to this program, a hundred thousand Russian Jews entered the United States, adding to the numerous Jewish immigrants already residing there. And although it resulted in a relative failure when the concentration of immigrants in Galveston proved impossible, this enterprise was the only one that the ITO carried to its conclusion. With the onset of the Great War, Zangwill, who was a pacifist, tried to resolve the Jewish problem by force in Palestine. He saw a chance to succeed in the conflict between the British and the Ottoman Turks, and went so far as to demand the transfer of the Arab populations. Neither the World Zionist Organization nor the European powers were ready, though, to endorse such a measure.

But when the Zionists actually got interested in the land of Israel, they did not all always have the same conception of it. This conception changed over time, adapted to certain realities, but was seldom unitary and seldom intangible. Ahad Ha-Am (Asher Ginzberg) thought the heart of the people was the real foundation upon which the land would be constructed, so it was necessary above all to work on reforming the spirit of the nation. The land could not serve as a refuge for all the persecuted Jews, and even if it could, not all of them would emigrate there. If only with respect to this point, we should render homage to the farsightedness of this great Russian Jewish publicist. On the other hand, Ahad Ha-Am thought that Palestine could serve as a national cultural center, able to renew the spirit of Jews everywhere. He wanted to save Judaism and not just the Jews. He reproached Herzl's *Der Judenstaat* for having nothing Jewish about it. And while he rejected the Diaspora, it was not so much because, like Herzl, he feared the assimilation of Jews, as because he feared that they could no longer live as Jews there, since they were henceforth defenseless in the face of an open society. In fact, he sought the best way of assuring the spiritual survival of the Jews where they happened to be living and envisaged a compromise reminiscent of the status of the land of Israel in the time of the Second Temple, with the difference that it would be by intellectual works and by a renewed and secularized culture that the national Palestinian homeland would give the Diaspora the means of survival. The spiritual center would not have the mission of making the periphery disappear; on the contrary, it would serve it by taking over the task from the religion that until then had served the dual role of national homeland and spiritual center. The return of a Jewish elite to the Holy Land would thus paradoxically allow the whole of the people finally to get rid of the vestiges of an outmoded religiosity.

For his part, Aaron David Gordon, a contemporary of Ahad Ha-Am's, defined life in exile as a form of parasitism, which was quite susceptible to being perpetuated in the land of Israel. In effect, he feared that when placed under the thumb of the religious, the latter would be transformed into a new exile. Productive work had a redeeming force for him. Self-realization came about through work on the land of Israel, since the land belonged to those who lived in it and made it fruitful.[39] Work put the Jew in contact with the land as a whole, and with

Heaven, too, of course. Gordon combined a Tolstoyan inspiration with a mysticism about the land of Israel that took much of its flavor from Jewish tradition. The Jews would rediscover their origins by renewing their ties with Mother Earth,[40] and it would suffice for a minority of them to decide to live in Palestine for the Jewish people as a whole to regain vigor. In 1918, Gordon would evoke the historic rights of the Jews to this land—a notion that would end up triumphing over that of work on the land.

Ber Borochov, for his part, maintained that the solution to the Jewish problem would come with the territorialization of the Jewish people, meaning its transformation into a nation that was master of its own territory.[41] It was by making Zion into an independent, unconditionally sovereign political entity that the Jewish people could escape the danger of extinction and break with anti-Semitism. For him, Zion did not begin in the land of Israel but in the necessity of freeing the Jewish people and finding a remedy for its physical and cultural distress. It was the destiny of the Jewish people that lay at the center of the Zionist consciousness. The settlement he advocated in Palestine was of a socialist type, and his Zionist project was articulated around three inseparable themes: the redemption of the people of Israel, the renaissance of Hebrew culture, and the return to the ancient homeland. On the issue of settlement in British East Africa, he made himself the spokesman of the "Zionists of Zion."

Max Nordau, another key leader of Zionism, expected that a return to the land would allow men and women who had lived too long in the dark and humid alleys of the ghettoes of eastern Europe to regain their equilibrium.[42] Deprived of a native land, deprived of a land of his own, the Jew was in effect condemned to an instability that could only have harmful repercussions on his mind and body. For Nordau, as in fact for all the theoreticians we have looked at, regardless of their different nuances, the Zionist enterprise had all the appearances of a therapeutic movement, a treatment for the Jewish sickness, in which the land and the pioneering spirit were the essential ingredients.

A synthesis between Orthodoxy and political Zionism was taking place at the same time in the person of Abraham Isaac Kook, who was in the lineage of religious pre-Zionists like Kalisher and Alkalai. Kook called the refusal to seize the opportunity to return to the Holy Land a "profanation of the name" of that land. Palestine was for him the spatial center of holiness in this world, vertically radiating toward the Jews who lived there and horizontally radiating toward other peoples and the rest of the globe. He took it as guaranteed that residence in the Holy Land alone was able to foster a renaissance of the prophetic spirit.[43] His specifically kabbalistic approach allowed him to accommodate secular Zionists. God used mysterious ways to bring redemption to the world, and, without knowing it or even recognizing it, the nonbelieving pioneers of the Holy Land were playing an essential messianic-historic role. The return of the Jews to their ancestral soil would mark the end of an era of darkness for the whole world and pave the way for the redemption of all of humanity. There was thus a universalist message at the heart of Kook's redemptionist particularism. The land of Israel incarnated the hope of redemption, but this hope was now inserted into a pragmatic context. Kook thus developed a religious Zionism adaptable to the nationalist awakening that was beginning to spread across a small part of the Jewish world in the second half of the nineteenth century.

Thus it was only very gradually and often uncertainly that the land of Israel became a concrete option in the minds of some people. The land and its borders were both shifting. In fact, the debate it aroused would not end even with the foundation of the state of Israel—far from it. Always in a register of instability, both enticing and alien, evasive and elusive, the land did not easily offer itself up for reconquest. Has it ever really been reconquered? Is it not doomed to remain an abstraction, constantly enriching itself with the imaginations of those who dream of it, as well as of those who have decided to live there? For the secular founders of political Zionism, it was first and foremost a means that served a project, an instrument much more than an end in itself, and still less the object of some pious obligation. As a symbol, as an abstraction, Zion indisputably became something that could strongly mobilize the Jewish national movement.[44] Only this name had a sufficiently powerful echo to be able to assemble a great number of Jews across the world around collective action (social, political, and economic), whether they participated themselves in the foundation of a new society as emigrants or were content to give their material and moral support to the movement. Other choices were envisaged— Uganda, the north of Sinai, Argentina, the Jewish Soviet republic of Birobidzhan—which always raised important controversies within the Zionist national movement. However, these options were set aside as non-Zionist. Although these territories might seem easier to obtain, and their colonization appeared less problematic, they could never rival Palestine. Political Zionism was constructed at the dawn of the great period of European colonialism, at a time when Europe thought it had a natural right to territories quite outside its geographic and cultural sphere. But Zion had not been chosen as a land for the Jews in the way lands were chosen for colonization: by reason of its advantages, its natural resources, and its political accessibility.[45] Zion had been chosen because it was the only land able to arouse in the Jewish world the emotion and enthusiasm necessary to the success of a kind of immigration totally different from the migratory waves for the purposes of individual and familial salvation of the type that took people to North America. Without Palestine, Zionism was condemned to failure as a national project. To create a new society from a people dispersed across the world who were ethnically and culturally heterogeneous was a task not incumbent on other nationalist movements. Zionism was not only going to reconquer a symbol but also navigate among its different interpretations. Above all, it would have to recreate the land of Israel from scratch.

Six The Recreated Land

The Jewish past and history were apprehended as major elements in justifying Zionist claims to the land, while local Arab populations set themselves up as the legitimate owners and occupants in the face of those claims.[1] In their desire for rootedness, Zionism and the Jewish pioneers who settled in Palestine from then on would try to restore to the land of Israel its strictly earthly character, to be valued in and of itself.[2]

To Whom Does the Land Belong?

For the Zionists, the land of Israel was the "homeland" of the Jewish people, *moledet* in Hebrew, meaning "native land," "birthplace," from which flowed its historic right to it. On this level, Zionism drew the principal ingredients of its doctrine from within the religious heritage, but it secularized them, nationalized them, and adapted them to its requirements. The past was partially reconstructed and reinvented in order to justify the prospect that history and the desired future could be harmoniously combined. The land's "Jewish past" legitimized the settlement enterprise. But the link between the Jewish people and the land of Israel that the Zionists wanted to recover in the biblical account is not really what that story recounts: it was in the desert, in fact, that the People was born, in a no-man's-land that would never cease to haunt the Israeli native, right up to the present day, as a child of this "conquered" land that is never totally possessed. Scriptural literature recounts, moreover, that Israel's settlement on its land was really a result of conquest from its first inhabitants. The Hibbat Tsion

152

(Love of Zion) movement and the Zionists therefore strove to rewrite the biblical account to try to demonstrate that this conquest was ultimately merely the return of this territory to its natural masters, because only a portion of the Hebrew people had sojourned in Egypt and the remainder had stayed in place. The land of Israel was therefore well and truly the homeland of the Jews, and the Bible was the cultural expression of a people established on its soil. It was Zionism's responsibility to restore the Promised Land as the motherland. A restoration that would have to come about through physical acquisition of the land: those who considered themselves as belonging to this land knew in point of fact that it did not belong to them.

At the beginning of Zionism's history, the land of Israel was perceived as a free land,[3] but those who established themselves there in the last decades of the nineteenth century in reality settled in a place where little land was without heirs. At least until 1947, someone else had first possessed each parcel of land that passed under Jewish control, and so this transfer of property carried an economic, political, and social price. When members of Hibbat Tsion arrived in Palestine, it was still hoped that the lack of available land could be overcome, that it was merely a financial problem. The region's very destitution was attributed to the fact that it was in Arab hands. The struggle over the land was in fact going to be at the heart of the conflict that pitted Jews against Arabs, and to be so for a long time.

However, it did not suffice to find the necessary money in order to assure full control over these parcels of land: it was also necessary for them to be transferred from one national possession to another. The First Zionist Congress in 1897 tried to give shape to a program for land acquisition that conceived that the buyer could never be dispossessed; the land could never be sold to individuals, but would only be rented to them for the limited duration of forty-nine years. This proposal, made by a rabbi, was put into operation in 1907 with the creation of the Jewish National Fund, responsible for supervising the application of these rules governing the land it acquired, which would remain the property of the Jewish people. It is not surprising to see rabbis inspiring such a practice from the start: for them, buying land was a prior stage in the redemption of the land and of the Jews who settled there. Pre-Zionists like Kalisher and Alkalai had said nothing less.[4] In the ideal relation between people and land, God was in effect the sole owner, the only veritable possessor of the land, with humans having only the usufruct.

The Zionists took up and inflected the major themes of religious thinking about the land. The whole debate about the status of the land of Israel thus oscillated between a religious discourse and one that was secular and national. The movement applied to the land rules inherited from the sacred domain, which were subsequently institutionalized and brought under state control. The land thus never totally acceded to secular status, which partly explains the turbulent period that opened after the Six Day War, when the borders of the Jewish state now included territories pertaining to the heart of ancient Israel and hence to the holiness of a mythified land. Henceforth, the Promised Land was once more on the agenda, arousing debates of an uncommon violence. The landmarks shifted: the annexation of these new territories, "promised lands" to some, was rejected by others, and it was vigorously combated by the dispossessed Arab inhabitants.

Arab opposition to the acquisition of lands by the Jews and to Jewish immigration had preceded the first Zionist congress, and in time it would be transformed into veritable resistance. In addition, one may wonder about the exact boundaries of these lands coveted by the Jews. The land of Israel was primarily a concept rooted in historic awareness reinvigorated by Jewish nationalism—much more than it was an area with clear geographic limits or stable political boundaries.[5] In the course of the historical and cultural upheavals that the real Palestine has known, its boundaries and its status in the region often varied. Its very name had undergone many changes. In the contemporary period, this lack of clarity finds its best expression in the dozens of publications that appeared on the eve of World War I proposing various frontiers for the land of Israel. The territory mentioned in these publications ordinarily included upper and lower Galilee, the hills of Judea up to a line running from the Dead Sea to Rafah, and the region east of the Jordan extending from Mount Hermon to the Arnon River, which empties into the Dead Sea. These borders do not correspond to those imposed after World War I. It was in fact the British Mandate that for the first time in the modern era fixed boundaries that were clearly defined. The British revived its ancient designation and opted for the name of Palestine, following European Christian tradition. The war of 1948 and the armistice that followed would give birth to the State of Israel (Medinat Yisrael), a new denomination saturated with ancient overtones. And the Six Day War would, in fact, as in well as in people's minds, accentuate the imprecision and fluidity of representations; it was as if, because of history just as much as people's ideas about it, this coveted land were condemned to elude a concrete definition that stable frontiers should have offered. It belonged to fluidity and change, side-stepping whatever could give it a solid basis that alone was able to make it truly concrete. Was the land of Israel more resistant than any other to this passage from historical consciousness to the reality of history?

Starting in the final decades of the nineteenth century, the purchase of lands by the Jews was concentrated in the valleys. Almost no land was acquired in the mountainous regions, although they were the heart of ancient Israel, and thus they remained outside the sphere of the new settlers. A gap arose between the Israel of the religious imagination and the one that was being constructed. The "true" Israel did not resemble idealized Israel, and this dissonance has haunted its inhabitants right down to the present. Toward the end of the 1930s, except for the south, meaning the Beersheba area, Jews had bought approximately 5 percent of the total land of Palestine and 10 percent of the area thought suitable for cultivation. By 1947, this total had scarcely increased by 2 or 3 percent.[6]

The need to acquire lands and to keep them under Jewish control favored the creation of institutions integrated into the social structure of the new Jewish colony of Palestine, such as the Palestine Land Development Company Limited, dating from 1908, whose primary mission was to buy land for the Jewish National Fund and for private investors. But it was not sufficient to buy these lands; one had to safeguard the right to settle them, so quasi-military establishments were set up. Thus, too, arose the figure of the pioneer, much glorified in the first period of colonization, who assumed an important role in legitimizing a collectivity that was continually confronted with conflict that threatened its existence, faced as it was with the former owners of the acquired lands. This period of incubation, stretching from the 1880s to 1920, saw the appearance of the kibbutz, an agricultural collective characterized by self-defense, voluntarism, simplicity, and the desire to be economically self-sufficient.[7] The formative period 1920–40 later saw the rise of the *moshavim:* cooperative farm–villages first founded on lands abandoned by Arabs in order to prevent their return.

It was the left wing of Zionism, carrying on from Hibbat Tsion, that launched the settlement venture during the last decade of the nineteenth century. These settlements were meant to impose the Jewish presence on the territory, to erect a barrier against infiltration, and to guarantee local security, while permitting the dispersal of the population across the countryside in order to avoid concentration in towns. In effect, the urban condition ran counter to an ideology advocating the development of a new type of Jew, radically different from his homologue in the Diaspora.

In the period preceding sovereignty, Jewish settlement called for the creation of artificial boundaries. By releasing lands belonging to the Arabs and by converting capital into land, these settlements assured a territorial base for the establishment of a Jewish political and social entity in Palestine, even if the amount of purchased land represented only a small part of the region initially claimed by the Zionists. In 1948, there were 291 rural settlement sites. Given the demographic inferiority of Jews, their presence in the territory, though it crystallized Arab opposition, remained of scant significance. With independence, boundaries were opened up by recourse to military force and all the other means at the disposal of a sovereign state. Between 1948 and 1964, 432 additional settlements were created.

This new period was marked by the restructuring of the large towns, the institutionalization of the frontier, and the construction of development towns, second-tier in the urban system, which were designed to receive immigrants. Institutionalization in this case also involved the state's promotion of the rural cooperative and the substitution of the state itself for local initiative. The Jewish Agency became responsible for the founding and operating of farm settlements, including stockbreeding. Indeed, land was at the core of the new sovereign state's concerns; it continued to rent and distribute it according to its own geopolitical and security criteria. The lack of free land contributed to reinforcing this paternalistic regime; land management was left to state control. The Six Day War, finally, dramatically placed the territorial issue at the heart of Israeli debate once more, where it became the subject of negotiations and brought the colonization issue back to center stage. The cycle was now complete; the land was well and truly a founding myth, always present to the point of obsession—a horizon always beyond reach. Space still obsesses Israel.

The Cult of the Land

The agricultural fundamentalism of the young state of Israel from its beginning drew upon a current that quickly came to dominate Zionist ideology.[8] The preference accorded to work on the land had a precedent in economic thought: the eighteenth-century French physiocrats had thought that agriculture alone was able to create wealth and new values. A pragmatic ideology, Zionism aimed to establish a Jewish society and a state in Palestine. From this perspective, it stressed the necessity of rejuvenating and restructuring Jewish society by means of a return to the land and an inversion of the pyramid of occupations, with an enlargement of the pool of workers and, principally, peasants and a reduction in activities linked to commerce and money.[9] This theme grew in importance with a spectacular rise in the pioneering and socialist forces within the Zionist movement after World War I.

The absence of other economic alternatives in the 1950s in Israel reinforced the tendency to idealize agriculture. An agricultural model based on equal distribution was created within the framework of an interrelation between sources of production (land, water, and capital) and personal work paid symbolically for the use of national land, water, and capital. Agriculture continued to be not only an economic enterprise but also a way of life. The house and the farm formed an organic whole. Farmers gained in influence within the population and determined the country's image, its defense, and its political elite. The agricultural sector, an integral part of the economy and the society, was the foremost representative of the values inherited from the first Jewish pioneers.

In the 1880s, the new arrivals had found the "old Yishuv" already in place, an ensemble of communities founded on philanthropy and depending for subsistence on financial aid from the Diaspora (the *halukka*).[10] At the time, these communities formed the majority of the Jewish population in the country. They were heterogeneous and did not speak with a unified voice. Jerusalem was their center. They never developed a relationship with the land comparable to that of the modern nationalists;[11] when they encouraged agriculture, it was not within the framework of mystical romanticism but as a pragmatic response to the economic distress of the poorest sectors of the population. The name "new Yishuv" was reserved for institutions and settlements born of the efforts of Hibbat Tsion and principally financed by Baron Edmond de Rothschild. The pioneers of the new Yishuv, settlers coming from this first wave of immigration, made Israel's renaissance their goal. It was expected they would lay the basis for a powerful national movement and the reconstruction of the nation.

In the mouths of these men and women, the name "old Yishuv" had very negative connotations, since it referred to a social reality perceived as a continuation of Diaspora existence. The new Yishuv aspired to renaissance, rejected the norms of the way of life inherited from exile, and for the same reason considered the old Yishuv to be another form of ghetto. Of course, for ideological reasons, some historians later argued that the return as such of Jews to the Holy Land, whether they were Orthodox or nationalist, had been the expression of a rupture with exile, meaning with what was provisional, insecure, and a rejection of rootedness, and that this return as such aimed at creating a new Jew, living on his land and making a living from it. The reality was quite different, however, and there was a profound gap between these two worlds.

Emancipated European Judaism was not mistaken, moreover, when it considered the Palestinian Jewish community to be a simple branch of traditional Jewish society, which had to be "regenerated" all the more carefully because it was located in the Holy Land. All financial aid grants were subject to the acceptance of this principle by the beneficiaries. At the same time, the Holy Land, and more precisely its

Ashkenazi component (the Sephardic and oriental Jews adopted another attitude) had set itself up as an orthodox bastion of resistance to modernity. It was in this context that the arrival of the first nationalists took place—a paradoxical context in which they would try to play the role of an avant-garde. It should also be remembered that even after the pogroms in Russia and Romania in the 1880s, when thousands of Jews headed for Palestine, very few of them were animated by a national consciousness. The old Yishuv was therefore enriched with new recruits and continued for a long time to represent the majority of the country's Jewish population. Founded within a Zionist perspective, the new Yishuv aimed to create and strengthen the economic base of the Jews of Palestine, and also to furnish labor and give a livelihood to the masses. The agricultural colonies were exclusively inhabited by its members. But like the old Yishuv, they remained dependent on external forces. Some of them were sustained by Baron Edmond de Rothschild; others by Hibbat Tsion and later by Zionist bodies. The members of the new Yishuv, however, furnished labor in exchange for the money they received and considered this aid to be temporary. In contrast, the assistance from which the old Yishuv benefited was well established and built into a justified ideological institution: its members saw their immigration to Palestine as a religious act and wished to devote themselves entirely to the study of the Torah.

Two realities thus opposed each other in this Palestine that was now open to new projects: the traditional one, incarnated by the old Yishuv, and that of a modernity devoted not only to a national renaissance but also to the creation of a new way of life, meaning a productive one, for the Jew of the future. Manual labor and in particular work on the land were, in the eyes of the new Yishuv, capable of transforming in depth the image people had of the Jew and that the Jew had of himself. The birth of the modern and productive Jew was inseparable from the land. This was not the first attempt at agricultural colonization; there had been precedents in Russia, Austria, and in America.[12] But this time, the chosen land was the land of a Book, and not just any book. The first settlers and their descendants after them would never cease oscillating between this land and this Book.

Even in its concreteness, powerfully affirmed by the pioneers, this land remained that of a Book; it remained holy. Everything concerning it was clothed in holiness. The agencies responsible for acquiring it and those who worked it were participating in a sacred task. The blue collection boxes of the Jewish National Fund and the figure of the pioneer-settler, both redeemer and hero, were woven into a Zionist mythology. The glorification of the peasant, a figure familiar to the intellectual elite of Russian Jewish youth from which the first pioneers had come, the influence of the writings of Leo Tolstoy, and a certain romantic vein all combined to crystallize a whole movement aspiring to social reform, founded on an idealization of the simple life. In the press and literature of the time, the prominence granted to rural themes and to the figures of Jewish laborers plowing their furrows in Palestine's soil eloquently testified to this nostalgia for the land, and to a desire for the normalization of Jewish existence. Agriculture was in effect an activity of prime importance in the absorption of the Jewish masses who were destined to immigrate to the country. The conquest of the land of the ancestors (*erets*) was based on the creation of a mythology of the cultivated land (*adama*). It was as if only this work of mythologization, and hence of abstraction, could paradoxically make palpable to the Jews a land too long caught inside dreams of exile. Nationalists and Zionists always had recourse to founding myths that were capable of grounding their ideology and were alone able, it seemed, to allow real access to the land; the simple purchase of areas for cultivation was not sufficient to guarantee a national appropriation of the territory.

The Symbolism of Pioneering

The land of Israel, the Hebrew man, and the Hebrew language were the heart of the Zionist credo of national renaissance.[13] The redemption of the people necessarily came about through redemption of the land. The pioneers expected colonization to lead to individual and collective salvation. To build, and in building to rebuild themselves— this was the existentialist philosophy (before its time) that the settlers promoted, a philosophy taken up in popular songs of the day, which themselves contributed to strengthening the pioneer myth. Colonizing is the pioneering activity par excellence, both the guarantee and the proof of rootedness. The founding of a settlement was the ultimate realization of the ideology that the Zionist youth movements were inculcating into their members.

"The conquest of labor" was the battle cry of the second wave of immigration that began in 1904, following new pogroms in eastern Europe, and would continue until the outbreak of World War I. Its members combined socialist ideals with concepts of national renaissance.[14] The Hebrew word used, *kibbush*, "conquest," has a military meaning, implying possible recourse to force to guarantee control over labor (as over territory). This slogan applied initially to the transfer of labor in the colonies from Arabs to Jews. The land of Israel in effect would not be Jewish unless it was worked by the Jews themselves. The Zionists thus manifested their desire to distinguish themselves from the Arab community by establishing Jewish territorial entities, a policy they maintained during the period of the Mandate. It was thought that in this way, two separate communities would be able to develop, one Arab and the other Jewish, concentrated in distinct regions, each enjoying real autonomy. Such a settlement strategy was perceived as a pragmatic and political necessity, and over time the colonization effort would enable the zones involved to accede to national sovereignty.

When the first attempts at "the conquest of labor" ended in failure, the initial dogma took on a new meaning. The word *kibbush*, independently of its military connotations, also evoked moral force, strength of character, and thus the possibility for each person to surmount the difficulty of manual labor, to find satisfaction in it without caring about its ultimate objective. The land and its care were therefore both invested with material and ethical meanings. Since by its nature, the land existed in these two registers, it was inevitable that its conquest, attributed to the merit of labor, was seen in the same light. To work the land was a victory over oneself, not just an act of transferring property.

The writings of Aaron David Gordon strongly contributed to this evolution in the credo of the conquest of labor. They tightened the link between the physical and spiritual dimensions of work and underlined its sacred character, helping to develop the concept of the religion of work (*dat ha-avoda*). The land certainly did not manage to elude its status as Holy Land. Those who worked it acceded through it to this holiness: the founding of a Hebrew settlement demanded absolute engagement and devotion and a great willingness to sacrifice. Abraham Shlonsky, whose writings reflect the experiences of pioneers of the third wave of immigration (1919–23), evoked the sacred work of the pioneer in terms borrowed from Jewish ritual. The Zionist settler was substituted for God as creator.

The Hebrew word for "pioneer" is *halutz*, also borrowed from military vocabulary. The *haluts* is a warrior, one of the vanguard. The same discipline is required of him as of a soldier. He is also a hero who dies to defend his land. The episode at Tel Hai in Galilee in 1920, mythified and later recuperated by the revisionist tendency in the Zionist movement, in which Joseph Trumpeldor and five of his men were killed in unequal combat against Bedouin attackers, therefore became the symbol of national renaissance, the sign of an awakening of authentic Jewish patriotism, though it was not the first clash of this kind with the Arabs. In this period of colonization, when the Jewish presence in Palestine remained quite small, such symbols were necessary in order to galvanize people's energies. In 1855, there had been only 10,500 Jews in the Holy Land, of whom 5,700 lived in Jerusalem. With the organization of Hibbat Tsion and the Biluim, the first wave of immigration (1882–85 and 1890) brought in 1,500 people a year. Yet in 1898, the number of Jews in Palestine was estimated at only 50,000. There were 75,000 at the start of the second wave of immigration in 1907, and by the outbreak of World War I, the number had reached 85,000, but it fell to 65,000 during the conflict. In 1922, with the third wave of immigration, the Jewish community resumed its expansion and attained a total of 165,000.[15]

Faced with the new and exalted figure of the pioneer and the masculine values it promoted, it is remarkable to observe that the image of womanhood within the Zionist movement remained totally traditional at first: her place was in the home or school or office.[16] Among the dozens of Zionist leaders, there was not a single woman. There was no place for women on the farms of the Zionist laborers, except for kitchen and other domestic tasks. During the first wave of immigration, the wives of settlers were turned into housekeepers in the new settlements, and there were few women farmworkers. It was during the second wave of immigration that a new image took shape, that of the working woman, the *halutza*, the pioneer who found the meaning of her life in work on the land. Women's aspirations, though, were opposed by those who allocated labor on the farms, who balked at opening up this field to them. The will of women themselves to participate alongside the men in work on the land, as well as an awareness of the fact that they were essential to the rural economy, finally opened the way to the creation of a women's farm in lower Galilee in 1911. Its principal role was to train women for agricultural work; the stress was on working the land and not on domestic labor. In 1917, the farm shut down, but of the seventy women who had shared in this venture, only two left the country, while the others remained and continued working in agriculture. Women's stability, along with their capacity for farmwork, contributed to ensuring men's stability in relation to the land and to the place. Now the pioneer woman could finally exist—so that the man could devote himself faithfully to his land. The *halutza* as such had no right to the sacralization of *halutz*, but she had a share in it insofar as she sustained the pioneering effort.

As essential actors in the enterprise of national renaissance, the settlers saw themselves as engaged in an act of creation. The religious metaphors used to describe it were secularized, and biblical images were employed to characterize their contribution to a new religious era. As we have seen, Jews were living in Palestine well before the arrival of the pioneers, while very many others continued to live elsewhere, enjoying a prosperity much more evident than could be hoped for upon the ungrateful soil of the homeland. In order to mark the importance of their act, the pioneers felt constrained to make a tabula rasa of the pre-Zionist Palestinian Jewish community, who seemed so exilic to them. The new Yishuv incarnated the present and future, as opposed to the past, to which the old Yishuv was relegated. The new Yishuv and the pioneer were one; the two images were interchangeable. By adopting the figure of the pioneer, the new Yishuv inherited all its characteristics. Such a society could not be unjust. The struggle with nature in which the pioneers were engaged in order to transform the landscape and to improve their surroundings also strengthened their right to live on this soil. Zionist literature complacently described these people building towns along a sandy coast, draining marshes, and digging wells. These reborn people could not be content with what was old; they were ambitious to change the face of the land and its climate by planting forests.

Planting trees was, in fact, a veritable rite, indispensable to entering into contact with the land.[17] The Jewish National Fund and the Jewish Agency saw it as a sacred act leading to the redemption of the land. Hebrew educational institutions supported these bodies' activities; their children raised money for this purpose. The Jewish festival of Tu Bishvat, the New Year of Trees, in January/February, was an occasion to speak about trees and to promote the fund's mission to reforest. The planting of trees became the central patriotic ritual of this festival within Hebrew secular culture. Thus the religious and the secular intersected when it came to the land; any act concerning it took on highly religious significance. Before the birth of the State of Israel, the tree symbolized national renewal, the people's taking root in the soil of the mother country. In Zionist memory, the land of Israel, which had been covered with forests in antiquity, had become a desert during the absence of the Jews. Only their return would allow this desert to be transformed anew into cultivated land. The planting of trees symbolized this legitimate taking of possession.

The forest was also invested with a memorial function for the living. Forests were named after individuals or groups. Memorializing the dead and reviving the nation, past and future, were united in order to confer a supreme significance on the act of planting. Knowing the religious significance of the memory of the dead in Judaism enables one to measure the importance accorded to reforestation. Such memorialization also naturally had a pragmatic side, since it sustained the planting activities of the Jewish National Fund. These forests, bearing the names of great figures in the movement, became Zionist historical landmarks. And they reached the status of living memories when they were planted in honor of soldiers who had died during Israel's wars or as memorials for victims of the Holocaust. The forest/book of history, the forest as text, is thus spread out before the living so that they will remember, never forget.

The forest took its place in the pioneer's struggle to overcome his own history, a history marked by exile, the Holy Land's desolation, and by the hostility of nature, climate, and Arabs. In planting forests, the settlers advanced their combat for the conquest of the land. The forest was their victory. Literature itself clearly echoed this symbolism. Eliezer Smally's novel *The People of Genesis*, published in 1933, in the midst of the pioneering period, and Abraham B. Yehoshua's *Facing the Forests*, dating from 1968, after the creation of the State of Israel, both exploit this theme of the forest and its destruction by the Arabs (increasing their authors' celebrity in the process). In the context of the Jewish-Arab and then the Israeli-Palestinian conflict, the uprooting or the burning of trees and forests—bearers of national memory, symbols of collective identity, markers of ownership of a contested land—were inevitably acts of war.

This type of sabotage was quite frequent in the years of the Arab revolt between 1936 and 1939. Later, in the 1980s and 1990s, forests and orchards once again became important factors in antagonisms between Israelis and Palestinians within the context of the appropriation of new territories. Israel and its settlers planted trees to mark their settlements, and so did the Palestinians to avoid the confiscation of their lands by Israeli authorities. The stakes were the same as at the start of colonization: possession of the land, of a land that always slipped away. And if one side opted for a strategy of reforestation, the other initiated a counterstrategy of destruction: the Intifada against the trees. As in the past, the Jewish National Fund relaunched its planting campaign, which it called "Tree for Tree." On Tu Bishvat in 1989, after the burning of the forests of Carmel, it called for the replacement of a million charred trees with the planting of three million new trees. Conversely, the Israelis uprooted 170,000 trees on the West Bank between 1987 and 1994.[18] Forests remain on the front line in the long historical struggle for the conquest of the land.

Of course, the strategies for mastering space varied from one period to another, but the principle remained constant: a close combination of the symbolic and the pragmatic, as if the former always had to come to the rescue of the latter and compensate for the material insufficiency of the lands actually possessed by the Jews. The glorification of the land as such was overblown compared with the reality of the land. Did salvation really depend upon it? The pioneers had arrived in Palestine with a narrative as their luggage: the biblical story. Their profound desire was to move from the symbolic to the real through contact with the land and to create a new place where that would be possible. This explains their estrangement from the spiritual center of Jerusalem, their distrust of towns, and the tropism that pushed them irresistibly toward new lands: wild and uninhabited lands.[19] A real (re)birth could only take place in an elsewhere not occupied by the idea, not deflowered by the founding story. At the same time, though, this story nourished the pioneering act, irrigated it, guided it, and rooted it in a land that until then had been known only through the narrative.

For some people, in fact, the land of Israel remained largely an idea. This was the case with Ahad Ha-Am, for example, who thought the pioneer ideal was impracticable because of the Arab presence; for politics and economics, he preferred America. But this was also true of the pioneers themselves, since it was largely from the idea that they drew the strength necessary to renew ties with the land. It was through the Bible that these new conquerors took possession of their territory; this is why they tried to find the remains of ancient Hebrew settlements behind the Arab names of villages. The pioneers, then the native residents who succeeded them, regilded the Bible's blazon and brought it back to center stage as a source of inspiration. They thus broke with the centuries of religious tradition in exile that had focused on the Talmud and its study—and invented a secular religiosity oriented toward Scripture. The Bible entered the school curriculum of the Jewish Palestinian community.

David Ben-Gurion did not consider himself only a politician, but also a propagator and interpreter of the Bible. According to him, only a Jew living on and working Israel's soil could truly understand Scripture.[20] Only intimate familiarity with the geographical, climatic, and historical specificity of this land, only the lived experience of the bond with this land, could offer the means for a clear understanding of the text. For Ben-Gurion, the Bible was neither simply the source of a Jewish philosophy or ethics, or of a universal humanism, nor simply a document endowed with scientific authority about the land and its inhabitants. In addition, the Bible was the common denominator of the construction of the renewed Jewish state, able to serve the unity of a Jewish people returned to their land. It was a purveyor of heroes. It taught the future of the Jewish nation.

And so new settlements were given ancient Hebrew names. This Hebraization was a ransom, a redemption, but it also contributed to assuring the primacy of the language and of the word, and hence resulted in deterritorialization, the possession of the land through the word. For example, in the Negev, a desert region, devoid of a historic tradition really able to furnish any inspiration, between 1949 and 1950 Hebrew names were given to some 533 geographic sites, between Eilat in the south and the Ein Gedi–Gaza line in the north.[21] Of these, 120 took historical names and 50 were named after biblical characters; for the remainder, Arab names were translated or given a Hebrew form according to phonetic resemblance. Also translated into Hebrew were Arab names for topographic features, for plants and animals, and anything else intimately linked with the land and landscape. The language of the Bible, a resuscitated language, thus redeemed and sanctified everything that could not be inserted into historical continuity. It purified the land and guaranteed its conquest via naming, as if physical conquest could not suffice. The name transformed the place into a text.

In the process, the Bible acted naturally as a screen, paradoxically preventing spontaneous contact. New stories were superimposed on the initial story, recreating a territory that was not at all separate from the mythical land. Born of the Book, Zionist patriotism in turn fabricated other books, produced other readings in order both to support the primal myth of the land and to signpost the territory when it was still only at the planning stage. The territory itself was in turn wholly impregnated with these stories, penetrated with a spiritual and historical depth that would become an integral part of it. This entanglement of the idea and the concrete weaves through the whole history of the land of Israel from the last decades of the nineteenth century on. It has also shaped the perception that Israeli society has had of itself down to our own day. Literature, cinema, songs, posters, history, geography, archeology, and textbooks—everything conspired in this ideational reconquest of the land.

The Myths to the Rescue of the Land

The literary evocation of the Hebrew worker living in a wooden hut, eating Arab bread dipped in olive oil, underlined three changes: he was a worker, he was the true son of the land, and he did not eat in the Jewish manner.[22] The green olives, the olive oil, the soft cheese, the welcoming ceremonies of local populations, and the kaffiyeh (Arab headdress) all acquired a primordial semiotic status. The adoption of elements of Bedouin and fellahin cultures by members of various Jewish immigration waves to Palestine also expressed the hold of nineteenth-century romantic norms and of stereotypes that confused Bedouin robes with those of biblical ancestors, for example. Engravings and illustrations reinforced this influence. The Bedouin offered a ready-made model for generating a positive attitude toward elements that would eventually be identified with the reality of the population and landscape. Non-Jewish Europeans visiting the region in the nineteenth century developed similar views. That immigrants would adopt this Western attitude toward the Near East is scarcely surprising, since they had already adopted a number of Western prejudices about the Jews themselves: that they were deprived of roots, physically weak, that they disliked manual labor, were alienated from nature, and so on. These generalizations and identifications were without much foundation, of course. But they allowed Zionists to advocate the transition, through agriculture, of the Diaspora Jew into the new Hebrew. Moreover, at the end of World War I, having done a good bit of work on the ground, the Zionists still believed they could create a national Jewish homeland in Palestine without arousing great opposition from the Arabs.[23] According to a theory then in vogue, the native fellahin were, in fact, no less than descendants of the ancient Hebrews who had been forcibly converted to Islam by the Muslim conquerors. Certain Zionist leaders thought it was possible to assimilate them or to develop a proselytizing program among them. This desire to integrate the non-Jewish populations of the region was intimately linked to the desire to create a new Hebrew identity. To conquer Palestine presupposed a mastery not only of space but also of time. The Bedouin were perceived as the true children of this land, and at the same time as an "inferior" and "savage" population. The Zionist settlers were there to regenerate the land that belonged to these people, whose food, habits, attitudes, and music simultaneously expressed courage, loyalty, roots, and an exalted "primitiveness." By seeking to resemble them, the pioneers were really appropriating a land that they knew only through an idea. Inversely, regenerating this land through Jewish work was another way of appropriating it while regenerating oneself. In a similar vein, women writers of the first wave of immigration to Palestine such as Hemdah Ben-Yehuda and Nehamah Pukhachewsky also preached in favor of an expansion of settlement and the emergence of a modern, liberated Jewish woman in this new setting.[24] The land and its men were endowed with all virtues, ancient and new. The land whose soil was beginning to be trod was still a Promised Land, capable of metamorphosing its men and liberating its women.

The characters of the "realist" and optimistic literature that developed in parallel with pioneering were quite naturally credited with the same qualities praised in biblical heroes.[25] Completely realized human beings, in perfect communion with nature, they looked toward the future. Zeev Javetz's young heroes in *Excursion to the Country* (1891), *Swords into Plowshares* (1893), and so on, frequently cross biblical sites on the hikes that bring them into contact with nature in the motherland. Descriptions of Palestinian landscapes lyrically idealize the land, giving meaning to the settlers' taking possession of it. They remodel space and time, transforming them into imaginary, timeless, atopian realms.[26] All these stories begin by describing the profound attachment of the pioneers to the soil they tread; plots come later. Jewish Palestinian writers of the second generation, weighed down with the baggage of literary traditions from eastern Europe even when they confess their uprootedness, express unbounded admiration for this land, which gives them a sense of being anchored and of belonging. Thus Meir Wilkanski in *Bi-Ymei ha-Aliyyah* (The Era of Immigration [1935]) evokes in almost prophetic terms the redemptive experience that the soil, sky, and language of this new land give him. With its naïve dramatization of pioneering, this literature (which prospered in the 1920s and 1930s, but also in the 1950s and later) is far from reflecting reality. Rather, it expresses the enthusiasm of young authors who had decided to live in the world of their dreams.

In the choice of plots and characters for their fictions, they responded to the requirements of pioneering Zionism and illustrated in some way the great themes of its propaganda. Writers were perceived as an organic part of the national body;[27] they were the principal creators of myths. People expected the literature they produced to sustain in a didactic sense the new settlers' confidence in their acts and their beliefs. Fiction and theater in the Jewish Palestinian community at its beginnings, and then in the 1940s and 1950s, were distinguished by their engagement and their documentary fidelity rather than by their universalism. The writers of this naïve tradition projected reality onto the framework of their vision, judging that it should be promoted in that way. They addressed their message to the Diaspora in order to enlarge the Zionist dream, as illustrated by the books of Aaron Abraham Kabak, *Between the Sea and the Desert* (1932–33) and of Asher Barash, *Gardeners* (1937–38). Readers, whether they lived in Palestine or in the Diaspora, discovered and interpreted reality through the representations this literature offered. Even journalistic accounts were permeated with enthusiasm for the land and its workers, and for the new conquerors' heroism in the face of the local inhabitants. And so life was probably more touched by the texts than the texts were by life.

Another literary current, later and quite different in nature, made the land of Israel the sole element in the new Hebrew identity. Led by the poet Yonatan Ratosh, a whole group of young writers, students, and journalists, called the "Canaanites," who had been active during the War of Independence (some had been members of clandestine right-wing organizations), expressed radical views about what was expected of a new Hebrew culture in their journal *Aleph*.[28] They were really advocating the construction of a Hebrew identity that was fundamentally dissociated from Jewish identity: while Jewish identity was perceived as essentially religious, with no link whatsoever with the land or its history, the Hebrew identity the Canaanites called for was shared, according to them, with all the inhabitants of the Middle East, by virtue of their past and their common local roots. The Hebrew nation had to define itself in terms of territory because it was perfectly identified with the land of Israel, with the past, and with the culture of this country. Inversely, what had no roots in this territory, or had not been nourished by it, like Islamic culture or the Jewish culture of the Diaspora, in no way belonged to it. Very critical of Jewish literature of the Diaspora and of its Palestinian disciples, the Canaanites accused the latter of betraying or ignoring the authentic Hebrew values of courage and strength, which were tied to the soil, to the people, and to the history of the land of Israel.

The return to one's roots came about through a voyage of initiation in childhood. A story by Benjamin Tammuz, "Between Eden and Ophir," which appeared in *Aleph*, tells of the return of the author to his childhood, which is at the same time a crossing of ancient Palestine and its landscapes. A number of other stories exploit the same theme. As land of childhood and as land of the past, the land of Israel fashions an identity that cannot manage to be satisfied with the land in the present tense. This dissatisfaction makes it necessary to travel, which is the antithesis of the rootedness demanded by the ideologists of the movement. As a rule, this thirst for the past overwhelms the real or symbolic appropriation of the land, a land that it paradoxically renders foreign to those very people who possess it, or who, like the Canaanites, aspire to a Greater Israel.

For the newly founded State of Israel was not going to suffice; the land remained incomplete, still promised. Of course, the Canaanites scarcely numbered more than twenty, but their social, cultural, and literary influence in Israel was important. The peak of their success occurred in the 1950s, when their position coincided with views then in vogue within the Zionist movement, at a time when, after the War of Independence, people were expecting a cultural renaissance supported by young people within the new national framework. After the Six Day War, the encounter with the "historical" land of Israel (Judea and Samaria) gave a new significance to this search for roots. Literature reacted in its own way, giving birth to a type of story centered on the land of Israel, written in colloquial Hebrew, set in the region's landscape and in the present, and linked to the land's history, as if conquest did not suffice to confer legitimacy on possession, as if the text always had to come to its rescue. The text was present both before the conquest and after it.

During the Arab riots of 1936, the posters of both left- and right-wing political parties in Palestine called for activism. The activism of the Jewish pioneers was highly praised and contrasted with traditional Jewish passivity. For the left, activism is the strengthening of colonization; for the right, it meant war and vengeance. The great revolt of the Jews against the Romans that had ended in 70 C.E. with the destruction of the Second Temple, the rebellion of Bar-Kokhba in 132–35 C.E., and the brave first generation of the Zionist pioneers were jointly exalted as illustrations of the people's past valor, as a guarantee for the future, and as an exhortation to current combatants. The goal of the struggle was the Promised Land. For the right, this land belonged to Jews in its entirety and not an inch of it should be given up; for the left, Israel was affianced to the land by an eternal betrothal. In the posters, the future was no longer historical but suprahistorical; it was an endless period during which the Jewish people would inhabit its land in security (for the left) and without renouncing the smallest patch (for the right). National identity and the historical past, focused on the land and now annexed by political parties, thus founded a national myth that was peopled with the heroes of yesterday, becoming a party myth for activism in the present.

In Palestinian Hebrew songs before independence, land and countryside were one. The songs' privileged setting was the agrarian colony. They were addressed to students as well as workers, sung to accompany both marches and labor. Centered on the summits of pioneering, this music quickly detached itself from the Diaspora, to which it conveyed the local ideal and in which attachment to landscape occupied a central place.[29] In her work before 1967, the singer Naomi Shemer, the heir of this tradition, exalted the land of Israel through the figures of the hiker and the soldier, and evoked the impatience and fears of a young lover waiting for her beloved soldier. It exalted also the work and memories of the generation of builders. Later, her songs took a more ideological turn, a change already perceptible in her "Yerushalayim shel Zahav" (Jerusalem the Golden), though it was written before the Six Day War. Her tone became more solemn: the land was no longer represented by the colors of its flowers or peaceful fauna; it became the portion of David and the heritage of Jesse's son. Thus even after the legitimacy conferred by the foundation of a state, even after victory, legitimation by the founding Text still proved necessary. In her late work, Naomi Shemer slid toward a pseudo-mystical tone that was almost messianic. With the conquest in 1967 of the heart of ancient Israel, the call of the sacred was heard once again—as if the real land, finally possessed, still eluded reality. In these songs, the authentic land, the exalted land of Israel, was not revealed on the ground, on the surface of things, or in the landscape, but rather in hidden depths. This evolution in Naomi Shemer's songs is in tune with that of Palestinian, then Israeli, Jewish society as a whole. Ineluctably, it seems, there was a slide from the concrete to the abstract, from the quotidian to the solemn, culminating in the apocalyptic. Listening closely to the work of this singer, whose themes and longevity are significant, one observes that the landscape itself does not appear as real but as a substitute for reality. One does not sense any real encounter with it, no adherence; landscape is scarcely more than a picture postcard. The land's reality is filtered through the Text, which does not support it. The Text is self-sufficient, whereas reality needs the Text in order to exist. The Text precedes the land, creates it, and obscures it.

But the culture of the native does exalt contact with the land. It is not by chance that the native is referred to by the Hebrew term *tsabar* (sabra) derived from Arabic and meaning literally "cactus." A plant growing out of an ungrateful and rebellious soil, emblematic of a landscape that the Zionists wanted at all costs for the new Jew to become an integral part of when he finally acquired roots, the cactus is a spiny plant, but it gives fruit with a creamy heart. Nevertheless, it is a plant of aridity, of the desert, of this non-place that is the site of the Book's revelation. . . . Could the sabra still be, despite or because of the name he bears, the Jew of the non-place, of the unsatisfied quest for a habitable land, for a land that could at last grip him by the feet and could also prevent him from gazing on high? The expectation was immense and the desire for an anchor very strong. The contemporary poet Saul Tchernichowsky wrote: "Man is only a little bit of earth/ Man is only the reflection of his country's landscape." The Promised Land had to become the mother country at all costs. Not only did the pioneers redeem the landscape, but they also wanted it to nourish their children, secure them to the land in a carnal, not abstract, contact. How could such a demand be satisfied, however, when the accumulated layers of symbolic sedimentation, enriched by the Zionists themselves as religious laymen, continued to interpose themselves between the land and humans?

Hikes were considered an essential educational activity. The famous *tiyul* (excursion), the only concrete way of knowing the country and establishing direct contact with its nature, was elevated into a ritual practice well before the creation of the State of Israel. Schools and youth movements soon gave it a prominent place, developing the custom of the annual excursion. In the 1950s, the Society for the Protection of Nature was founded, a sort of Israeli equivalent to the European Green movement.[30] It assembled Israelis of different political tendencies who were concerned about the quality of life and the preservation of the country's natural and historical heritages. It offered classes in geography and the natural sciences, and provided various services in the areas of tourism, environmental research, and the protection of nature. The hikes it organized became almost a national ritual. Its guides' "uniforms" recalled those of the Palmah[31] and later those of the youth movements, enabling these guides to feel rooted in the environment and also letting the hikers they accompanied share in this sentiment. Similarly, the guides used Arab words in their commentaries, baked Bedouin bread (*pita*) in the open air, prepared herbal tea, and told their audiences stories borrowed from Bedouin folklore. Although the Bedouin were people of the desert, and originally nomads, it was, moreover, by imitating their way of life—already so privileged, as we have seen, by the first pioneers—that these Israeli guides and hikers persuaded themselves that they were fixed in this soil that they were traversing in all directions. Are we still witnessing here the no-man's-land as land of belonging, and the voyage as a sign of being anchored? In periods of tension, the hike continued to strengthen the bond with the land and to assure a Jewish presence in regions actually uninhabited by Jews. Its other aim was to show the Jewish presence in the land of Israel as an overall historical reality to those who practiced it; it reassured the Israeli about his right to this land. It gave individuals an occasion to underscore their personal identities as well as their national identities and to mark their territory. From the beginning, this practice, like other rituals, reinforced the connection between people and land, and reaffirmed its legitimacy without ever really erasing its ambiguity. This ambiguity equally marked the relationship established between culture and nature.

For identical reasons, geography occupied a central place in education. For a long time, the geography of the land of Israel had remained the prerogative of non-Jews, and the first sign of Jewish interest in this discipline dated in fact from the work of Abraham Moses Luncz, who starting in 1882 published a series of thirteen volumes entitled *Jerusalem*, consisting of articles on history and geography of the land of Israel (including topography, archeology, the history of the Jewish community in Palestine, etc.).[32] Over twenty-one years, Luncz also published the *Luah Erets Yisrael* (Almanac of the Land of Israel), designed for a wider audience. In 1918, at the end of World War I, the Hebrew Society for the Study of the Land of Israel and Its Antiquities was reestablished.

In fact, from the beginning of colonization, geography was a prime educational concern of the new Yishuv. During this first period, ending in 1918, the geography of the land of Israel, like the study of the Hebrew language, became, in the hands of these idealists, one of the major tools in the education system.[33] It was studied through the length of the school curriculum: in elementary classrooms, it was integrated into the general curriculum; in intermediate classrooms, it was tellingly called *moledet* (homeland), and it became geography properly speaking in higher grades.[34] This teaching was based on experience, on direct observation, field trips, and the *tiyul*—but in its content, as in its pedagogy, it remained marked by a strong European influence.

A second period, running from 1918 to 1948, was characterized by the subject's politicization and by the strengthened ideological orientation of Hebrew-Zionist education. The land of Israel now lay at the core of education. An educational ideology of "knowledge of the land" (*yediat ha-arets*) was developed, bringing the child to experience the land as homeland on both intellectual and emotional levels, making it an essential element in the development of the child's personality. The New Hebrew had to feel rooted. This rootedness was procured by excursions and instruction in the nature, population, and history of the land of Israel. The *moledet*, or "homeland," course became the kernel of the educational system and other disciplines were subordinated to it. At this time, professional geographers began to appear, but the teaching they helped shape aimed at relaying the pioneer and Zionist message. During the British Mandate, the *moledet* was no longer merely a discipline but an overall educational ideology. It dealt with the natural aspects of the countryside (the soil, flora, and fauna), combined with the history of man's interaction with his environment (forms of colonization or agriculture)—all laden with strong nationalist connotations. The stress was placed on the link between the succession of seasons, the different times in country life, national festivals, and sometimes certain sites and national historical events. Classroom study was complemented by practical experiments, such as growing certain seasonal vegetables in the school garden, or by excursions to significant sites on dates of symbolic importance. This course aimed to instill a strong emotional relationship between the pupil and the spatial and temporal dimensions of collective identity, to strengthen the children's love for their nation and, after 1948, for their state. The essential objective was to anchor young Jews solidly in the soil of Palestine, simultaneously the land of their ancestors, the site of the birth of the Hebrew nation, their mother country, and the natural place for creating an authentic Jewish material and spiritual culture.

Land and homeland were united to prepare the terrain for the foundation of the future state. The teaching of "homeland" and geography was not a simple transmission of knowledge from one generation to another; rather, it relayed the values and social norms of the Zionist movement, whether from its right wing or its left wing. It was not until the 1970s and 1980s that "homeland" acquired the status of a systematic discipline. When one analyzes the textbooks used over one century in Zionist education, one finds four types of author. First, there was the European, who looked at a Levantine land with the eye of a colonist. Next came the Zionist idealist, who insisted on the return of the Jews to the land of the patriarchs and on nostalgia for historical sites and for the text, and who wanted to link students with the remains of the past scattered on this land, which he described as fertile, and thus as it had formerly been, in the hope that the immigration of millions of Jews would restore it to its ancient grandeur. A third type of author, the practical Zionist, who came after the preceding one, was attached to this land's present and emphasized what was being built under Zionist influence, which had the power to modify the landscape and to create something from nothing—often stressing the importance of the return to agrarian work and to the rural life. The man of science, finally, who elaborated textbooks according to objective scientific criteria, appeared only rather late in the sweep of time.

In the search for roots, archaeology played a role no less important than geography. The digs were a descent into the inmost depths of the earth, a means of finding oneself there, *under* the ground, a means of finding one's kin and reestablishing the chain that had been broken *above* ground. Archeology helped to put names on sites and to rediscover concrete places behind names charged with a powerful symbolic and historic significance.[35] In the 1930s, archaeology was used in political debate, since it was now a matter of demonstrating the continuity of Jewish settlement in the land of Israel, of proving the Jewish character of areas that a land-sharing plan would have left to the Arabs, of confirming the Bible's historicity, and especially of highlighting the bond between Jewish inhabitants and their land, underlining the territorial aspects of Jewish life in the land of Israel. Until recently, archeological research was essentially devoted to those periods in which the Jewish presence in Palestine could easily be demonstrated.[36] Thus it served to confer a new historical depth on modern Jewish settlement. Sites dating from the period of the Second Temple, the key period when Palestine still remained the center of the Jewish world, despite the existence of a significant Diaspora, were essential from this standpoint: they furnished the needed symbols. Significantly, the first Jewish dig took place in Tiberias in Galilee—because Galilee had become the heart of Jewish Palestine after the Bar-Kokhba revolt. And while archeologists and historians were actively devoted to the study of the Davidic kingdom and the periods of the Second Temple, of the Mishnah and the Talmud, they were in contrast, not particularly interested in later periods, which were parenthetical, in a sense, in the history of the Jewish people on its land.

Another essential cultural product that was mobilized was the cinema, whose mission was to explain the experience of the Palestinian Jewish community to the outside world, to the Jews of the Diaspora, to world opinion—and to educate the young. Cinema sustained the efforts of the nation builders and transmitted something of this new contact with the land to those who were constrained to live the experience through someone else and at a distance. It was a privileged vector of Zionist propaganda. The Zionists were, of course, not the first to resort to the cinema to promote their cause; nationalisms of all stripes have done the same. But any originality in Zionist cinematic propaganda lies in the fact that it crystallized precisely around the land. People wanted at all costs to believe, and have it believed, that the land was effectively primordial for those Jews who had freshly arrived on a land that had only been promised and was still to be conquered. The less the land is there, the more fervent the quest for it. The less it exists in reality, the more it is represented. *Eretz Israel Resurrected*, directed by Yaacov Ben-Dov in 1921, curiously stresses the land and not its redeemers:[37] there are no human faces, but only distant figures, people who exist only as members of a group, in images dominated by the landscape, which is the true protagonist of the film and furnishes the context for any dialogue. A few years later, in 1927, in *The Pioneer*, Natan Axelrod placed the *halutz* at the center of his film. But in *Oded the Wanderer* dating from 1933, the directors Hayim Halahmi and Natan Axelrod were once again more preoccupied with the landscape of the Jezreel Valley than with the main character's tormented face. In 1933, *The Pioneers*, directed by Alexander Ford, exalted the Spartan virtues of the *halutzim* as against a café society so alien to these people of the land. The first talking film in Hebrew bore the title *This Is the Land* (1935); this documentary by Baruch Agadati is about the history of the Jewish Palestinian community since the arrival of the first pioneers in the 1880s. It has its characters enter a biblical landscape, shows the difficulties faced by the settlers, and calls on exiles to come back. Another film of this period, *Labor*, takes the search for water as its theme. It ends with a victory, the pioneers marching together behind the flag.

In 1935, the year of the Nuremberg Laws, a Zionist propaganda film was shown in Berlin: *The Land of Promise*. Subsequently, it toured the world, and in the early years of the State of Israel, it was still being shown to schoolchildren and immigrants in transit camps. Even today, most of the documentaries dealing with the pre-state history of Israel make use of this film, in which the land is introduced in biblical terms, youth is a dominant element, and the songs emphasize a bond with the land that is at the foundation of everything. A land in decline, separated from its people, is tamed by the descendants of this people; it is revived by water and by the work of their hands, culminating in scenes of harvest. The formula "long-neglected fruitfulness" recurs in the English version. All these films center on the land, on agriculture, and "productivization of the land" through work. This profound desire for symbiosis between land and inhabitants continued to be expressed well after the state's foundation. In a documentary produced in 1965, *In Jerusalem*, the population is depicted as living in full harmony with the nature of this city—because it is an integral part of it. Nature, history, and myth are repeatedly interwoven.

The Land of Historians

History was also an indispensable tool in the (re)creation of the land. Here again, the Zionists' approach was no exception: many other peoples have made use of history, and we know the role played by historians in general in forging national communities. In this instance, though, it was not just a matter of glorifying a people's past, of exalting its exploits, of drawing the map of its memorial sites. Zionist historiography organized itself around a national territory from which the national community had been physically removed for centuries, and in which it was trying once more to take root. History's role was to help to establish a people on soil that was foreign to it, to legitimize this settlement, to make its contours and borders more precise, and thus to sketch a new national identity. Founded upon reminiscences and symbols of a fundamentally religious nature, it was articulated around a double negation: negation of the Arabs, another people, who were already present, and negation of the Diaspora, the unjustified absence of the Jewish people from their land.

It was through the Idea that the land had to be (re)born. It was scarcely possible to deny outright the Arabs and Palestinians, who were well and truly there and possessed a large part of the territory. Instead, it was necessary to make the Jewish presence go back into the mists of time and to assert that it was uninterrupted. Primacy, antiquity, and continuity lent legitimacy to the conquest and resettlement that were under way. In spatial terms, Jewishness had to be seen as naturally linked to Zion and, in temporal terms, as a continuous, eternal entity. It was not sufficient to buy parcels of land; the land still had to be appropriated and internalized so that it was an integral part of the identity not only of new immigrants but also of Jews still in the Diaspora, who could be considered future settlers or future Zionists. It was necessary to transform the Jews into a nation in the modern sense of the word. History and historiography were mobilized to achieve this; historians engaged in this enterprise did not have to act under the orders of some official leadership or established regime— which might have made possible the emergence of a counterculture. On the contrary, they were themselves active Zionists, writing history with their convictions. It was Zionist historiography's responsibility to establish the existence of a nation before nationalism and to demonstrate the unity and continuity of this national existence in all times and places. Contemporary Jews were the direct successors of the ancient Hebrew nation, and the land of Israel was their cradle. Their return to the land of Israel was at the same time their return into history, since to the Zionist mind, exile also meant exile outside history.[38] Historians were charged with (re)creating the land of (re)rootedness. One of the striking traits of Zionist doctrine was the preponderant role it gave humans as creators both of their land and of their destiny: a divine role, yet secularized. The historical "school" of Jerusalem in the 1930s therefore tried to reconstruct the history of the people of Israel around a fixed center: the land of Israel. Thus, in 1935, there appeared in Jerusalem the first issues of the Hebrew scholarly journal *Zion*, still today the symbol of the historiographic establishment. Its opening declaration asserted the centrality of historical study. This journal quickly became a means of cultivating a new kind of thinking. Jewish history was by no means only that of an ethnic or religious group, but that of a unique nation, born on the soil of the land of Israel. Zionism needed history to prove that the Jews really did constitute an entity and that there had been no break whatsoever between ancient Israel and Judea and modern Jewry.

Antiquity, in Zionist collective memory, was that privileged moment in history when the Hebrew nation flourished on its soil and enjoyed an autonomous political, social, and cultural life. It was exile that introduced the decisive historical break. The new historiography therefore adopted the traditional articulation between Zion and exile, corresponding to two types of Jewish experience that were clearly differentiated. Rabbinic Judaism, however, used other forms of periodization, based on the evolution of the Law and the succession of its masters. Moreover, while from a traditional perspective, the two concepts had once been interdependent, Zionism turned them into irreducible opposites. The land as an absolute positive could only exist *against* exile as an absolute negative. And so Zionism emerged as the negation of exile. Whereas ancient times had been those of ties to the land, exile was the loss of those ties. Antiquity was the Golden Age of the nation to which the Zionists aspired to return. The authentic roots of the people were buried there and could be recovered: the national spirit, the Hebrew identity, the Hebrew language, the homeland, and all the attributes of an independent nation. In Zionist historical memory, the ancient Hebrews had formed a proud nation, solidly anchored in the land of their fathers. They tilled its soil, understood its nature, and were ready to fight for their liberty and to die for it if necessary. A beautiful romantic image, constructed as the counterimage of exile, the source of inspiration for the new day and age.

Secular Hebrew culture was particularly interested in the Second Temple period, with its wars of liberation against the more numerous forces of the occupier, like the Maccabees' war against the Syrians or the Judeans' wars against the Romans. Figures of antiquity like Judas Maccabaeus or Bar-Kokhba, even when the revolts they led had ended in bloody failures, were set up as historical models for settlers and pioneering youth. Disaster and defeat were obscured; only heroism was remembered. These fierce battles were the proof that Judea had not fallen through indifference or for lack of patriotic zeal, but that until the last moment the Jews had desperately fought for their soil and for their liberty. From now on, commemorations of these ancient wars of liberation tended to attenuate their religious dimension in order to advance their national and political significance, with which Zionist settlers could identify. Had they not left exile of their own free will to return to the land of their ancestors and to free it from the foreign yoke? In the light of these ancient examples, the Judeo-Palestinian conflict took on eminent meaning. The pioneers were today's secular redeemers.

Zionism turned toward ancient heroes who had been traditionally deprecated; it rehabilitated the Zealots, the Sicarii,[39] and the Biryonim.[40] By reviving a dormant memory, it counted on triumphing over exile and its bad influence. It offered these examples as models to pioneer youth, while marginalizing Jews of the Diaspora who could not claim this heroic ancestry. The new Palestinian Jew was a re-creation: he had to adopt a genealogy in line with his aspirations. He referred to himself as an *ivri* ("Hebrew") precisely in order simultaneously to attach himself directly to the ancient Hebrew past of this land and to dissociate himself from the *yehudi*, the Jew of exile. Now there was only *Hebrew* youth, *Hebrew* literature, and *Hebrew* language. Hebrewness was the natural fruit of the refound land. The sabra, the native, knew no fear, timidity, or, of course, weakness; he was the antithesis of the Diaspora Jew, the opposite of the exiled Jew. He was Hebrew and not Jewish. He had returned to the land; he had roots. This was a largely imaginary construction, of course, since the new Hebrew culture could never totally emancipate itself from exilic influences. The new immigrants were pressured to abandon their original languages and cultures and to accept the values and norms of the new Hebrew culture. The famous melting pot that was long the Zionist credo had nothing to do with multiculturalism; on the contrary, it implied acceptance of a single, sovereign model. And the failure of the enterprise would be as great as the hopes it had aroused.

Of course, Zionist aspirations for renewal and homogeneity were not fundamentally different from those that fed other nationalist movements or other nation-states. In this case, what attracts attention is the zeal applied to erase exile, as if the only thing that counted was the reality and continuity of the presence of the people on their land. The Zionist periodization and reconstruction of Jewish history, clearly selective, were very revealing from this point of view. For example, Ben-Gurion maintained against all evidence that the Jewish tribes had never gone to Egypt, that they had remained loyal to their soil, that only Joseph's family had left for a while, that the founder of the new faith, Moses, had forged monotheism in the desert, that it was Joshua who then spread it among the tribes of Israel that had remained in Canaan. . . . Interest in the ancient history of Israel, so strong in Zionist historiography, accommodated itself to much deliberate ignorance: about the exile of the ten tribes of the northern kingdom in 722 B.C.E. and about the long periods in which Hebrews and then Judeans lived under Babylonian, Persian, Greek, and Roman domination. Similarly, the case of Jewish self-defense in the Middle Ages, during exile itself, was elided. In the Zionist vision, the long, dark night of exile was preceded by a luminous, flourishing pre-exile (antiquity) and was followed by an equally luminous and flourishing post-exile (the national renaissance). From dispersal resulted the loss of contact with the land, from which originated spiritual and political degeneration. Exile was purely negative: the absence of land. Inversely, from this essentially binary perspective, once the link with an ideal antiquity had been renewed, there could be nothing more positive than return to the land of Israel.

From this perspective, to reduce the historical length of the exile, seen as a parenthesis, was a necessity. Thus, in his monumental work in several volumes, *Yisrael ba-Golah* (Israel in Exile [1926–66]), Benzion Dinur, one of the leaders of the Jerusalem historical school, resolutely distanced himself from the commonly admitted periodization of Jewish history in order to make the exile begin in the seventh century, at the time of the Muslim conquest of Palestine. Generations of historians would follow his example. Far from admitting, as is ordinarily the case, that the dispersal began with the destructions of the First and then Second Temple and with the end of Jewish sovereignty, Dinur attributed to the Arabs the responsibility for the historic uprooting of the Jews from the Holy Land—and so Zionism had a natural justification for the legitimate return of this despoiled property to its first owners. At the other end of the chain, Dinur made the era of renewal begin, not during the Enlightenment or during the French Revolution, but in the second half of the seventeenth century, in the time of the Sabbatean crisis and the immigration to Palestine of Yehuda Hasid Ha-Levi and his disciples. We know that Zionism clearly distinguished itself from the messianic fevers of the type initiated by Sabbatai Tsevi. But by making this the point of departure, Dinur stressed the popular nostalgia for Zion that for him preceded and prepared the way for political Zionism. The objective of similar manipulations was to contract the period of exile (now reduced to ten centuries) and to stretch the periods in which the nation actively manifested its tie with the land of Israel. For Dinur, the most stable point, the nodal point, in Jewish history was really the land of Israel. The interpretation he gives of this history centers on the nation and seeks to demonstrate that the establishment of a national homeland in Palestine was merely its natural and predetermined consequence. All of Jewish history is presented as preparation for this ultimate stage, and aspects that do not fit the mold or that are judged secondary are simply erased.

After the foundation of Israel, the educational curriculum was adapted to the ideological presuppositions of Zionism in its state version. Textbooks described Zionism as the most powerful and oldest current in the history of the Diaspora and tried to demonstrate that there had always been a Zionist course of action.[41] Dinur, minister of education (1951–55) in the new Jewish state and supervisor of the writing of the curriculum, declared that Israel's specificity was its particular historical consciousness, now the heritage of the whole people, in addition to ethnic kinship and linguistic community.[42] For him there was no doubt that the consciousness of Jerusalem, the image of the Holy City and the links it had with Israel, constituted one of the organic elements of this historical consciousness. In classical and then medieval Jewish literature, he recalled, Zion and Jerusalem functioned as synonyms for Israel. Among the Prophets and in the Writings, they commonly referred to the nation. Zion was Israel's "mother." This image, frequent in the Talmud, is unchanged, he tells us, in the writings of Jewish thinkers of the Middle Ages. And the integration of this theme into liturgy itself proves to what extent, according to him, it really forms part of the consciousness of even the broadest social strata. What was more natural than for the modern national Jewish movement to have taken the name of the emblematic site of the nation (Zion/Zionism)? Any indication of the permanence of a Jewish "nationalism" active throughout history was thus piously pressed into service. Any other option, a Jewish Enlightenment movement or a non-national solution, was seen as a deviation.

In the state period, however, this representation of history was enriched with a new dramatic dimension: the Holocaust was presented as the undeniable proof of the validity of Zionism, and the foundation of the state in the land of Israel as the ultimate realization of historic Jewish nationality. As a historian and educator, Dinur helped to set up this system. His interest in the pedagogy of the Holocaust also came from his wish to fix clearly the boundaries of Jewish historical memory in the new state. After the state's foundation, classroom texts stressed more than formerly the historic right of the Jews to Palestine, while denying the least right to the Arabs. Retrospectively and anachronistically, Zionism was considered the cornerstone of modern Jewish history, and the whole course of Jewish history was seen from this angle: the State of Israel was the telos of Jewish history, its happy end. The discourse current at the time clearly distinguished between victims and heroes: the former in the Diaspora, the latter in the land of Israel. This dichotomy would recur, not only in textbooks, a monopoly of the Ministry of Education, but also in rituals commemorating the Holocaust. The Israeli parliament decided in 1951 to dedicate a day of national commemoration not only to the victims of Nazism but also to Jewish resistance fighters. The history lesson they wanted to draw from these events was that Jewish passivity had had fatal consequences, whereas self-defense and resistance had been the glorious expression of national vitality. This juxtaposition served to strengthen the hierarchy of Zion, prime site of heroism, over the Diaspora, the prime site of shameful suffering. This retrospective projection would also profoundly affect the writing of Jewish history in the Diaspora, inasmuch as it became a

valley of tears, a sinister succession of persecutions, pogroms, and op-
pressions. Even today, this lachrymose perspective marks the work of
many historians and often dominates the interest of Jews and non-Jews
alike in Jewish history.

No doubt, Zionist historiography was far from being as monolithic
as these pages might imply. Nationalist historians have not been the
defenders of a single line of interpretation. But with the exception of
Gershom G. Scholem, a specialist in Jewish mysticism, all have placed
the nation—and the land—at the center of their studies. The creation of
a new nation demanded the writing of a new history able durably to
support the existence of Israel on its recovered land, a land that people wanted to have been—and wanted to see become again—eternally
Jewish, in a quasi-religious and ahistorical aspiration to the absolute.
To this end, historians adopted convenient concepts. Thus, systemi-
cally, it is the Hebrew name Erets Yisrael, literally, "land of Israel," that
is used to refer to the region in *all* historical periods, including those
when there were no longer any Jews in Palestine or when the territory
was administered by other powers. Another concept constantly pressed
into service is that of *aliyah*, literally, "ascent," a term that in Hebrew
refers specifically to the migration of Jews to the land of Israel. This
became the word used to refer to the five waves of Jewish immigration
to Palestine approximately between 1882 and 1939 that are officially
counted by historians. There is, in fact, a neutral term for emigration
and immigration in Hebrew—*hagira*—but its use is reserved for non-
Jewish migratory movements or Jewish migrations that do not have
the land of Israel as their destination. But the primary meaning of
aliyah is religious. It referred first, in the ancient period, to the pilgrimages made by Israel three times a year to bring offerings and sacrifices to the central sanctuary of Jerusalem. After the dispersal, *aliyah*,
which is also the "ascent" of the believer to the reading of the Torah
during synagogue services, refers to the departure of someone who out
of religious concern wants to visit the Holy Land, or to die and be
buried there. In taking up such terminology, Zionist historiographic
discourse established a direct link between past and present and inex-
tricably mixed the sacred and the profane. Any act of immigration to

Palestine took on, a posteriori, an ideological and Zionist significance—although we know that many immigrants never saw themselves in this way, even if over the course of time they would eventually integrate certain elements of Zionist ideology into their identities.

Even if the Jews had lived outside the land of Israel for two thousand years, for Dinur, it had never ceased to be the axis of national identity. Of course, in one period or other, other communities besides the one in Palestine had played a preponderant role in the Jewish world. But the land of Israel continued to be for all of them "a center of authority." Finally and especially, in the hearts and minds of Jews, the land of Israel retained its unshakeable centrality, source of an inextinguishable nostalgia. Its symbolic status was always kept high by a continuous Jewish presence on the soil of Palestine: a presence that depended on financial aid from the Diaspora, and that became ipso facto the common project of all Jews, whether they were inside or outside the land. This part of the nation that obstinately kept on living on ancestral soil was both the most persistent and the most resistant part.

Negation of Exile, Negation of Self

In such an approach to Jewish history, there is scarcely any place for the Diaspora. The negation of exile is, in fact, inseparable from Zionist discourse, but it really began to express itself well beforehand, in the Haskalah, the Jewish Enlightenment movement, as it developed in eastern Europe in the nineteenth and twentieth centuries, which reflected an unflattering image of traditional community life, with its observant Jews studying the Talmud and speaking Yiddish. The same tendency to self-denigration was also found in the Sephardic world when it began Westernizing in the final decades of the nineteenth century. In the Hebrew literature written by proponents of the Enlightenment, which was studied in progressive Jewish schools in Europe and, of course, in Palestine at the beginning of the twentieth century, exile makes a sorry appearance. This bleak portrait reinforced the negative attitude of Zionist youth toward the Diaspora. As a result, Zionism set itself up as a countermodel to exile—and as a solution to exile. In the collective memory that Zionism constructed over time, exile was the site of suffering, humiliation, fear, and precariousness. Indeed, the first pioneers had arrived in Palestine as a result of pogroms, so it was difficult for them not to associate persecution with life in exile—hence, no doubt, a projection of this negative memory of exile onto the Diaspora as a whole. It is in this climate, however, that the Zionists sketched a typology of the exiled Jew—largely inspired by anti-Semitic stereotypes—as weak and fearful. Opposite this personage, who served as a foil, there stood the Jew regenerated by contact with the land of Israel, possessed of all heroic and noble virtues. Only the land of Israel could create this new person. The Jew of the Diaspora was an anti-model, and against him was constructed the new Hebrew. The rejection of the Diaspora became a favorite theme in education, and the Diaspora Jew, especially starting in the 1930s, was denounced as a passive victim, the object of history rather than its active subject—since, after all, he was outside history.

This rejection of the Diaspora aroused criticism, however, especially among members of the group Brit Shalom,[43] such as Samuel Hugo Bergmann, Gershom G. Scholem, Martin Buber, and others, who did not believe that Zionism or Palestine had the power to solve the Jewish question.[44] Besides, for these nationalist Jews of central Europe, it was an error to separate Zionism from the general course of Jewish history in this way. Zionism should be understood as another link in the long chain of struggles fought by the Jews for their existence and for their essence. The construction of Palestine was a battlefront, a front of prime importance. The land of Israel was called to become a beacon for Diaspora Jewry and the creative center of the Jewish renaissance. Strongly attached to these precise aspects of the Zionist effort, faithful to an inspiration that could be traced back to Ahad Ha-Am, some of these men still rejected the idea of a Jewish state for practical reasons, above all, the Arab question. For Bergmann, "the fact that the whole of the Diaspora is building the land of Israel by its own efforts serves as one of the primary sources of the land of Israel's influence over the Diaspora."[45] To him, the Jewish center of Palestine should not be built at the expense of the Diaspora or its creative strength.

In addition, Ahad Ha-Am and Gordon observed the extraordinary vitality that the Jewish people had manifested throughout its history in the Diaspora. The simple fact of its survival proved this sufficiently. Ahad Ha-Am had formulated a moderate version of the negation of the Diaspora, distinguishing between a subjective negation of exile that expressed a personal dissatisfaction derived from life in exile and its imperfections and an objective negation tied to the fact that, with emancipation having demolished the protective wall that surrounded it, the Diaspora was in great danger of dissolving. Ahad Ha-Am foresaw, in fact, that the Jews of the Diaspora would benefit from the positive influence of the spiritual center of Palestine. For his part, Gordon saw exile as much more than the condition of the Jewish people; it was also the condition of the individual and of humanity—in fact, it was the existential experience of modernity itself. However, these nuanced and complex analyses of exile and the relative necessity of its negation did not win the adherence of partisans of political Zionism, especially of practical Zionism. For the pioneers of the second and third waves of immigration, the success of the Zionist enterprise in Palestine clearly depended on the concentration of all the nation's energy in this country alone.

The negation of the Diaspora nevertheless contradicted the Zionist affirmation of a historical continuity between the ancient Hebrews and contemporary Jews. It appeared to be a sort of self-hatred. The pioneers themselves came out of this Diaspora that they were contriving to repudiate. They could not so easily erase their past, especially in a country that by the nature of things was becoming a land of immigration, a land where each person arrived with the baggage of his own Diaspora culture. The negation of exile or the exilic *condition* (*shelilat ha-galut*) often took the form of a condemnation of the *Jews* living in exile (*shelilat ha-gola*). But even the most virulent critics of the Diaspora were not in favor of a total break with it. In fact, at the beginning of the twentieth century, texts and schoolbooks still devoted an important place to the history of the Diaspora. Teachers themselves had come from exile. The works of the historians Dubnov and Graetz were still studied, the former reducing the Jewish nation to a cultural entity, and the latter seeing it as both cultural and spiritual. There was nothing exceptional in this, since other precursors of Jewish historiography, such as Isaac Marcus Jost in the nineteenth century, had maintained that the Jews' perception of their own identity varied from one place to another, and that the history of Jewish communities had been molded by the history of the countries where they had been established and the attitudes of the host societies. For Jost, the land of Israel had not played any particular role in the history of the Jews—except for those who had lived there themselves, under non-Jewish regimes. Abraham Geiger, his contemporary, father of the Reform movement, defended a comparable position. So in the interim, young people, even if they absorbed the negative image of exile constructed by the literature of the Jewish Enlightenment, remained confronted in schools with visions of the history of Israel that were not very centered on Palestine. The lack of educational resources accounted for much of this. The Hebrew educational system and historical memory took a while to establish themselves.

The historians of the Jerusalem school would in time, of course, reject the historical perspectives of these precursors who, with the exception of Graetz, did not consider the Jews to be a political entity. Still, neither Dinur nor Yitshak Fritz Baer, the two colossuses of this new historiographic tradition, totally adopted the hard line of the militant Zionists about the Diaspora. They contrived despite everything to weave a solid link between the past and the present, and endeavored to bring to light the dialectical relationship between Jewish memory and the history of Jews in the modern era. It was not until the second generation of the Jerusalem School historians that their predecessors' Palestine-centered tendencies were reinforced, at the expense of the history of exile. Long cultivated subsequently, the negative image of the Diaspora did not fade until much later, in textbooks published after 1967, at a time when insistence on productive agricultural work and the merits of communitarian life was also abating.[46] This final reversal was due to the major changes that occurred in the cultural expressions of Israeli society, with a renaissance of religious sentiment, other ways of perceiving the Holocaust, and the marked erosion of the socialist Zionist heritage.

Looked at closely today, and notwithstanding these variations in attitudes, the central—even "autarkic"—construct of the land, as much
the work of the Zionists as of Zionist historians, appears largely imaginary and out of touch with historical, political, and economic realities. The longevity of the Israeli system still depends at least in part on
the existence of the Diaspora.[47] However, the Jews who continue to
live outside Israel are still perceived as Jews of the dispersal (*yehudei
hatefutsot*). This attitude clearly implies that the State of Israel is the
center of world Jewry, and that Diaspora Jews are defined by their relation to that center, meaning that they are peripheral. Israel envisages
the Diaspora as its hinterland, as a source of human, economic, political, and moral support.

But the Hebrew state is a small country, even if one includes the occupied territories. Without really numbering among the great powers,
it is nevertheless placed among the important Western countries. This
is by no means due to the wealth of its natural or human resources. The
strength and perhaps the existence of Israel depend upon a solid Diaspora that is well integrated into the local sociopolitical system. To this
should be added the economic aid from this Diaspora, and American
political support, which guarantees the position of Israel on the international chessboard. Conversely, world Judaism, in constructing its
identity, grants a prime place to the existence of Israel, which comforts
it—though not, of course, in the way the Zionists had imagined. Emotional links are what unite the Jews of the Diaspora with Israel. From
this point of view, the Hebrew state is crucial to them, but it certainly
does not constitute the center of gravity the builders had foreseen.

Largely founded on a denigration of the status of the Diaspora as
an autonomous source of Jewish values, denying its capacity to assure
the survival of the Jewish people, and regarding the state as a national
and cultural vanguard on which everything depended, Zionist ideology could not help but engender difficulties and tensions in the symbolic aspect of the relations forged between Israel and Jews abroad.[48]
As the years went by, these tensions diminished as the Zionist doctrine of negating exile was eroded, and especially as a result of economic and political necessities. There had been, on the one hand, an

aspiration and, on the other, a reality that had long been obscured. The myths had been necessary in order to create this land: they had always been its alma mater.

To create these myths and sustain them, it had been necessary to erase or rewrite certain historical facts that did not fit the claims of identity and nation. For example, until the 1930s, the Phoenicians and their history had no place in the image of Israel's ancient past entertained by modern Jewish national consciousness.[49] Some authors presented the Canaanites and Phoenicians first as enemy peoples of the Hebrews, and Jewish historiography long devoted itself to underlining the essential differences between Canaanite and Phoenician cultures, on one hand, and that of the people of Israel, on the other. But in the 1930s, the Hebrews, Canaanites, and Phoenicians again became useful to different mediators who were anxious to offer historical representations of the past that were able to inspire the future. Seeking to attract attention within the revisionist Zionist movement to the need for a maritime force, a group of young people appealed to the Phoenician model. In the glorious imagery of the Phoenician maritime empire, the Hebrews appeared as equal partners. Ben-Gurion himself shared this historical vision, created from whole cloth, and elevated to the rank of historical truth, this myth would serve to develop an awareness of the Mediterranean in the pioneer mind. Zionism saw in the Mediterranean much more than the western frontier of the land of Israel: it was its natural extension. Besides, by implying that the ancestors of Israel had taken part in one of the most fascinating maritime adventures of the ancient Middle East, the theory of Ernest Renan, which made the Hebrews a desert people who lacked the imagination and aptitude for national existence, was undermined. But when the Phoenicians ceased once again to be of use to the revisionists in their interpretation of the history of the Hebrews, they were dropped without compunction. Now, one wanted to show that the people of Israel had developed in reaction to their environment, and so cooperation between Hebrews and Phoenicians no longer had any importance.

On the other hand, the final moments of Israel's ancient history were invested with eminent significance. The fall of the Jewish fortress of Masada in 74 C.E. (leading to the collective suicide of the besieged population) and the catastrophic revolt of 132–35 C.E. were thus quite simply associated with the values of an active heroism, with no attention to the somber events and their fatal outcome. Armed resistance to the enemy was in itself considered a victory, regardless of the sad historical truth. The tragic episode of Tel Hai in 1920 similarly furnished material for a comparable mythification: the ferocious struggle of a small band against more powerful and numerous assailants was stressed, not mentioning the flight of other members of the colony—who were the only ones to survive.

Between 1882 and 1931, there was much interest in buying land at El-Medieh, a village in the southwest part of Samaria, near the town of Lod. El-Medieh was identified with Modi'in, the place in ancient Palestine where the priest Mattathias around 167 B.C.E. had given the signal for a revolt against the Hellenistic sovereign of Syria, Antiochus IV Epiphanes, which would lead to a liberation of national territory and the restoration of Jewish political autonomy.[50] Starting in 1911, pilgrimages were organized to Modi'in. Between 1925 and 1931, Zionist men of letters and institutions worked to "redeem" this site. It was thought in Palestine that such a "redemption" might serve as an educational model to arouse the enthusiasm of Hebrew youth, to breathe the heroic spirit of their ancestors into them, and to strengthen the tie between the Jewish people and their homeland. Modi'in was thus invested with a mythic dimension and became a national symbol and the destination of a Hanukah (Festival of Lights) pilgrimage. Since 1945, a torch has been lit there whose flame is carried to different parts of the country, and since the foundation of the State of Israel, it has been brought to the president's residence. Modi'in and the cult that surrounds it are very symbolic of the ardent aspiration of Zionists to find in the past their inspiration for the present and the mixture of the profane and the sacred that characterizes the myths they have produced. These myths are witness to the nationalization of a religious celebration like Hanukah.

In fact, as a general rule, the founders of Israeli society have given a new meaning to traditional Jewish festivals by associating them with a nationalist mythology. The divine is replaced with the human. As models and exaltations of the principle of national renaissance, these celebrations, now Hebraized, stress their rural bases, so that they recall the centrality of the land of Israel and of nature within the national culture. Their religious significance is relegated to the background, and people insist on the conflictual aspect at the origin of several of them. At Hanukah, the accent is on the victory of the Maccabees over foreign oppressors rather than on the miracle of the small phial of oil that allowed the Temple to be reconsecrated and worship to be resumed. Purim commemorates a collective salvation, the fruit of the strategies of Mordechai and Esther, who succeeded in thwarting the criminal projects of Haman. Passover evokes the liberation and national renaissance under Moses' and Aaron's leadership. At the same time, Israel commemorates its wars against the Arabs. Holocaust and Heroes Remembrance Day recalls Nazi atrocities. Ancient and modern celebrations contribute to constructing and perpetuating a whole mythology: from slavery at Passover to victimization at Holocaust Remembrance Day, via the national struggle (Memorial Day for Israeli soldiers who died in combat) and independence (Israel's Independence Day).

The land of Israel was thus largely reborn through myths and symbols. But was this new birth really synonymous with reappropriation?

Seven The Impossible Land

A Culture of Rootedness

The obsession with the land characteristic of the Zionists is not satisfied with acquiring the land or reconfiguring its symbols; it is accompanied by a rejection of the city. The founding fathers of Zionism, including Herzl, were not opposed to urban development in Palestine.[1] However, the actual settlers would manifest indifference and often hostility toward the city. Their principal center of interest remained the land, which they thought themselves able to appropriate through labor, to the point of becoming one body with it. From this point of view, negation of the Diaspora and negation of the city arose from the same attitude. It was the *erets*—land as opposed to exile—and the *adama*—land as opposed to the city—that would enable the new Jew to become the new Hebrew and finally acquire roots.

The leaders of the colonization effort contrived to prevent urbanized Jews of the Diaspora from settling in cities once they arrived in Palestine. They did not always succeed, but the general tendency at the time favored the foundation of agrarian communities, whether the kibbutz, the collective village, or the *moshav*, the cooperative farm–village. While the rural sector concentrated the most attention and was governed by national institutions, there was no comparable effort to develop the urban environment. Zionist leaders did not make official declarations about city policy or explore the desirable forms of future urbanization. In any case, the future lay with the revolutionary structures of rural settlement, and not towns. For a long time, the village dominated the town, not only ideologically but also politically. Moreover, in utopian literature there is no positive reference to the city; rather, it is the source

195

of all social evils and the cause of the disintegration of the healthy and happy rural communities of the preindustrial era.

The Zionists' total lack of interest in the city flagrantly contradicted reality, since the great majority of the Jews of Palestine were urban. In fact, the rural sector never surpassed the level of 30 percent of the Jewish population, and it currently accounts for only 15 percent. The total rural population began to decline in the second half of the British Mandate, dropping from 29 percent in 1941 to 26 percent in 1945. This tendency was accentuated under the state. And in the 1960s, the figure fell to 18 percent.[2] However, during the formative phase of the Jewish Palestinian community, no new town was founded, with the exception of Tel Aviv in 1909, at a time when the pioneer and agricultural ethos had not yet totally dominated local Zionism. This ideological negligence could not help but affect urban development in contemporary Israel. The city and the country took off in contradictory directions; the cleavage between agriculture on the left and towns on the right (particularly Tel Aviv) created the conditions for conflict between rural people and urban people on the country's political scene. Problems of all kinds—material, economic, social—were left neglected.

The town was abandoned to its fate; it developed under the pressure of immigrants who, owing to limited economic opportunities and limited availability of land, did not want to (or could not) be absorbed into the rural sector. In a planned and centralized society undergoing rapid growth, to neglect the planning of an essential sector of society could only be the source of many difficulties. Thus a city like Tel Aviv haphazardly grew in all directions. Israeli towns in effect lacked an urban image. The leaders of the pioneer effort were less concerned about what happened in the cities than they were worried at seeing urban growth drain resources necessary for rural development. And so the urban congestion, slums, memorable traffic jams, and many other problems that are often denounced today are by no means new: their origin lies in the period of the Mandate and the beginning of the state. Lack of interest in the city was even more harshly felt in the immigrant towns established in the middle of collective settlements developed and inhabited largely by veterans. These immigrant towns constituted islands of destitution amidst prosperity. Nor did the so-called development towns, also peopled by immigrants, but more recently created, follow the general current of Israeli society; they remained isolated, and their most fortunate inhabitants soon abandoned them and left behind the most deprived residents.

However, from a sociological point of view, the absence of ideological direction with regard to urban development did not only have disadvantages. Left to himself, and thus less subject to ideological pressures, the city resident could use his initiative in domains left fallow by the agricultural pioneers. In the 1950s and 1960s, the kibbutzim themselves became aware of the changes produced in society by urban activities and institutions and tried to follow the times by introducing industry into their villages and by professionalizing their activities, by sending their members into higher education, for example. Still today, collective settlements are oriented toward the large cities, even if they continue to affect some indifference to them and to dominate the new towns created nearby. But on the whole, the town was truly sacrificed on the altar of the land, so sacred and so desired.

Nevertheless, this veneration of the land and its pastoral overtones did not lead the Zionist movement to indulge in pure romanticism. On the contrary, it had early on stressed progress and modernity, and it consigned enormous efforts to innovations enabling Jewish agriculture to be competitive. The Jewish farmer quickly became the most progressive farmer in the Middle East. Recreating the imagined land and making it real presupposed both method and planning.

The various philanthropic organizations that engaged in the settlement of Palestine conceived of it as an educational enterprise whose objective was the moral betterment of those selected groups who were capable of getting settlements under way that would serve as an example to Jews of the Diaspora.[3] With the founding of the World Zionist Organization in 1897, a new attitude appeared that saw the Jewish peasant as the basis for an autonomous national economy. And so a group of experts emerged: specialists in settlement with the technical and management skills necessary for the realization of definite objectives. These were the first engineers of settlement, its first architects. They came largely from the German cultural area, influenced by the tendencies prevailing in that area. Max Bodenheimer and Herzl developed colonization programs, but they did not manage to put them into effect. After Herzl's death in 1904, Otto Warburg, a botanist with the German colonial office, initiated a certain number of projects for research and development in Palestine. And after 1909, a second contingent of eastern European Jews appeared who had received a German education and were linked to the Labour wing of the Zionist movement; they took jobs with the settlement institutions of the Zionist Organization.

While French philanthropists saw founding a rural colony as a moral act of "regeneration," the engineers considered it to be a means to economic independence and social reform. They maintained that a technically advanced agricultural sector could guarantee a stable, healthy national economy, able to absorb the immense Jewish proletariat that had formed in the final decades of the nineteenth century, which was barely tolerated where it was currently living. For the Zionists, this proletariat ought to be settled elsewhere, and when they undertook to direct this resettlement, they did not fail to stress that it was imperative to avoid the defects of industrial society spreading across the new Jewish homeland.

The engineers were also inspired by the principles of colonial agriculture, believing that the government should be the agent of rural progress. However, there were clear differences between German-style colonization and the kind encouraged by the Zionists. The Germans constituted an imperialist power that controlled and exploited its colonies for the benefit of the metropole and its government, whereas the Zionists used an international organization in order to create an autonomous homeland. Moreover, in imperialist practice, only the colonial rulers had access to sophisticated technology. Among the Zionists, on the other hand, the transfer of technology was constructed by and for the Jews. It goes without saying that Zionist colonization projects gave little consideration to the possible consequences for the Arabs. The Jewish community of Palestine, however, wanted to share Western technology with a population they considered to be indigenous, in the hope that it would manage to overcome its own feeling of hostility and end up accepting the Jews as brothers. Even so, many Zionists were sensitive to Arab and Ottoman opposition during the final years of World War I. The engineers, for their part, merely saw this as yet another obstacle to be overcome, like any other. An examination of the division of lands in

Palestine shows that the Jewish Colonization Association (ICA), which was non-Zionist, owned 54 percent of the rural Jewish domain. Private companies controlled another 27 percent, and the institutions of the World Zionist Organization only 4 percent.[4] The engineers of the World Zionist Organization thus had to work within a narrow compass. However, their influence far exceeded the tiny sector directly subject to their activities, and it stimulated the whole community.

Like the disciples of the Jewish Enlightenment movement, the Zionists had internalized the critiques of the eighteenth-century thinkers who had denounced the Jews for their lack of productivity and had called on them to abandon commerce for agriculture and industry. From this perspective, technical competence was an essential attribute of the new Jew, a man of the land. In 1948, the kibbutz became a national label and a formidable means of education and mobilization for the Zionist idea. On the model of the farmer and the soldier, the technician of the land was raised to honor in the Zionist pantheon as an incarnation of the pragmatic spirit that Zionist ideology wished to infuse into the new Jewish society then being formed.

What was the result of all these efforts focused on the land, of this ardent desire to redeem it and to incorporate it into the experience of the new Jew? To what extent did this land come to truly belong to the new Jew, at least symbolically? Was it possible to hold the land both as mother country and as Promised Land?

Interminable Exile

In the literature of the Jewish Enlightenment, the land of Israel was a coveted land, yet dreamlike, distant, and unknown. It was regarded through the lens of eastern European realities. However, once they had trod its soil, immigrants from eastern Europe developed a nostalgia for the countries they had left behind them, as if the land of Israel could never become theirs. Even when it did, it carried an exile inside it. And exile within the land of Israel was even more difficult than exile among the nations of the world. Yet, had it not been expected to bring about the end of exile? A Jew who stepped onto the soil of Israel necessarily did so with his or her exile as baggage. It was an enormous dream to think that one could create a Hebrew nation by ignoring this "strangeness" of the land, a "strangeness" that would later pursue the natives themselves. And so exile was transmitted from generation to generation. Did the Jews have the capacity to move beyond this and to become a people established on its land at last? One thing is certain: the idea of the land never ceased to dominate the reality of it.

Many writers of the first waves of immigration confessed their uprootedness in their new environment—meanwhile vowing admiration and boundless love for it. This tendency was especially clear among authors belonging to the second wave of immigration (1904–14). The adaptation of the pioneers to the Palestinian landscape was quite difficult, which is reflected in the writings of those who lived this experience in their bones. The hope of regeneration and the apprehension of despair gave rise to quite distinct characters.[5] On the one hand, the writers sketched a glorious portrait of pioneers and heroes, and on the other, they related the somber fate of protagonists on the edge of madness. All these books are traversed with a sort of incapacity to cross the threshold of the idea in order to confront reality. Their authors lived in Zion, but their hearts had stayed in eastern Europe. They were still simultaneously describing the shtetl and its problems and evoking the destiny of uprooted Jews, at once pious and heretical, and expressing a desire to be rooted in the coveted land and to build a new reality there. This time, it was the shtetl and the European metropole that formed the horizon of the colonies, of the collective farm or of the Levantine village. The object of nostalgia was no longer the Holy Land but the abandoned land. The bucolic vision cultivated by the Jewish Enlightenment in the Diaspora, the ideal land with its olive trees, doves, and brooks, gave way to a hostile reality in which the newly arrived intellectual felt exiled anew.[6]

Disheartened by the harshness of his new life, Yitzhak Lamdan avowed that he missed his European home, while still believing (like other writers) that there was no other choice for the Jews. He sang of pioneering and enthused about the Palestinian landscape, but he also lamented the difficulties of existence in this new milieu, smitten by heat and blasted by the desert wind, the *hamsin*. We have come a long way from the eternal spring and the pastoral landscapes evoked in Diaspora literature. Lamdan nostalgically recalled scenes from his past in the Diaspora, when the idea of Palestine had been so sweet and harmonious. Other writers followed suit. The magnified landscapes of their ideal Palestine were replaced by those of the countries they had left, which were now behind them. The cedars and olive trees and their mythical descriptions gave way to birches and fields scorched by sun and snow. They escaped into a past that was now perceived as comforting—but still that of exile.

This renewed feeling of exile was liable to engender a conflict with the Promised Land and to prevent it from becoming the hoped-for motherland. Even writers who became monumental figures in contemporary Hebrew literature, like Saul Tchernichowsky and Leah Goldberg, evoked the difficulties of their encounters with the Promised Land. Leah Goldberg fondly remembered her former town in Europe. A poem of Tchernichowsky's whose first verses are often quoted as emblematic of the desire for rootedness—"Man is just a little piece of earth/Man is just a reflection of his homeland's landscape"—ends on the theme of wandering.[7] Hayyim Nahman Bialik, the national poet, remained the poet of exile even after his immigration to Palestine: his writings would not describe the land of Israel. Nostalgia for the abandoned country is sometimes expressed in details borrowed from the cultures of origin: in pioneering literature, the Cossack and the Ukrainian are transformed into the Bedouin or the fellahin, the kaffiyeh replaces the clogs, and the Palestinian song "How Beautiful Are the Nights in Canaan" replaces the sentimental songs of the steppes.[8]

More contemporary writers, even those who were active protagonists in the War of Independence, are not immune from this melancholy about the lost land. For example, while Yehuda Amihai expresses his love for the Israeli landscape and for Jerusalem, his native town of Germany (which he left at the age of twelve) plays a no less mythic role in his work, notably in his poem *The Voyages of the Last Benjamin of Tudela* (1963). Some are not content with expressing their homesickness: they make the return voyage. Thus, in order to exorcise the call of the Diaspora or to become definitively attached to the land of Israel, it is necessary to leave once more and then come back again. For example, S.Y. Agnon's novel

A Guest for the Night (1938–39) is the story of a man's return to his native village Shibush, in Galicia, after a long absence.[9] At the heart of this voyage is the desire to find the past again and to relive it. The narrator left as a youth and now returns two decades later when he is forty-one; his house in Jerusalem has been destroyed and he has neither the strength nor the motivation to rebuild it. He turns toward the past in the hope of regeneration, to find moral support, and to redeem himself. To this end he leaves—in the same state of mind in which the pioneers themselves had made the trip to Palestine. The narrator's departure implies that the land of Israel cannot resolve the spiritual crisis he is going through—but his native town will not suffice either. Perhaps we see here an accomplished expression of the insurmountable dilemma of the Israeli—or of any Jew. The character's return to the land of Israel at the end of the novel is a return to family, to the national homeland, to himself.

The travels of Agnon's hero are reminiscent of the almost ritual voyage made today by many young Israelis after their military service. This trip abroad, which may last up to a year, has become a custom in contemporary Israel. It usually ends with a return to Israel. A comparable phenomenon may be observed among Israelis going to visit their countries of origin, thanks to the opening up to Israeli tourism in recent years of many Muslim and eastern European countries.[10] It is a sort of search for identity in a distant place, both spatially and temporally. These travelers find the roots of their Israeli identity (or they believe they find them) by returning to a past that is not directly their own but that teaches them about their history: returning to the soil of the country of origin, they feel themselves in exile from Israel. . . . Israel, land of exile or mother country? The spectacle of the *yordim*[11] who leave voluntarily and definitively settle in the United States, who are incapable of integrating into their country of adoption either, unfailingly raises the same question: Does the land of Israel need other lands in order to exist, including in the eyes of its native citizens? For his part, the narrator of *A Guest for the Night* returns to Israel overcome by nostalgia for an era when everything will be immersed in the unity of creation, when name and form will be perfectly one and will reveal their intrinsic perfection in complete redemption—a nostalgia for a land that has once again become Book.

In the work of Devorah Baron, although she lived forty years in Palestine, the concrete and real land then in formation is nonetheless practically absent.[12] The impossibility of the land is expressed in its being occulted. Baron's land of Israel is the Bible's land of Israel, the one evoked by the Talmud and tradition, to which are linked certain religious practices. Baron was shaped by the Lithuanian *musar* movement.[13] She soaked up a cultural atmosphere in which knowledge of the Hebrew language was associated with reading modern Hebrew literature and with political activity. Baron's land derives from all her literary sources; it synthesizes the Book and the idea of Zionist realization. It is Scripture that bridges existence in the Diaspora and the dreamlike, sensitive reality of the land of Israel. For Baron, biblical myth furnishes the key to contemporary reality, and the Zionism of exile needs just as much as does the Zionism of the Holy Land to be anchored in the Book. Outside the Book, no land is possible.

The Book/land is omnipresent in the work of Isaac Bashevis Singer, who won the Nobel Prize for Literature in 1978.[14] Undoubtedly, his case differs from those of the other authors mentioned up to this point because he is a Jewish American writing in the Yiddish language, not an Israeli, and so he offers the Diaspora perspective on Israel. However, his work also shows that, even after the foundation of the state, the land of Israel has not lost its status as Promised Land. Exile is everywhere, even in Israel, because exile is inside each of us. It is inside each Jew for whom exile cannot end with a concrete state. Singer clearly distinguishes the Holy Land, the spiritual Zion, the eternal hope of redemption, from the State of Israel, in which he sees the work of a secular Zionism and the contemporary realization of restoration. All his stories set in Israel are told in the first person by a narrator who has affinities with Singer himself. The setting is always Tel Aviv. The desert wind blows sand around the city, making life uncomfortable. Not only the climate but also the rest of nature is hostile. The narrator finds it strange that people everywhere speak and write Hebrew. He perceives a profound and destructive tension between the sacred roots of the language and the profane usages to which it is put. He is embarrassed that this reality is constructed by humankind and not by the Messiah. And so, is the land of Israel condemned to remain a Promised Land? The modern political accomplishments of Zionism have rendered ambiguous the messianic promise of the reestablishment of Zion. Throughout their long exile, the Jewish people had dreamed of a spiritual restoration of the biblical Holy Land. After their emancipation, they had worked energetically for the material reconstruction of a political homeland. What emerged was inevitably founded on principles that appear to Singer more profane than sacred. He explores some of the distortions of secular Zionism in a story called "The Captive" (English translation, 1973). Since human nature remains unredeemable, the places where people live are interchangeable after all: to be here or to be elsewhere amounts to the same thing. In *The Family Moskat* (1950), the popular market of Tel Aviv, the Shuk Ha-Karmel, evokes the Krochmalna Street of the author's Polish youth. In Singer's writing, the land of Israel, like Egypt, is not a geographical locale but a spiritual condition. The Israeli Agnon himself can be counted among these writers who were alarmed when they saw the state appropriate a messianic dimension.[15] Ben-Gurion considered in fact that the state was much more than the product of a concrete history, that it was the realization of prophetic visions. In his eyes, the Jews of contemporary Israel were on the same level as the Hebrews of Joshua's time! In contrast to Ben-Gurion, whom he did not hesitate to oppose, Agnon clearly distinguishes himself from those intellectuals, historians, researchers, and archaeologists who devoted their time to fashionable subjects and helped to plaster a biblical mythology over the accomplishments of the modern State of Israel.

When the land *is* present, certain Israeli writers of today, such as Aharon Megged, prefer to evoke the sea that borders it or the desert that devours it.[16] Megged associates the sea with a feeling of freedom, of liberation from the yoke of ordinary life. In recent years, though, it almost disappears in favor of the desert, symbol of both freedom and death. The desert is the crucible of the Jewish people. But it also evokes solitude, a feeling of alienation, and the desire for annihilation. This feeling of alienation faced with the land one inhabits curiously dominates the work of this author of the Palmah generation; this alienation pertains to the very fact of being an Israeli. One is not really where one is; one wants to be elsewhere. In the Promised Land, one still dreams of a promised land, even when the dream has become a real land. Upon his arrival in Palestine at the age of six, Megged first lived in a collective village, then in a kibbutz, later reaching the city where he spent the major portion of his life. In books written in Tel Aviv, the author devotes little space to description of the city as compared to that reserved for the kibbutz and the village. And after 1965, mention of the kibbutz yields to the village, place of childhood and adolescence. He criticizes these two modes of life, but they are still omnipresent in his oeuvre. In Tel Aviv, one dreams of what one has lost, as one probably dreamed of the big city when one was still on the kibbutz or in the village. Moreover, Megged is little interested in the physical structure of the kibbutz or in its spatial organization. Most of the passages concerning the kibbutz are the expression of a position about it, a judgment of the life lived there. As for the village, Megged scarcely describes its landscapes; he prefers to dramatize his characters, so he avoids foregrounding the setting. The Holy Land transcends the limitations of space; this is the only way for it to remain promised. By ignoring the links between people and land and their boundaries, Megged's desert (reminiscent of the place Sinai occupied after 1967 in the Israeli consciousness) escapes the fantasy of the circumscribed land as coveted object. The sea and the desert, as well as the nostalgic memory of the kibbutz and the village, now imaginary, enable a flight from the oppression of a land in conflict, fought over by two peoples.

The impossible land of Israel is not so only for intellectuals. Orthodox Jews also have some difficulty in apprehending a fundamentally new but hybrid reality like the State of Israel.[17] They ask an obvious question: to what extent can modern Jewish activism on the stage of history coexist with persistent metahistorical aspirations and not by its very nature deny the fundamental concepts of Jewish faith? This ambiguity is already present in the language. Hebrew has certainly been secularized, but it remains no less freighted with an ancient religious charge, always liable to be awakened. Even the name "Medinat Yisrael" (State of Israel) is problematic. At the beginning of the twentieth century, the anti-Zionist rabbi Elyakum Shlomo Shapira of Grodno asked how it was possible to tolerate the existence of a "State of Israel" without the Torah and without observation of the commandments; he was the first to use this formula. Herzl had spoken of a "State of the Jews" to refer to a concrete people and its actual situation. The term "State of Israel," on the other hand, is charged with metahistorical and theological associations. Shortly before 1920, Abraham Isaac Kook, the foremost theorist of religious Zionism, proposed a combination of the two dimensions by making the nascent State of Israel into the stepping-stone to God's throne on earth, thereby conferring on it an exceptional messianic and metaphysical status. It is unlikely that those who in 1948 chose this name for the new state were fully conscious of its religious overtones. Whether Zionist or anti-Zionist, Orthodoxy expresses an uncompromising demand for utopian perfection. For it, the question was whether the Zionist renaissance was simply a rebellion, a rejection of the Covenant, a substitution of the earthly and national for the spiritual and religious, or whether, on the contrary, this earthly return was precisely just the preparatory phase for a religious and spiritual redemption.

Some ultra-Orthodox leaders gladly demonize the Zionist enterprise as the anti-messianic work of Satan himself. The Holocaust and the birth of the State of Israel belong to the same process for them: the final eruption of the forces of evil as a prelude to redemption. They energetically oppose the development of the Holy Land by secular means left in the hands of sinners. Some quote an ancient medieval tradition that the very sanctity of the land of Israel requires of its inhabitants a particularly high level of spirituality. Common mortals cannot settle there without incurring the greatest danger. The Holy Land is the place of residence of the ideal Jew, certainly not of the average Jew. Hayyim Eleazar Shapira of Munkacz, a Hungarian Hasidic master, reiterated early in the twentieth century that the land of Israel was exclusively designed for prayer and spiritual activity. He opposed any development of agricultural or manual labor there. Repeated assertion of the sanctity of the Holy Land thus resulted in a paradoxical denial on his part of its materiality. Redemption could only come from heaven, and only authentic "fighters" against the forces of evil, meaning the ultra-Orthodox, could envisage living there.

When it is anti-Zionist, as are the "Guardians of the City" (the *Neturei Karta*), the ultra-Orthodox camp in Israel (those who are called *haredim*)[18] posits that life in the Jewish state is an exile. Because its creation is a betrayal of the messianic vocation of the Jewish people, because it is a fundamentally secular reality, this state has not put an end to exile at all. In entering into the kingdom of the Torah, the Jewish people have left the ordinary course of history. But the Zionist movement has undermined the transcendental law that in principle governs their destiny, and so the catastrophes befalling the Jews are sanctions against their sins. The Holocaust itself can be interpreted as punishment for the Zionist temptation of breaking the "vows" that Israel has to observe, making it hasten the end by rebelling against the nations and against divine government. Moreover, Zionists are putting in danger the life of the Jews of the Holy Land by arousing confrontation with the Arabs. The more Zionism realizes its objectives, the more the ultra-Orthodox and anti-Zionist camp insists on an ideology and historiosophy of passivity. Thus to live in exile becomes a true confession of faith.

For ultra-Orthodox non-Zionists, too, the creation of the State of Israel is not the end of exile, despite the physical deliverance and despite the initial gathering of the dispersed tribes that this creation has enabled. In their eyes, a world that is not totally messianic is by definition an exile. This conception contains the theological and metaphysical notion that exile means exile from the Divine Presence; exile is a world that is not purged of sin. In 1948, nothing fundamentally changed, either for the Lubavitch leader Menahem Mendel Schneersohn or for his adversary Rabbi Eliezer Menahem Schah, head of the network of Lithuanian *yeshivot*, who declared that the people of Israel would remain in exile until the arrival of the Redeemer, even when they were in the land of Israel, and that neither redemption nor the beginnings of redemption lay there.

For the ultra-Orthodox, nothing distinguishes Israel from a non-Jewish environment, hence from the Diaspora. They experience exile in the land of Israel as an even more difficult exile because they are living under a Jewish government, because what was supposed to be a welcoming homeland has been revealed as strange and hostile. Some go so far as to identify their condition with that of Jews persecuted by the Gentiles and to see a punishment for their sins in the simple fact of living in a land of Israel given over to secular power. Exile in the Holy Land is dual: first, general and metaphysical exile, the absence of redemption; second, particular exile in this secular reconstruction of the Holy Land under a Jewish nationalism detached from the Torah and from its commandments.

By this logic, as Rabbi Schah asserted, the State of Israel is at best one solution among others to the problem of the Jewish people's survival, of which exile and the dispersal are even the best guarantors since they avoid the concentration of Jews on a single territory.[19]

The Return of the Promised Land

After the Six Day War and the conquest of Jerusalem, and all of the Holy Land corresponding to the boundaries of the divine promise, Israel, particularly its religious wing, was transported by an immense spiritual exaltation. The Jewish people suddenly enjoyed renewed contact with holy places like the Western wall and the tombs of patriarchs and matriarchs. This reinforced the conviction of many that redemption was on its way, a belief that touched even the most anti-Zionist fractions of Orthodoxy. However, the conquest of these "historic" territories and the hope of seeing religious law applied there paradoxically disengaged Orthodoxy from its ties with the state, a modern concept, by putting the land back at the heart of the debate. The accomplishment of secular—and hence heretical—Zionists, the state as such had no affinity whatsoever with redemption. With its entirety now under Jewish sovereignty, the land of Israel was given back to the heretics as well as to the devout. While until then Orthodoxy had considered life in Israel as an exile, it now exerted pressure to keep the conquered territories; any restitution to the Gentiles of the smallest parcel of land would be a violation of religious law. While it denied the legitimacy of the State of Israel because it was a state of the Jews and not a Jewish state, Orthodoxy still considered this enlargement of the land of Israel as a highly positive thing from a religious point of view.

Lands previously only promised because not yet conquered, the domain of the Book and the imagination, the "territories" therefore brought the land of Israel to the center of the political arena. Vocabulary varied according to the speakers' preferred options. For the Arabs and the extreme left, they were "occupied" territories, and for the annexationists, "liberated" territories. Official terminology shifted from territories "administered" by the army to "Judea and Samaria."[20] Detaching itself from the cultural, political, and social aspects of Jewish existence, the country's center of gravity shifted to the land, its holiness and its integrity.[21] Before 1967, political discourse focused on the State of Israel (Medinat Yisrael); after 1967, it crystallized around the land of Israel (Erets Yisrael).[22] The former is a political concept; the latter a national and religious one. There were now a State of Israel and a land of Israel; this change reflected the shift from a collective identity founded on political symbols to an identity founded on traditional religious symbols.

A breach opened up, and Orthodoxy could now find a way to an accommodation with its principles. In parallel with a secular nationalism, incarnated by the Likkud,[23] an activist religious nationalism developed in the years following the conquest. In fact, it occupied the terrain. The land coming back to the center is a divided land; the currents that form around it are split between annexation and restitution. The peace movements fight for restitution and their adversaries for annexation; the debate is over a land not inhabited by Jews, a desert land, which reinforces its immateriality. It is quite another land; it does not resemble the one in which Israeli life takes place. Given the intensity of the debates surrounding it and the passions animating them, it is difficult to see this as a debate simply over "territory." Rather, it is about the Book/land, invested with metahistorical holiness, from the other side of time, beyond the real. All the hatreds and all the hopes, even messianic ones, converge upon this non-place of desire, symbol more than reality. A sort of return to the earliest times is taking place. Those who fight for restitution reject this Book/land as the antithesis of the land their elders wanted to bequeath them, on whose soil they were born. This Book/land brings them back to the Promised Land and reactivates the experience of the impossible land.

The peace movements manifest their vitality in Tel Aviv, profane, urban, and open to the sea and to Otherness, exempt from symbols of the Book. It is a city created from nothing in 1909, a city of pioneers, a city without history. On the other side is Jerusalem, the arena—and stake—in the fight for the land. It is a very alien city to the non-religious Israeli, where closed worlds lie side by side, such as the ultra-Orthodox district of Me'ah She'arim and the Arab old city surrounded by walls. Many barriers remind a secular Jew that this land does not entirely belong to him, and that other autochthonous entities live there, in exile, as he himself feels when faced with them.

Jerusalem is a city above daily life, an area that jealously preserves its spiritual character. The conquest of Judea and Samaria linked it to the rest of Greater Israel, to the Promised Land never before conquered; it now dominates Judea. The mythical land lies there, assuaging the need for a Promised Land, a land whose frontiers are restlessly pushed back. As soon as the land starts to become concrete, the dream of a symbolic land is reborn, which people buckle down to making concrete again—as if they feared missing a Promised Land. The land of daily life must constantly be nourished by the Book in order to exist—hence this infinite quest to annex the symbolic.

The Gush Emunim ("Faith Bloc"), founded in 1974, plunged into this breach. This extraparliamentary movement presented itself as an organized fraction of the national religious party.[24] Its goal was to prepare groups to settle in the "territories"—including right among the Palestinian Arab population. Likkud's arrival in power in 1977 conferred legitimacy on this movement, which possessed not only large human and organizational resources but also rationally justified its activities within the framework of Jewish messianic expectations. It drew much of its inspiration from the doctrine of Abraham Isaac Kook, the first great Ashkenazi rabbi of the land of Israel (1921), the original religious Zionist thinker, and especially from the teachings of his son, Zevi Judah Kook, the charismatic figure whom this movement recognizes as its spiritual master.

For the Gush Emunim, the occupation of Judea and Samaria during the Six Day War was part of the long messianic process that began with the birth of Zionism. It developed a doctrine of the land of Israel's holiness that held the Jewish people and their whole land to be one. This "complete" (*shelema*) land of Israel exceeded the frontiers enlarged after 1967: it was identified with the land of the Covenant described in Genesis; its frontiers were those of the promise, including the occupied territories, most particularly Judea and Samaria, the heart of "historic" Israel. The Gush thus returned to a mythic and ultimately boundless land, to an always-incomplete conquest. For its members, it was a sacred duty to remain firm, to oppose American and foreign pressure in general, to prevent the establishment of an Arab entity inside the borders of the land of Israel, and to continue to participate in the long process of redemption.

The Gush Emunim presents itself as the "movement for the renewal of Zionist accomplishment." It considers itself to be a renaissance of historic Zionism, which had died out in the 1950s and 1960s. Its members perceive themselves as the true heirs of the creators of the new Yishuv, the new Palestinian Jewish community founded upon colonization of the land, manual labor, and personal example. Gush settlements arise from the purest Zionist activism. On the model of the earliest pioneers, its believers take up combat for the land's redemption. In both cases, setting aside their ideological differences, the desire to appropriate the Promised Land is foremost. One appropriation having been insufficient, the Gush takes up the torch. So is the land of Israel only ever promised? As soon as one part is redeemed, another arises to await redemption. However, one thing distinguishes the Gush from its predecessors: the land that it wants to redeem is part of the divine; it is the Book/land par excellence. And for it, the Palestinian question is not a national issue but a problem of individuals; the Palestinians are only *gerim*, non-Jewish residents of the land of Israel, who, according to the Torah, should be treated by the Jewish people with tolerance and respect—but no more.

In fact, in the period following 1967, Zionism was not in a position to respond creatively to the problems posed by the Israeli occupation of the territories. This ideological paralysis contributed to a prolongation of the indefinite status of these territories, which provoked the Intifada and correspondingly diminished Zionism's influence over Israeli society. Zionism had used religious symbolism to bring the Jews back to Palestine; the Gush now used Zionist practice in relation to the land in order to substantiate the symbolism of the Promised Land.

Even in its most asserted concreteness, the Gush's land was keeping its specificity as Promised Land and hence as a symbol. How could a symbol be negotiated with the Arabs once it had given the now-limitless land an absolute value? In effect, to touch a morsel of this symbol, a parcel of this territory, was necessarily to harm the symbol as such—and hence it was intolerable.

The Coming of Post-Zionism

Zionism has ceased to be a mobilizing force in numerous sectors of Israeli Jewish society, without any other ideology or world vision capable of a large consensus being able to replace it as a means of legitimating the state. The situation in Israel resembles that in countries where strong ideologies like socialism and communism have crumbled. But unlike the crises that have hit those countries, the Israeli domestic crisis is not unanimously recognized. Strong social pressures continue to underpin a rhetorical allegiance to Zionism. Some spokespeople of this "post-Zionist" era violently attack the founding myths of Zionism, among which the issue of the land and its colonization naturally plays a central role. By getting rid of everything that stands between the land and them, the "post-Zionists" (or those who claim to be such) aspire to accede to a land "purified" of its symbols, and hence negotiable with the Palestinians. A "neutralized" and "normalized" land becomes a land like any other, at the opposite extreme of the resanctified and hence indivisible land of the Gush Emunim.

The term *post-Zionism* applies to critiques that tend to problematize Zionist discourse as well as its account of history and the social and cultural representations that Zionism has produced.[25] In their zeal to defend the dominant Zionist position and to protect the cultural space from external incursions, some people have been tempted to see post-Zionism as a form of anti-Zionism, if not anti-Semitism—but they are wrong. Coming from a different perspective but destabilizing Zionist discourse in their own way, people such as Anton Shammas, a Palestinian writing in the Hebrew language, and Imil (Emile) Habibi, a Palestinian who writes in Arabic (and who won the prestigious Israel

Prize for literature in 1992), have shown (in Shammas's case) that Israeli and Hebraic culture is not merely Jewish, and (in Habibi's case) that Israeli culture is not solely Jewish and Hebraic. Moreover, the latter's writings have been made accessible to an Israeli audience thanks to Shammas's translations. Apart from their own literary merit, the discourses of these two authors from Israel's Arab minority also offer a counternarrative of events—for example, of the 1948 War of Independence, in Habibi's case. While he does not aspire to neutrality but rather wishes to give the displaced Palestinians a voice, his argument nonetheless approaches that of the post-Zionists, who for their part, in an essentially academic and "objective" discourse, have endeavored to revise the official narrative.

Similarly, if one is willing not to stick with an overly conventional definition of post-Zionism and willing to see it as a new stage in Zionism itself and in the Israeli population, then one must realize that the large-scale immigration since 1989 of Russians has also shaken a number of conceptions of Zionist ideology and indeed its very foundations, quite apart from any militancy on the part of those involved. For many of them, emigration was not identified with an *aliyah*. Their choice of Israel corresponded more to a desire for the West. We are far from the sacralization of *aliyah* and the "saving" role of the Jewish state. These immigrants of a new kind reject neither their native language nor culture. Their intelligentsia in particular usually shares a feeling of having historic roots outside the space and time of their host country. Russia remains their cultural "homeland," and paradoxically, their relations with it continue to be those of a "diaspora" with its center, thereby inverting the equation in the Israeli nationalist narrative of a return to the mother country. For members of this fourth Russian immigration, exile is ultimately inside Israel, where Russian cultural particularism has every chance of developing.[26] The notion of unilateral assimilation into the Hebrew nation is blown apart in favor of more pluralist avenues; such attitudes readily flout the idea of a mythified land, emblem of a past that used to give its whole meaning to the Jewish presence in contemporary Israel.

To come back to post-Zionism as ordinarily understood in intellectual circles, it is generally identified with those who are called "new" historians. Their novelty essentially lies in their rereading of the history of Zionism and of the state of Israel. Their way of writing history is not revolutionary from a methodological standpoint, however. In recent years, their interpretations have aroused lively controversy both in the Israeli press and in academia. The historical debate, long confined to the university, is thus conducted in broad daylight and privileged in the media. On many points, the arguments advanced were not totally unknown to those interested in Zionism and its history. But the echoes they now produce are an additional proof of the democratization of intellectual debate in Israel and the pluralism that now obtains there. There has even been a television series, titled *Tekuma* ("Renaissance"), recounting a history of the State of Israel quite different from the conventional mythology, which was transmitted while the country was celebrating its fiftieth anniversary. This, too, provoked animated public debate, showing that an Israeli national identity is still in gestation and that its myths, even if durable, are beginning to crack seriously.

It goes without saying that these questionings by the "new" historians are endogenous; they are the expression of preoccupations inside the country, remote from those of the Jews of the Diaspora, which are absolutely not taken into account. While the new Israeli history criticizes preceding historiography as typical of nationalist historiography, closely dependent on the isolation in which it developed,[27] it still centers exclusively on Israel, although it now takes the Arabs into consideration. While the "Jerusalem School" had given pride of place to the land of Israel, the "new history" has chosen Israel as the exclusive subject of its attention. Despite its revisionism, it is no less invigorating, at least because less edifying.

In the light of Palestinian claims, new questions have appeared about the right of the Jewish people to the land of Israel.[28] Faced with the messianism of religious Zionism and with the radicalism of the traditional right wing, which implies that widespread Jewish settlement is alone capable of performing the duties of the Jewish people toward their land, weighty feelings of guilt are being expressed within the secular left, to which the historians espousing post-Zionism (if not postmodernism) belong. The regrets engendered by the Six Day War conquests are gradually provoking a reexamination of previous conquests. Has Zionism not been imposed from the outside in order to realize the historic right of the Jewish people over their land at the expense of the concrete rights of the Palestinians who have lived there since time immemorial? Was there any legitimacy, even any significance, in making such a right prevail? Has Zionism not from the beginning committed a colonial injustice against the historic inhabitants of Palestine? Posed on an ethical and political level, these questions did not emerge in this form before the Yom Kippur War. But these second thoughts are also directly linked to the recent vicissitudes of Zionism. Since 1948, it has shifted its focus from land settlement and construction to state security. The pioneer movement has been replaced by the armed services, and the defensive war has been transformed into the principal symbol of Zionist achievement. This attitude has shaped the encounter between members of the "generation of the State" and the Arab-Palestinian population.

Historians and sociologists of the post-Zionist school like Baruch Kimmerling and Gershon Shafir subject the beginnings of political Zionism to reinterpretation. They make considerable effort to avoid using words with connotations like *aliyah* for Jewish immigration, Erets Yisrael (the land of Israel), *geulah* (redemption), *geulat ha-karkaot* (redemption of the land), and *meoraot* (events), for riots and Arab demonstrations in the 1920s and 1930s. Breaking with a terminology that is fundamentally Judeo-Israeli, they reproach the sociologists and historians of the university establishment for not taking into consideration the Judeo-Arab conflict in general and Palestinian society in particular.[29] This new generation of intellectuals was formed toward the end of the 1980s, marked by the publication in English of books by Simha Flapan, Benny Morris, Avi Shlaim, and Ilan Pappe, comprising a historical critique of the War of Independence, which they prefer to call "the 1948 War."[30] These authors, who were soon joined by others like Tom Segev, maintain that the Jewish population of Palestine was not threatened by destruction in 1948, and that the victims of the period of civil war from November 1947 to May 1948 were actually civilians. They also discuss the secret agreement between the Jewish Agency and the kingdom of Transjordania to neutralize the

Arab Legion. They advance new arguments to explain certain mas-
sacres committed by Jewish forces, discuss the lost opportunities for
peace, denounce the idea of a universal plot against Israel, and, as in
the case of Yael Zeerubavel, revisit founding myths of political Zionism. This enterprise of reinterpretation arouses virulent attacks, testi-
fying to how deeply it touches sensitive points in the Israeli national
consciousness. The post-Zionists' reflections reopen the problematic
of the land and of Jewish settlement in Palestine, to which many naturally hesitate to rally, for reasons that are both ideological and emotional. In any case, critique and countercritique manifest the centrality
of this problematic for everyone.

The characterization of the Palestinian Jewish community and then
of Israel as a colonial society is probably as old as the Zionist idea itself.
But as a sociological perspective, it has only recently been formulated,
in consequence of developments after the Six Day War in 1967.[31] The
idea that Israel is a society of colonial-type settlements was the very
core of Arab and Palestinian views at the end of the 1960s. In general,
the Israeli public sees such a description as a calumny. To speak of Israel's
colonization implies in effect that the Jews conquered a land and that
they despoiled and exploited the natives. This scarcely fits with the
image that Zionism traditionally projected of itself as acting on behalf
of a "people without land" returning to "a land without people." For
Gershon Shafir, Zionism is a typical colonial movement, born in the
era of colonialism, despite its particular characteristics: the absence of
a metropole, the marginal role played by capitalist considerations of
profit, and its nationalist discourse and motivations.[32] Zionist historiography conceives of the colonization of Palestine without reference
to colonialism. For Shafir, on the contrary, Zionism is a quite remarkable example of colonialism that succeeded in founding a state despite
its lack of military and financial means. Collective establishments like
the kibbutz and the *moshav*—the pride of Zionism—are presented as
typical pioneer colonies. The "conquest of work" necessary for the creation of the new Jew, emancipated from his Diaspora models, around
whom the Zionist dream crystallized becomes a colonial plan to ex-
clude the native from labor and land markets.

The Zionist Left rejects this kind of interpretation, having always professed self-liberation and redemption through work on the land. The Right, of course, does not recognize itself in it either, since it asserts that "the whole land of Israel" is the inalienable property of the Jewish people by virtue of a historic right, if not a providential covenant. The settlement initiative developed by the Gush Emunim after the Six Day War has been wholeheartedly supported by the government. Since then, Israel has established a hundred colonies, with some 100,000 residents, in the "territories." This new settlement movement is distinct from the one prevailing until 1948 because it is sustained by a significant coercive force on the part of the government and the army and is legitimated on religious grounds. Despite this difference, it has espoused the pioneering ethos of Labour Zionism of the pre-state period, freed from its secularism and its socialism. This compromising kinship disturbs the Labour party somewhat, which makes a distinction between its tradition of *hityashvut* (settlement) and the *hitnahlut* (colonization) of Gush Emunim—the latter term coming from a Hebrew root already present in Scripture, where it is used to describe how the ancient Hebrews took possession of Canaan. This being so, even the Labour movement recognizes—in order to fight it—the sacred dimension of the Gush's activity. *Hitnahlut* evokes the taking of a "heritage" (*nahala*), the restitution to their legitimate owners of the "property" and of the "land of ancestors" (*nahalat avot*).

The 1967 conquests created an overlap between the limits of the Israeli system of control and the theological land of Israel.[33] Neither religious nor non-religious people could ignore this return to a "land of the patriarchs." Most of the Jewish settlements had until then been situated on the periphery of Zion, along the coast and in the valleys of Mandate Palestine. With the exception of Jerusalem, the mountainous region, and hence the sites of the biblical kingdoms of Judah and Israel, had remained out of bounds. The Jews had not been able to buy land or establish colonies there before the 1947–48 war. And even during this first conflict, the heart of the "historic" land of Israel had not been invested. The upheaval introduced by the 1967 conquests thus had profound theological and political repercussions, as much among religious people, who saw the state of the Jews becoming a Jewish state, as among the non-religious, who were traditionally attached to a secular definition of that state. The political and demographic situation created a sentiment of domestic siege, which redoubled the feeling of external siege and prevented the inclusion of the "territories" within the political frontiers of Israel. The authorities still considered this new space to be a fortunate opportunity, a sort of territorial reservoir, furnishing the state with useful strategic depth in the face of a possible military attack. The land recently conquered was thus very differently perceived by different sectors of Israeli society.

Not all the inhabitants of "Greater Israel" benefited equally from the situation, and while Israel's spatial borders seemed to have been pushed back, new ones took shape that crisscrossed the collectivity. Only 18 percent of the colonists of the "territories" affiliated with the Gush Emunim were oriental Jews; the rest were Ashkenazis.[34] Unlike the latter, who profited from this extension of the territorial frontier by acquiring land and developing settlements, the oriental Jews, who were frequently middlemen, benefited more from the enlargement of the economic market that followed the conquest. The integration of the occupied territories into the Israeli economic system created interdependence and instigated change in the Palestinian society of the West Bank and Gaza. The proximity of Israel opened vast economic possibilities to disadvantaged strata, while weakening the control exerted by traditional elements. The line of demarcation between the West Bank and Israel continued to constitute a limit for the traditional and cultivated Palestinian elite, whereas for the most disadvantaged, who could try to find work in Israel, it was more of an employment frontier. Thus in Palestinian society as in Israeli society, the borders were differently perceived according to social milieu. Israelis and Palestinians developed different visions, depending on their expectations and needs, of both Israel and the "territories."

Much more imaginary than physical, the borders of Israel therefore suggest an astonishing fluidity. Israel cannot experience its territory the way some countries in Europe and elsewhere have learned to do. Here other questions are posed; the land is not yet fully acquired as a stable given that raises no more doubts. Here identity is not constructed within the limits fixed by immutable space. The land does not yet belong to the native like the air he breathes. For the Jew as much as for the Israeli, but also for the Palestinian, the land is never acquired. The expansion of Jewish settlements in the occupied territories has favored the rise of the Palestine Liberation Organization. The Intifada was the first mass mobilization against Israel since 1930, and this phenomenon has deeply affected Israeli society. In the wake of these changes, an open questioning of Israeli colonialism has resulted in many theories.

Baruch Kimmerling, one of the principal representatives of post-Zionist sociology, rejects the idea of the uniqueness of Jewish experience as able to account for the events of history and the foundation of Israel.[35] He prefers to substitute the paradigm of colonialism, which approaches Israel as a society of immigrant colonists comparable to other societies of that kind. The need to acquire land, at a time when the Jews had so little, gave rise, as we have seen, to the creation of institutions and the constitution of an ethos that has profoundly marked the character of the society in formation in Palestine since the beginnings of Zionism.[36] Institutionalized by the Jewish National Fund, a purchasing policy had the objective of assuring the transfer of Arab lands to Jews and preventing their return to Arabs through resale—which amounted to taking them out of the free market in which they had initially been acquired. The lands bought were maintained under national responsibility; the Jewish National Fund could rent them but not sell them—and rent them to Jews only. Thus the transfer of land from Arab nationals to Jewish nationals simultaneously consecrated its passage from private property to national property. The model of colonization had a collectivist effect. In the social and national context that prevailed in Palestine, the purchase of land guaranteed little more than de jure control; for hold over it to become effective, it had to be accompanied by settlement, by de facto control. The collectivist model of settlement was thus an inseparable component of the nationalization of the land. Similarly, under pressure from a group of workers who considered employing Arabs to be insulting to the spirit of Herzlian project, Arabs workers were replaced by Jews. Kimmerling even maintains that the Jewish colonists would have expelled or decimated the locals if they had been in a position to do so. Shafir, who develops a Marxist-leaning interpretation, argues that the segmentation of the labor market by the exclusion of Arab competition determined a separate Jewish national identity. With the independence and victory of 1948, Israel's territorial base was enlarged well beyond the land available to be bought and to receive settlements. The state imposed its sovereignty over all land situated inside its frontiers—a change that Kimmerling calls the "Israelization" of the land. In 1962, about 75 percent of all the land of Israel belonged to state bodies, about 18 percent to the Jewish National Fund, and only 7 percent to private individuals.[37]

In the period after 1967, Shafir identifies three phases. A first, military, phase was dominated by the Labourite current that was in power until 1977; a moderate colonization of the "territories" was then justified by security considerations. A second phase belonged to Gush Emunim; the justification was religious and messianic. In the final, economic, phase, the Likkud sought to attract Israelis from the lower middle class to the "territories" in order to stimulate the economy. Each of the three, one after the other, contributed to exacerbating border conflicts.

In Shafir's eyes, Israel is indeed a society of a pioneer/colonial type, on the model of the United States or South Africa. Shafir explains the genesis of this colonialism by means of economic data. The immigrants from eastern Europe in the 1880s established the first agricultural settlements, *moshavot* like Rishon Le-Zion ("First in Zion") and Zikhron Ya'akov ("Memory of Jacob"), and created a stratum of farmers. Given the economic hardships, these colonies were placed under the protection of Baron Edmond de Rothschild and became colonial-type settlements, employing unskilled Arab labor on a seasonal basis. Rothschild's system ceased to be viable, however, after the first decade of the twentieth century. The settlements then passed under the control of the Jewish Colonization Association (ICA), and an economic policy of rationalization displaced labor power. The second wave of immigration, starting in 1904, saw the entry into the market of a wave of poorer Jews, who briefly entered into competition with Arab workers by lowering their own standard of living. But by 1905, the struggle had begun for the "conquest of labor" through higher salaries and the exclusion of Arabs from the labor market, meaning from the settlements. Employers responded by importing Yemeni Jews, who, it was hoped, could be got to work for Arab wages. This, Shafir believes, might have determined the hierarchical status of different Jewish ethnic groups; it explains the place of the Yemenis at the bottom of the social scale, and by extension, the place of other oriental Jewish immigrants in the social structure of Israel.

Around 1909, a new concept emerged as a solution to the problems of the land and work in the framework of Zionist colonization: the model of cooperative settlements. At this stage, national identity was centered on the Ashkenazi Labour movement, which excluded Arabs and included oriental Jews—but with second-class status. When the Zionist movement did not manage to attract enough private capital or capitalist pioneers, the only group it could recruit for settlement were agrarian workers. Far from striving to realize a socialist utopia, these engaged in a purely colonial type of settlement. The kibbutz movement that began in 1905 was the driving force. The socialist component in kibbutz ideology, Shafir argues, is merely the retrospective legitimation of what was at the start a purely colonial strategy. The kibbutz became the spearhead of colonization by driving from the labor market any threat of competition from Arab Palestinian workers; its success also belongs to the role it played in the national seizure of the land. Shafir was also the first historian to take advantage of Palestinian historiography—which does not, of course, mean that he has completely taken over Palestinian collective memory and history. The profile of Israeli society and the positioning of its various ethnic strata that he sketches are once again drawn around the issue of the land.

It is clear that arguing their case, the post-Zionists have not always avoided generalizations or shortcuts. Their adversaries remind them, for example, that the Jews who returned to Zion did not perceive themselves as ordinary colonists. To this, Kimmerling and others reply that the Boers in South Africa and the French in Algeria did not perceive themselves as colonists either—or at least not like the British in Australia or in America. Another post-Zionist weak point that is underlined by their detractors is that they have not wanted to admit that, since the first wave of immigration in the 1880s, the Jewish settlement in Palestine is the clearest expression of the modern Jewish national movement. It was a matter of a struggle, similar to those of other ethnic and national groups, to create a political entity in a place they considered to be their historic territory. One of the original aspects of the Zionist movement was simply that in this case, the creation of a national state required the emigration of the population from one place to another. For the Jews, this combat implied a "return to history," in other words, their ceasing to be a passive element among global and regional forces and themselves becoming an active and influential force. The Arabs were also outside history, and it was their encounter with Jewish colonization that reintroduced them into it. The creation of Jewish settlements emanated only from the desire to be separated from Arab society and to construct an entirely autonomous system, an economic, political, and cultural structure that would not be dependent on the Arab population.

There is no lack of objections to the post-Zionist reinterpretation of Zionism's history. Of course, the "new" Israeli history has little place for the tale of the return of the chosen people to its empty homeland, soon transformed into an earthly paradise, in the face of a generally anti-Semitic and hostile world. Zionism is no longer a unique case of nationalism. It can be analyzed as a colonialism among others, with its own particularities. Another challenge is to continue to counteract the idealization of Zionist history by deconstructing the myth of the melting pot, one of the basic ideals of Zionism.

Some people directly link Zionism's attitude in the Middle East with the attitude it adopted toward the history of the Jews and of the traditional Jew. Thus Amnon Raz-Krakotzkin explains that the concept of "negation of exile" engendered the movement's insensitivity and lack of openness to the Other in general, whether Jewish or Arab. He proposes an alternative and positive approach to the notion of exile, liable to encourage tolerance of different types of "new Jews," guarantee them legitimacy in contemporary Israeli society, and reintegrate them into the collective memory.[38] He suggests seeing the Dias-

pora experience as a form of existence deriving from Jewish excep-
tionalism, which he defines as a situation of constant symbiosis, in opposition to the actual reality of Israel. To choose to be a Jew is to
choose exile, and it means nothing else. Conversely, by seeking to
recreate a national territorial reality for the Jews and make them capable of a total Jewish experience, Zionism implied the rejection and repression of other options for Jewish existence. In fact, Raz-Krakotzkin
aspires to renew the sense of exile in Israel itself, without forgetting
those who are still in a state of veritable exile, the oppressed of the
Third World and the inhabitants of refugee camps. In his eyes, the historiography fabricated by Baer and Dinur, founded on the idea of historic continuity and presenting Jewish history as a national history,
simply adopted the historical model of the victors. The "negation of
exile" is at the same time a refusal to recognize the tragedy that the
foundation of the State of Israel was for the Palestinians.

The adversaries of the post-Zionist school roundly denounce the
postmodern inspiration of such analyses, in which there are no longer
events, peoples, or reality—only texts and their interpretation, a sort of
metahistory. Of course, not all the post-Zionists are postmodernists.
And the proponents of the old historiography themselves consider
that these attacks on Zionism and the way in which its history is written are, in fact, launched in the name of modern values like humanism, equality, and democracy, and that they are far removed from any
kind of nihilism. The post-Zionist discourse is said to tend to reduce
historiography to a chronicle of injustice and misery. It supposedly
turns into sentimental description in which the historian is asked to
identify with the vanquished and criticize the victors. It is as if Zionism's victory sufficed to make it immoral. In fact, the post-Zionists
(and the postmodernists along with them), who have incorporated
postcolonial, poststructuralist, and feminist analyses into their critical
approach to Israeli realities in the journal *Teoria u-vikoret* (Theory and
Critique), have succeeded in making heard alternative voices to the
usual Zionist voice that is all-powerful in the country's cultural space.
And their discourses have joined others, just as discordant, like those
of Palestinian writers of Israeli nationality such as Anton Shammas and

Emile Habibi, who are shaking up the dominant representations of history, nation, and culture, and demonstrating the cultural violence exerted by Zionism upon the Palestinians.

Without entering into the meanderings of this national debate, and keeping in mind that only a tiny fraction of Israeli society recognizes itself in post-Zionism, one has to realize that this discourse betrays a confused desire to return to origins, to a pre-Zionist situation, to a time when the land of Israel was still only a Promised Land. The celebration of life in exile as a metaphor for moral sensibility and openness to the Other only reinforces this impression. And if one is alert to the fundamentally ethical requirements that inspire the post-Zionists, one may ask whether they do not simply express a rejection of a land "dirtied" by the tribulations of two peoples throughout the past two centuries and an aspiration to a land that is "purified," situated beyond contingencies, on the edge of the sacred.

Gush Emunism also aspires to a "purified" land, but purified of the Other, the *goy*, to a Book/land beyond the state, to the rediscovered land of ancient Israel. If the holiness of the post-Zionists is secular, that of the Gush is religious. While the former projects itself into an anteriority close to the Promised Land, the latter, paradoxically taking up the Zionist ethos, rejoins the phase of conquest, pioneering, and the era when Zionism on the march wanted to appropriate the land and make the Promised Land a reality.

The Wandering Israeli

The aggravation of the country's conflicts tends periodically to reactivate the search for a promised land. Another aspect of this search is the appearance of the figure of the wandering Israeli in a nation that was expected to put an end to centuries of Jewish wandering. The blurring of landmarks is not alien to this dream. Israel is one of the rare countries to judge the emigration of its citizens to other places so severely. It is significantly the word *yeridah*, literally, "descent," that is used to refer to voluntary departure, whether the emigrant is in search of better economic opportunities or quite simply wants to escape the tension that dominates the daily life of the average Israeli. *Yeridah* is in some sense a negation of the very fundamentals of Zionism, which had aspired to make the land of Israel the land of all Jews. This objective was not attained, of course, since the majority of the Jewish people still live in the Diaspora. But could one not at least hope to permanently fix the presence of the Israelis themselves?

Whether as fantasy or as reality, wandering preoccupies even the native-born. In Zionist ideology, the sabra is the opposite of the wandering Jew of the Diaspora. It was generally acknowledged that in arriving in the "Promised Land," the Jew had reached the end of his historic journey, that he would cease forever to wander in distant and foreign lands. But, as we know, once they complete their military service, young Israelis have a habit of traveling for several months, if not a whole year, to distant and, of course, foreign countries. The defense of the homeland is thus extended by a departure. But even in Israel, the Jew remains a nomad; his wandering is part of his life.

That it has become possible to leave definitively, even simply to dream of it, testifies to a crumbling of the fundamental values around which the Zionist doctrine crystallized in the first years of Jewish colonization in Palestine, and which remained ideologically central in the nation's first years.[39] This crumbling of values is itself the consequence of Israeli society's lack of preparation to recognize the contradiction between the dreamt-of homogeneity of the Zionist idea and the reality of a society of immigrants. Until the middle of the 1960s, the media and communications networks tried to prevent any information liable to undermine this ideal of homogeneity from reaching the public. The failure to absorb oriental Jews, and more specifically those from North Africa, and the economic polarization of classes, which was becoming sharper, were therefore carefully masked. The melting pot remained the Zionist credo, vigorously proclaimed at every opportunity.

After the Six Day War, the disparity between the different social strata became quite evident. The fresh and painful awareness of this disparity was best expressed in the Black Panther movement, whose violent demonstrations clearly illustrated the failure of the Zionist ideal of homogeneity. It was not until the end of September 1997, at the approach of the Jewish New Year, that Ehud Barak, the new leader of the Labour party and direct heir of the Zionist socialism that had dominated the country until 1977, solemnly asked for "pardon" from Israel's Sephardim for the way in which they had been treated by his political family, saying:

> The Labour movement was responsible for the creation of the State of Israel. This process was accompanied by the uprooting of entire communities from North Africa and the Arab countries, whose members were scattered first in transit camps and then in "development towns" and in *moshavim*. They have played a pioneering role of prime importance in building the country. But they have never been given the recognition that is their right. I proclaim today how decisive their contribution has been. In the course of the uprooting of communities, families have suffered serious damage at the human level, damage that has left in people's memories deep scars associated with the name of the Labour movement. For the suffering thus inflicted I ask pardon in my own name and in the name of the history of the Labour party.[40]

At this turn of the century, there was a taste for repentance everywhere. This declaration, though, aroused many reactions, whether it was described as a sincere statement or an electoral maneuver, as an act of justice or an insult to the country's founding fathers. Whatever its import, it correctly reminded people that Israel was not a promised land for everybody, and that many have experienced it even as a new exile in their own land, as a redoubling of their old exile. No doubt, the oriental Jewish communities were not the only ones to have seen their native cultures denied. But they were placed in the front lines, because power was concentrated in the hands of Ashkenazim. The vanity of the hope of integration has recently been expressed in the public's intense interest in the ethnic past, folklore, and customs of the Diaspora. This interest results in the recycling of native cultures: oriental songs, for example, are very popular. So is the trip to the Diaspora in search of roots, often linked to the Holocaust. The reawakening of the Zionist dream is thus accompanied by a rehabilitation of exile—although Zionism had originally made its negation one of its major doctrines.

The wars of 1967 and 1973 marked a turning point. From the ruins of Zionist values thus arose the figure of the wandering Israeli. The Gulf War in the winter of 1991 only strengthened this process. During this strange conflict, the Israelis realized that they were not protected inside the nation's borders, that they were exposed to missile attacks. Awareness of this vulnerability penetrated the private sphere. Behind the realistic fear, an apocalyptic terror gripped the population, which drew a masochistic satisfaction from images of its unstable existence, which became a marker of its identity.

Recognition of the weakness, the crack, as a recurrent model of the history of the Jewish people is related to the interest manifested in recent years by many Israelis in the Kabbalah, according to which the creation of the world is the culmination of a process of contraction of the divine and a "breaking of vessels," and its existence an exile. People passionately reread Jewish authors like Moses Mendelssohn, Franz Rosenzweig, Martin Buber, Edmond Jabès, and George Steiner, who dissociate Jewish existence from the land. A return to talmudic models is apparent in the theater, for example. People try to comprehend contemporary Israeli reality in the light of the norms of the ancient Jewish world. In this spirit, the foundation of the state after the Holocaust and the subsequent arrival of waves of refugees are perceived as one more chapter in the cyclical history of the wandering Jew.

Wandering Israelis have become a recurrent theme in Israeli literature,[41] involving both those who leave the country and find a temporary or permanent home abroad and those who stay but continually dream of life elsewhere. One finds them in various books published in recent years: *Masa' be-Av* (The Voyage of the Month of Av) by Aharon Megged (1980); *The Mixed Tendency* by Yotam Reuveni (1982); *Menuhah nekhonah* (translated as *A Perfect Peace*) by Amos Oz (1982); *A Distant Land* by Yitzhak Ben-Ner (1982); *Pesek-zman* (translated as *Borrowed Time*) by Amnon Jackont (1982); *Gerushim me'uharim* (translated as *A Late Divorce*) by A. B. Yehoshua (1982), and *Mascarade* by Arie Semo (1983). In the 1980s, this tendency grew in correspondence to the post–Yom Kippur War period and the arrival of Likkud in power. A sort of disenchantment appeared, coupled with a desire to wander.

The characters in these novels are sabras. The gravity of the problem of wandering is underscored by the fact that the authors have chosen sabras who are taken to be part of the elite: Ashkenazis whose parents had come to Palestine as pioneers and who are now politicians or educators. They have received the best Israeli education, have volunteered for fighting units in the army, have excelled at their studies. They appear solidly rooted in Israeli life, and so their wish to leave the country and try a new life elsewhere reveals even more clearly the seriousness of the personal and ideological crisis they are going through. But in the context of the country's culture, it is more the desire to leave than the actual departure or the specific destination that furnishes the dramatic basis and the emotional tension in this kind of literature.

The hero of *A Distant Land*, Shuvali, is haunted by the desire to leave with his extended family for New Zealand. In his imagination, they will all live a utopian life there and work the land together on a farm. It is not without irony that this vision is described in rigorously Zionist terms: Shuvali dreams of a different promised land, which he will go and redeem elsewhere. The first Zionists dreamed of the Mediterranean sun; the wandering Israeli prefers Nordic countries that will relieve him of the heat and pressure of Israeli life. In *A Late Divorce*, Israel is marked by ageing, madness, and confinement, whereas the Diaspora is associated with youthfulness, creativity, and fertility. The wandering Israeli expects a change of environment to allow him to organize the personal space that is lacking at home. Israel often evokes imprisonment and suffocation for him. This whole literature reflects the current social and ideological crisis that Israeli society is undergoing: conflict between generations, disillusionment with myths, the oppressive feeling of confinement associated with a continual state of siege and amplified by the strong demand for conformity in a small, cramped society.

The land of Israel is too real, it stifles and devours its inhabitants. Contemporary Israeli fiction reveals the growing discomfort of a generation nourished on the romantic vision of sabras and their future in the land of pioneers, who must now deal with the gap between this vision and the sociopolitical reality of Israel. Do the Israelis of today, no less than the Jews of yesterday, still need a "there" to allow them to escape "here"? As if the Promised Land for which they are still searching could only be elsewhere? It is a fragile line that separates the sabra from the wandering Jew.

Notwithstanding that indigenous materials and subject matter directly linked to the country's nature remain central to the plastic arts in Israel, a movement arose in the 1970s around the School of Art for the Teachers of Art in Ramat Hasharon that lies outside an affinity with the land and its associated mythologies. The artist and teacher Raffie Lavie was the driving force.[42] Calendar photographs of Swiss landscapes appear in his works; in lieu of the nostalgia for the lost country of the writers from the beginning of Zionism, the artist offers images of a serene and snowy land, the opposite of Israel, which is neither the known country nor the lost one. There is a persistent desire for an imaginary country, similar to the dreamt of (but never seen) Palestine described by certain writers of the Jewish Enlightenment. There is a never-ending race after a land one does not have. The Promised Land, wherever it is, takes the place of the land that is lived.

Using the same approach, some artists subject certain images and national symbols to a peculiar treatment. For example, Tamar Geller uses a reproduction of Piero della Francesca's "ideal city" for his paintings of Tel Hai, the high point of national mythology. The tension between "here" and "there" is what preoccupies these creators. The images of "there," in which local ideas are reflected, are borrowed from tourist brochures or from classical art. An exhibition at the Israel Museum during the winter of 1991 was organized around works evoking the absence of roots and wandering, outside any anchoring in a given territory or given form. The myth of the exodus from Egypt is seen, not as the start of a voyage toward the Promised Land, but rather as a text of the generation of the desert. In accord with this choice and in the spirit of Buber, the language and syntax of these works stress the dimension of expulsion implicit in the order to leave given to Abraham ("Leave your country . . . ")[43] more than they do the promise of the land ("To your offspring I will give this land").[44]

Is the desert not, according to Jabès, the physical and mental space of any nomad? Many Israeli artists turn toward the desert and borrow certain traits from nomadic culture that are still preserved by the now-sedentarized Bedouin. These artists take the trouble to make the journey, to join Bedouin encampments on a road that then leads them to the camps of Palestinian refugees. Others find the desert in what is recounted in Jewish tradition and the texts that have preserved its mythic memory, such as the ritual tale of the exodus from Egypt that is read at Passover. Baggage, maps, and suitcases: all the elements of the journey as a quest for identity haunt the works of these artists of nomadism.

During one of his final interviews, Jabès said that even in Israel, the Jew is a nomad, that wandering is part of his thinking.[45] He added that wherever in the world and in the dispersal they find themselves today, Jews are always in a situation of exile in relation to the place they come from. "What are the dreams of the Israelis?" he asked. One dreams of Morocco, another of Poland. Ultimately, there is something that is the world. The Jew is the world. The land that is the Jews' is also the land of their exile. The Israelis are no different from other Jews. They carry within them not only exile from their parents, the reality of which was not recognized, but also their own exile, an existential exile, which pushes them constantly toward a "promised land," a Book/land. If the land escapes Israelis, they also escape the land, as if this land were promised to impossibility. Also, this land is impossible because the true place of the Jew, as Jabès said, is the Book. This is where he finds himself, where he questions himself; the Book is his freedom.

The land of Israel does not escape its destiny as a Book/land—one that can be read in many voices.

Epilogue

Nearing the end of this book, the reader might legitimately demand how it happens that a land occupying a unique place in the imaginations of believers in the three great monotheisms is still so diverse. That today the "new" Israeli historians are buckling down to deconstructing the myths surrounding Zionist Israel is additional proof that pluralism is starting to shake up the old Zionist rhetoric that, with the ideological zeal typical of all nationalisms, for a long time prevented any dialogue. Is this new diversity of discourses precisely the sign that we have entered a post-Zionist phase? Given the current effervescence, it would be vain to try to shackle this young country and stick simplistic labels on it. A shift from the Zionist era to the so-called post-Zionist one is not easy to discern. There is no single Zionist discourse, just as there is no single way of demythifying Zionist ideological constructions.

Those who came to settle in the land of Israel did not have a very clear notion of this land, and it was necessary to make it a mother country by bringing in Jews who had lived elsewhere for centuries. But Zionism did not succeed in erasing the representations that had sustained the Jewish people during the Diaspora. Israel could not become a land like any other, if only because people brought their own lands—those they had left, where their ancestors were buried—along with them. Each immigrant transported his exile with him. The less well he was integrated into the country, the more the nostalgia for exile surfaced, as it did for the Jews of North Africa, with their cult of the saints.[1] In their case, the cult of the tomb of a celebrated saint buried in Diaspora can be seen shifting to the practice of the same cult on an entirely new site in Israel, most often in a development town, generally full of immigrants, in a peripheral region. This phenomenon enjoyed a new upsurge especially in the 1970s. This migration of the saints brings integration to completion by importing what was lacking in the adopted land, thus securing an anchor. Some come with their country of origin, others with the Torah—but no one comes alone. And one should not forget the representations of the land of Israel handed down by previous generations and the echoes of liturgy buried in the immigrants' baggage. No ideological discourse, including the Zionists', could erase this multiple heritage. Even if it was somewhat stifled by the unifying rhetoric in vogue until quite recently, plurality existed well before it was loudly proclaimed. Diaspora, the Diaspora experience, would allow these Jews of the Maghreb to become Israelis without renouncing their ethnic specificity. Despite the famous ideal of the melting pot, people continue to be sustained by the soil of two homelands. People may also strengthen their Israeli allegiance outside the geopolitical borders of Israel: Moroccans returning to their country of origin for a limited stay find there the roots of their Israeli identity; young Israelis are taken on trips to the central sites of the Holocaust in Poland.[2] One no longer needs nearby sites in Israel itself to construct one's identity, since it also has resources outside, where the history of the Jews unfolded for better or worse. The history of the Jews is not separate from the history of the Israelis. It was only made so artificially, for ideological reasons, because it was believed that everything should happen on Israel's ground even if this implied forgetting what came before, forgetting the unforgettable. Now that the borders of Israel are fluctuating more than ever, that the voices of Palestinians are heard better than ever, and that an awareness that another people also have rights over this land is being asserted, horizons are being stretched and the obsessive attachment to the soil is giving way to other forms of rootedness.

If Israel is a problem, this is not only because its inhabitants never stop revisiting their land, infinitely multiplying the ways they look at it. The Diaspora, too, projects onto this country its own expectations and frustrations, hopes and disappointments, symbols and dreams. Israel is invested with so much holiness that in certain milieux it becomes impossible even to engage in a discussion on this subject. It is untouchable. Whoever criticizes it risks being denounced by someone as a blasphemer, even though within its borders, Israel is applying itself to a long and painful effort of demythification and self-criticism. Israeli governments follow one after the other, and there are always Jews in the Diaspora who approve of each of them without turning a hair, even when passions are unleashed in Israel itself. However, it is certainly erroneous to believe that all Diaspora Jews approve unconditionally of Israel, whatever policy it pursues. But this country is an integral part of the identity of a good part of world Jewry, especially since the Six Day War. Let us take the French case as an example. In France, there is an existential Zionism that is by no means monolithic, more a personal search than an ideology.[3] In some ways, the Jews of France incarnate a Zionism typical of postindustrial society: it is depoliticized, stripped of ideology, and brings the individual to the heart of its vision. Within this recomposition of identity, one can imagine the affective charge that is attached to Israel. This does not mean that identification necessarily implies some impulse to emigrate; one has to bear in mind the small number of those who go there. Moreover, the vision of Israel varies considerably according to the group—practicing or nonpracticing, secular or ultra-Orthodox. In France, Israel is a preferred field of study for the Jewish public, if only in terms of acquiring the Hebrew language, particularly in non-religious milieux. One learns Hebrew because of the relationship one has with Israel and not necessarily because one wants to plunge into reading Scripture. The trip to Israel is a modern form of the pilgrimages of old, and it is much more common among French than among American Jewry. The trip/pilgrimage plays a structuring role in identity, but like any pilgrimage, it involves more the pilgrim himself than the reality of the country he visits, the only aspects of which he remembers are those corresponding to his own expectations. Discordant voices have been raised here and there, especially in recent years, to denounce the policy of the government of the day. But for the Jews of the Diaspora, Israel still constitutes an important source of pride, especially since 1967. It remains a land endowed with many positive attributes, a land of refuge, in the face of memories of wandering in the black years of the German Occupation.

In the United States, after the Six Day War, Israel became the religion of Jewish Americans, the civil religion of organized American Jewry, as well as the supreme source of identity and community self-expression.[4] In this case, as in France's, there is no justification for seeing this as a phenomenon of double allegiance: far from it, since it is essentially a matter of a symbolic relationship with the land and with the very reality of that land. This relationship, as developed and expressed, remains largely detached from Israel in a concrete sense, more in the domain of metaphor, even when there is militancy in favor of Israel and financial support of it. In fact, Israel represents what one is not and what one would like to be—not to mention the ethical values it is supposed to incarnate. Close reading of contemporary American Jewish literature makes it appear that American Jews today define themselves as much with respect to Israel as to the past of their fathers, the Jews of eastern Europe or from old neighborhoods that were densely Jewish, like the Lower East Side of New York City. Any upheaval in Israel is liable to compromise their identity construct—hence the sacred aura invariably attached to it. In Jewish American schools, children are taught not to question Israeli policy; feelings of loyalty to the state of Israel are exalted.

This being so, and notwithstanding the teaching that is dispensed and absorbed in the United States, the phase of unconditional support for Israel has ended since the 1980s with the occupation of Lebanon. The Intifada in 1987 only reinforced this wave of criticism, which has continued to grow since then. Of course, large sectors of the American Jewish population still feel outraged by denunciations of Israeli policy by intellectuals like Woody Allen. The critical attitude is widespread in the columns of a Jewish progressive journal like *Tikkun* or a conservative one like *Commentary*. While it is true that many American Jews are critical of Israel, or quite simply indifferent to it, the organized Jewish community continues to support the State of Israel solidly, which is the case in France as well. Even if they do not adhere to Zionist ideology properly speaking, American Orthodox Jews associated with Agudat Israel—a political and religious movement that in the 1999 elections, along with its allies, won five seats in the Israeli

Knesset—defend the existence of Israel because that country is currently a great center of Orthodox Judaism, and because the hope of seeing it become a true Orthodox state has never been so great. As for the American Reform movement, it is entirely pro-Israeli.

These days, Western Jews plead in favor of integration into the Diaspora while manifesting a proud loyalty toward the "homeland"—a "homeland" where few Americans, French, or Britons would like to live. Dispersed throughout the world, culturally and religiously divided, the Jewish people still remain united in the support they lend to the *existence* of a Jewish state, where Hebrew is spoken, where a growing number of Jews live, and which many others visit to refresh their Jewish identity, even when they are not religious. After the Holocaust, attachment to Israel is laden with much sentimentality; the dominant figure of the heroic soldier or kibbutznik relegates to the background the painful memory of the victims of genocide. The Six Day War reinforced this glorious image, which was approved even by non-Jewish public opinion. The Jewish imagination of the Diaspora apprehended Israel and the Israelis in a romantic mode, which the latter did nothing to demystify. Still today, the Diaspora does not see Israel for what it is, which prevents a true encounter with this land and its inhabitants. This also partly prevents Israel from becoming what it truly wishes to be, since it must trail behind it these often impossible expectations. Israel as it is experienced day to day by its citizens largely escapes the Jews of the Diaspora, who prefer to see and find in it what they want to see and find there. Israeli post-Zionism is hardly preoccupied with the myths feeding on Israel in the contemporary Diaspora, since its first task is to demolish those of Zionism. The still rather guarded entry of part of the Jewish American population into the phase that is described by some as post-Zionist perhaps does not mark the end of its passionate relationship with Israel. Rather, it inaugurates the start of a more authentic relationship between the two communities. However, this is less true for France, where post-Zionism remains beyond the horizon of French Jews, with the exception of certain small elites.

Still, once may ask how this land, imagined and reimagined for centuries, could ever free itself from the sediment of images inseparable from its essence. Perhaps it is fated to exist through mixed and inter-posed images, even in its most immediate reality. Israeli Israel, so mul-tiple, scarcely resembles the Israel seen from the Diaspora, itself so plural—not to mention the Israel of the media, and many others. A singular land, the land of Israel still escapes uniqueness, and its myths continue to sprout in the furrows traced by the pioneers.

Afterword

In the autumn of 2000, the second Intifada took off, triggered by a visit on the part of Ariel Sharon—then an Israeli opposition party politician—to a site which, for the Muslims, is the Esplanade of the Mosques, and for the Jews, the Temple Mount. Even if this visit was not perhaps the principal reason for a return to hostilities between Israelis and Palestinians, it furnished a new proof of the profoundly symbolic value and the sacrality that both peoples attach to each parcel of this land claimed by both sides.

The gravity of the second Intifada and the hundreds of deaths it has provoked on each side will mark the future generations who will go on living on ground now saturated with the blood of martyrs. And the memory of the dead will long haunt the history of a partition of the land that, if it indeed comes about someday, will have been impossible for decades. That memory will naturally redouble the sacrality of this land, a land nourished with the blood of the dead, blood that offers the states constructed or to be constructed on this land a window on Heaven.

Sacrality and nationalism have never been incompatible—quite the contrary. As it happens, the sacred nourishes nationalism, because the sacred and the religious immunize the temporal and offer it innocence. Zionism itself, whose key players were deeply secular, cited the sacrality of the land of Israel and its place in the traditional Jewish imagination in order to give meaning and legitimacy to the establishment of a Jewish state on this land. Today, the Palestinians in turn drench this same land with such sacrality that men and women are willing to sacrifice

237

their lives for its sake. Such a sacrifice manifests their devotion to the land and illustrates and reinforces the sacred right they have to it. These holy warriors exalt the nation from which they have sprung and foreground the exalted nobility of the cause for which they are fighting. Henceforth, on both sides, it is bloodshed that time and again renews the unshakeable alliance between the people and its land. Less than a year after the attack on the Delphinarium discotheque in Tel Aviv on June 1, 2001, whose victims were mostly young Russians, a book of testimony by their relatives was published. One of the authors, Dimitri Radyshevsky, explains: "For the Russians, the Delphinarium was a mini-Holocaust. But if the terrorists' goal was to make them flee Israel, they have achieved exactly the opposite. These families will no longer be able to leave this ground bathed with the blood of their children."[1]

This blood tie can only further undermine the chances of a peace that each day appears more improbable. It establishes a genealogy of belonging; a Palestinian genealogy superimposed upon the Israeli genealogy. If the Bible is supposed to guarantee the historic right of Jews to the land of Israel, it is the blood spilled by the Palestinians that today endorses their right to the soil—an arid soil, watered with this blood, on which one day a "guiltless," purified state will spring up.

The Western imagination is caught up in this conflict. The space that the international press devotes to events in this part of the world denotes the inordinate symbolic importance of this land, ultimately sacred for everyone. Moreover, the conflict has burst forth elsewhere, in Europe, pitting Jews and Arabs against each other in places where previously cohabitation had been possible. Here again, the political dimension of events is bonded with a new significance. In Europe, it takes the form of a conflict between religious communities, between Jewish communities and Muslim communities. So has a "war of religions" begun, then, where it could have been avoided? The Arabs of France identify with their brothers in the Middle East, first with Muslims, and then with Palestinians. And the Jews of France identify with Israeli Jews, their co-religionists. Here, where politics should take precedence, it is the religious that comes up. Of course, not all the Jews or all the Arabs of western Europe identify in the same way with the protagonists of the Middle East conflict. But one scarcely any longer hears from those who remain (and want to stay) outside this new "war of religions."

How to untie the knots, spun in blood, between the political and the religious? One only need mention Israel for the subject, and even its political aspects, to take on strange religious overtones. Marked with the seal of biblical writings, of imaginary overinvestment, of religious emotion reactivated by nationalisms, this land cannot remain neutral and escape the grip of sacralized politics. The Camp David summit in the summer of 2000 failed over the question of Jerusalem and not over the problem of refugees.[2] French President Jacques Chirac, searching for a solution to the question of the Temple Mount, even dreamed of a division of sovereignty that was not horizontal but vertical: the Palestinians would get the Esplanade of the Mosques and a "certain depth of subsoil," and the Israelis, "a sovereignty beginning at the depth of the presumed ruins of the Temple."[3]

Of course, for believers, there is nothing surprising about the fact that this land of Israel bears the weight of its sacrality, but this is also sometimes true of laypeople. Even though he is not religious, when he was asked how he could let the question of the Temple Mount prevent an agreement from being reached, Gilead Sher, who led the negotiations for Ehud Barak from 1999 to 2001, replied: "We are not extremists, but we have a tradition, a site of worship where our ancestors prayed. One cannot sweep that away with the back of one's hand."[4]

The adoption of the theme by secular politicians arises from a manipulation that makes the situation inextricable. You can't negotiate over the sacred. So will it have to be God who puts an end to the murderous conflict that each day only grows more inflamed? How can one live in peace in this land of men and women while anticipating salvation from on high? The oversacralization of the land, which is just as much the case among Palestinians as Israelis, particularly since the second Intifada, can only fan the conflagration there, if not spread it elsewhere, to anywhere Jews and Muslims are in close contact with each other. For the politicians, the sacred has become a political weapon, which is, moreover, inevitably turned against those who use it.

It is time to disentangle the ideal Israel of those who observe the commandments from the Israel of compromise in which Israelis seeking peace want to live. And for the Palestinians, too, it comes down to uncoupling the sacrality of the imagined land from political self-affirmation. Only recourse to the political means (even if imperfect) that democratic countries know how to use will allow the Palestinians to found the state to which they aspire, within recognized borders. The sacred cannot be divided. The land can.

COLLEGIUM BUDAPEST, JUNE 2002

Chronology

This chronology aims merely to allow the reader better to situate in time a certain number of events of variable importance, to which allusions are made in the body of the text. It is neither a general chronology of the history of the Jewish people nor a general chronology of the history of Palestine or Israel.

END OF THE ELEVENTH CENTURY B.C.E. Establishment of a kingdom by Saul.

CIRCA 964 B.C.E. Completion of the building of the First Temple.

CIRCA 931 B.C.E. Death of Solomon. Schism between the kingdom of Judah to the south and the kingdom of Israel to the north.

CIRCA 722 B.C.E. Fall of the kingdom of Israel and deportation to Assyria.

CIRCA 586 B.C.E. Fall of the kingdom of Judah; destruction of the First Temple; deportation to Babylonia.

539 B.C.E. Cyrus's decree.

515 B.C.E. Completion of the building of the Second Temple.

332 B.C.E. Conquest of Syria and Palestine by Alexander the Great.

167 B.C.E. Start of the revolt of the Maccabees against the Seleucid sovereign Antiochus IV Epiphanes.

164 B.C.E. Liberation of the Temple by the Maccabees.

63 B.C.E. Roman conquest of Judea.

AD 66–74 Great revolt of Judea against Rome.

68 Yohanan ben Zakai flees besieged Jerusalem and negotiates with Vespasian his settling in Yavneh.

70 Fall of Jerusalem; destruction of the Second Temple.

132–135 Revolt of Simeon bar-Kokhba.

CIRCA 175 Judah the Prince settles in Bet-Shearim in Lower Galilee.

END OF THE SECOND CENTURY The Babylonian Exilarch Hunah is buried in the Holy Land.

CIRCA 200 Completion of the Mishnah.

THIRD–FIFTH CENTURIES Emergence of Babylonia as the main center of Jewish settlement and erudition.

END OF THE FOURTH CENTURY Completion of the Jerusalem Talmud.

END OF THE FIFTH CENTURY Completion of the Babylonian Talmud.

SIXTH–ELEVENTH CENTURIES The period called "Gaonic," dominated by the flourishing of Babylonian academies.

636–37 Conquest of Palestine by the Arabs.

1085 Taking of Toledo by the Christians. Significant advance of the *Reconquista*.

1096 First Crusade.

1099 Conquest of Jerusalem by the Crusaders.

TWELFTH CENTURY Voyages by Petahia of Regensburg and by Benjamin of Tudela.

1140 Judah Halevi leaves Spain for the land of Israel.

1180 Moses Maimonides, in Egypt, completes the Mishneh Torah.

THIRTEENTH CENTURY Immigration of French rabbis to the Holy Land; publication of the Zohar.

1267 Moses Nahmanides arrives in Acre.

1290 Expulsion of the Jews from England.

1394 Final expulsion of the Jews from France.

1488–90 Obadiah of Bertinoro writes three letters describing his voyages and his first impressions of the Holy Land.

1492 Expulsion of the Jews from Spain.

1515–16 Conquest of Palestine by the Ottomans.

SIXTEENTH CENTURY Jewish Renaissance in Galilee; development of a kabbalistic center in Safed; Jacob Berab's initiative to restore the Sanhedrin; reconstruction of Tiberiad; Joseph Karo's *Shulhan Arukh* appears; creation of Jewish regional and general authorities in Poland and Lithuania.

SEVENTEENTH CENTURY Sabbatean crisis.

START OF THE EIGHTEENTH CENTURY First book of general and Palestinian geography in Yiddish.

EIGHTEENTH CENTURY Birth of Hassidism; birth of Haskalah (Jewish Enlightenment) that is propagated in the nineteenth century in eastern Europe and in the twentieth in North Africa. Russian Jews are forced to settle in a circumscribed region, "the Pale of Settlement."

1760–70 Hassidic immigration to the Holy Land.

1790–91 Emancipation of the Jews in France.

1798 Voyage of Nahman of Bratslav to the land of Israel.

1799 Napoleon Bonaparte in Egypt and in the Holy Land.

STARTING IN 1808 Immigration of Perushim (followers of the Vilna Ga'on) to the Holy Land.

STARTING IN 1827 The British Jewish philanthropist Moses Montefiore makes seven trips to Palestine.

1830 Mehemet Ali, viceroy of Egypt, reclaims Syria and Palestine from the Ottomans.

STARTING IN THE 1830s Immigration of oriental Jews, especially from North Africa.

1830s–1880s Awakening of nationalisms in Europe; religious pre-Zionists urgently summon Jews to return to Palestine.

1840 The Damascus Affair.

1840s Millenarian revival.

1859 Digging of the Suez Canal.

1860 Foundation in Paris of the Alliance israélite universelle.

1860s–1870s Traditionalist groups, nationalist students, and philanthropists make proposals for agricultural colonization of Palestine.

1862 Publication of *Rome and Jerusalem* by Moses Hess.

1865 Creation in London of the Palestine Exploration Fund, a scientific society for research in Palestine.

1870 Foundation of the agricultural school Mikveh Yisrael in Jaffa.

1876 Publication of George Eliot's novel *Daniel Deronda* calling for a gathering of Jews in the Holy Land.

1880s–1890s Multiplication of European societies for the colonization of Palestine; creation of the first agricultural settlements in Palestine.

1881–82 Pogroms in Russia following the assassination of Alexander II; mass exodus of Jews to America, to western Europe and to some extent to Palestine; birth of the Lovers of Zion movement.

1882 Yehuda Leib Pinsker publishes *Auto-Emancipation* calling upon Jews to take charge of their destiny and redefine themselves as a territorial nation.

1882–1904 First wave of Jewish immigration to Palestine.

STARTING IN 1882 Edmond de Rothschild gives support to colonies in Palestine.

1890 Foundation of Baron Maurice de Hirsch's first agricultural settlement, at Moisesville in Argentina.

1891 The Blackstone Memorandum, a petition for the return of Jews to Palestine, comes from the American millenarian William E. Blackstone; foundation of the Jewish Colonization Association (ICA).

1894–1906 Dreyfus Affair.

1896 Publication of *The Jewish State* by Theodor Herzl.

1897 First Zionist Congress in Basel.

1903–5 Israel Zangwill leads the fight for a "Ugandan" solution.

1904–14 Second wave of immigration to Palestine.

1905 The World Zionist Organization rejects the Ugandan solution; Zangwill provokes a schism and creates the Jewish Territorial Organization (ITO); start of the "conquest of labor" in Palestine and the kibbutz movement.

1909 Creation of Tel Aviv.

1911 Creation of a women's farm in Lower Galilee.

1917 The Balfour Declaration.

1919–23 Third wave of Jewish immigration to Palestine.

1920–30 Activity by the Brit Shalom group, which does not believe that Zionism and Palestine are able to resolve the Jewish question.

1922 The Palestine Mandate is granted to Great Britain.

1924–28 Fourth wave of Jewish immigration to Palestine.

1926–66 *Israel in Exile*, a monumental work in several volumes by the Zionist historian Ben-Zion Dinur (Dinaburg).

1930–39 Fifth wave of Jewish immigration to Palestine.

1936 Arab riots in Palestine.

1947 Adoption of the division of Palestine by the General Assembly of the United Nations.

1947–49 War of Independence.

MAY 14, 1948 Proclamation of the Independence of the State of Israel.

1950s Massive immigration to Israel.

1956 Suez War.

1964 Creation of the Palestine Liberation Organization (PLO).

1967 Six Day War; the core of ancient Israel is occupied by the Israelis, and Israeli society is turned upside down; Zionism unable to answer the problems posed by Israeli occupation of the territories.

1973 Yom Kippur War; Israeli society loses confidence in its leaders and increasingly questions its identity.

1974 Foundation of the nationalist and religious extraparliamentary party Gush Emunim ("Faith Bloc").

1977 For the first time since the state's creation, arrival in power of the nationalist Right, which accelerates Jewish settlement in occupied territories; President Anwar Sadat of Egypt addresses the Knesset.

1978 Camp David Agreements between Egypt and Israel.

1979 Peace treaty between Israel and Egypt.

1980s Publication of the first works by a new generation of intellectuals formed around the historical critique of the War of Independence; they will be called "new" historians. A wide public debate continues around these historians' allegations and marks, among other things, the start of a post-Zionist era in Israel; birth of a literature whose principal theme is the wandering Israeli.

1981 Annexation of Golan by Israel.

1982 Israeli invasion of Lebanon.

1987 Start of the first Intifada, the "war of stones."

1991 The Gulf War; opening of the peace conference in Madrid.

1992 Return of the Labour party to power.

1993 Oslo Accords. Mutual recognition between Israel and the PLO.

1994 The Gaza-Jericho Accord authorizing the creation of a Palestinian authority in both of these autonomous zones. Peace treaty between Israel and Jordan.

1995 Agreement over the extension of Palestinian autonomy to the whole of the West Bank and Gaza. Assassination of Prime Minister Yitzhak Rabin, architect of the peace with Yasser Arafat, by an Israeli religious extremist.

1996 Recurrent Islamist attacks; Israel bombs south Lebanon; Benjamin Netanyahu of the Likkud is elected prime minister; tensions with Arab countries and with Palestinian authorities continue to be exacerbated.

1997 Protocol agreement on redeployment in Hebron. The new head of the Labour party, Ehud Barak, asks for "pardon" from Israel's Sephardim for the way they have been treated by his party.

1998 Fiftieth anniversary of the creation of the State of Israel. The Wye River Memorandum, signed by Israel and the Palestinians, aims to overcome the current impasse in the peace process.

1999 Legislative elections are anticipated in Israel and the Labour leader Ehud Barak becomes prime minister with 56.08 percent of the votes. The Sharm-el-Sheikh memorandum is signed by Israelis and Palestinians, who promise to reopen and accelerate negotiations over the permanent status of the "territories" with a view to a conclusive agreement. Fifth anniversary of the signing by deceased Prime Minister Yitzhak Rabin and the deceased King Hussein of the peace treaty between Israel and Jordan; during these five years, the two countries have done everything to apply the terms of this agreement.

2000 Ehud Barak is abandoned by some of his allies (notably religious ones); a government crisis ensues. Failure of the Camp David talks between Barak and Yasser Arafat under the aegis of the United States. The status of Jerusalem is the stumbling block, but voices are heard in Israel questioning the principle of the indivisibility of the capital. In October, after a visit by Ariel Sharon, leader of the Likkud party, to the "Esplanade of the Mosques" ("Temple Mount" for the Jews), a vicious cycle begins, and the dynamic seems to have shifted from peace to war. The "Intifada of Al Aqsa," by its sudden violence, both betrays the loss of legitimacy of the historic leader of the PLO, Yasser Arafat, and marks a turning point in Palestinian demands that breaks with their previous moderate line. The extremists of both camps play on the religious dimension to make the conflict insoluble. On December 9, Ehud Barak resigns.

2001 On February 6, the Israelis elect Ariel Sharon, the Likkud candidate, to the post of prime minister. The veteran Labour leader Shimon Peres becomes foreign minister in Sharon's government of national unity. On April 17, for the first time since the second Intifada erupted, Israeli troops seize back land controlled by the Palestinians in the Gaza Strip. On May 8, the youngest victim of the Intifada is killed by shrapnel from an Israeli tank shell at the age of four months. On May 14, Israeli troops kill five Palestinian policemen manning a checkpoint in the West Bank and launch a major bombardment of security targets in the Gaza Strip. On May 18, a Palestinian suicide bomber kills himself and five Israelis at a shopping mall in Netanya. Israel bombs the West Bank towns of Nablus and Ramallah. On May

21, in his report on the Middle East conflict, former U.S. senator George Mitchell calls for an immediate ceasefire and a freeze on expansion of Jewish settlements in the occupied territories. On May 22, Sharon rejects Mitchell's call for the freeze on Jewish settlement expansion and describes the settlements as "a vital national enterprise." On June 1, a suicide bomber kills nineteen young Israelis at the Dolphinarium discotheque in Tel Aviv. On July 19, three Palestinians, including a three-month-old baby, are killed by Jewish extremists near Hebron. On August 4, Israel's strategy of assassinating Palestinian political and military leaders moves to within one rung of Yasser Arafat, as two missiles narrowly miss a car carrying Marwan Barghuti, the man who rules the streets of the West Bank. On August 9, a suicide bomber blows himself up in a pizza restaurant in Jerusalem, killing fifteen people and wounding ninety. On August 12, a Palestinian suicide bomber blows himself up in a café near Haifa, wounding fifteen people. On August 14, Israeli tanks move into the West Bank city of Jenin and open fire on the Palestinian police station, which is strongly criticized by Washington. On September 11, suicide bombers in hijacked airliners destroy the World Trade Centre and part of the Pentagon. On September 12, Israeli tanks enter the Palestinian-ruled desert town of Jericho. On September 15, there is a major incursion of Israeli forces into the Gaza Strip. On September 16, Israel becomes as an early stumbling block to Washington's plans to recruit Arab states to a broad war coalition against Afghanistan as Prime Minister Sharon rebuffs U.S. calls for ceasefire talks and orders the invasion of Palestinian-ruled Ramallah. European countries fear that Israel is using the international focus on events in the United States as a cover for punitive actions against the Palestinians. On September 17, Sharon declares he will not sacrifice national interests for Washington's desire to forge a broad war coalition. On September 28, thousands of Palestinians mark the first anniversary of the second Intifada. On October 2, President George W. Bush says that he is prepared to back the creation of a Palestinian state. American relations with Israel plunge to their lowest point in a decade. On October 11, the Bush administration envisages Jerusalem as a shared capital for an Israeli and a Palestinian state. On October 15, Israeli forces withdraw from Palestinian neighborhoods in the West Bank city of Hebron, following a meeting of Israeli and Palestinian security officials. On October 17, the far-right tourism minister, Rehavam Zeevi, is murdered in Jerusalem. Violence intensifies across the West Bank. On October 19, Israeli forces seize large areas of Bethlehem, Ramallah, Nablus, and Jenin. October 17, bowing to international pressure, Israel agrees to pull out its troops from Bethlehem. On November 7, Sharon warns that he has a plan to bring one million more Jews to Israel. On November 22, five Palestinian children are killed while walking to school by a powerful explosion in a refugee camp in the southern Gaza Strip. On November 23, 59 percent of Israelis support the creation of a Palestinian state, according to a Gallup opinion in the *Maariv* newspaper. December 3, Israel helicopter gunships fire missiles at targets near Arafat's headquarters in Gaza City. Sharon warns Arafat that he is engaged in a war that could end in his own destruction. On December 4, Israeli helicopters and jets hit Palestinian Authority targets in the Gaza Strip and West Bank, as Tel Aviv takes further retaliatory action for the killing of twenty-five people in three recent suicide bombings. On December 5, the Israeli government agrees to a twelve-hour pause in the offensive against the Palestinian Authority as Arafat apparently bows to pressure to arrest senior members of the militant groups Hamas and Islamic Jihad. On December 7, Israel resumes air strikes against the Palestinian Authority. On December 10, one of Israel's few Arab parliamentarians, Azmi Bishara, goes on trial charged with undermining the state. On December 13, Israeli helicopters pound Palestinian buildings in the West Bank and Gaza, in a campaign of political and military retaliation for deadly Palestinian attacks. Sharon breaks off all ties with Arafat. December 16, U.S. Middle East envoy Anthony Zinni returns to Washington from an aborted ceasefire mission that produced the most spectacular surge in violence in the fifteen months of the Palestinian uprising.

2002   On January 5, Israel discovers a Palestinian ship loaded with fifty tons of arms. Arafat denies that the shipment was ordered by the Palestinian Authority. On February 1, Sharon says that he regrets not having "eliminated" Arafat twenty years ago during the invasion of Lebanon but denies he has any plans to harm him now. On February 11, Israel attacks Palestinian security headquarters in Gaza City in a second day of reprisals for an unprecedented Palestinian missile attack on southern Israel. On February 26, Israelis and Palestinians agree to resume peace talks as interest grows in a Saudi peace plan (Israel would withdraw from all the territories seized in 1967—the West Bank, Gaza, East Jerusalem, and the Golan Heights—and in return, all Arab states would offer normal diplomatic relations—including a peace deal recognizing Israel's right to exist and securing its borders). On February 27, Europe's foreign policy chief, Javier Solana, meets Crown Prince Abdullah of Saudi Arabia to explore the peace initiative. On February 28, the Israeli army storms the Balata refugee camp, the biggest in the West Bank and other strategic positions. Simultaneous invasion of the Jenin refugee camp. On March 2, a suicide bomber blows himself up in an ultra-orthodox Jerusalem neighborhood. Nine people are killed, including six children. On March 4, seventeen Palestinians, including five children, are killed in Ramallah as Israel steps up military pressure. On March 10, a Hamas member detonates a suicide bomb full of nails and metal screws in the crowded Moment Café in Jerusalem, killing eleven people and wounding more than fifty. Israel responds by destroying the Palestinian president's headquarters in Gaza City. On March 12, 20,000 Israeli troops invade refugee camps in the Gaza Strip and reoccupy the West Bank town of Ramallah. The United Nations Security Council for the first time endorses an independent Palestinian state and UN secretary-general Kofi Annan accuses Israel of "illegal occupation" of Palestinian land. On March 14, U.S. envoy General (ret.) Anthony Zinni arrives in Israel in the hopes of restarting the peace process after a week of unprecedented violence. On March 18, the U.S. vice president, Dick Cheney, arrives for talks with Sharon, and makes a qualified offer to meet later with Arafat. Meanwhile, Sharon makes a qualified offer to lift the travel ban on Arafat. On March 27, a suicide bomber blows himself up in a crowded hotel in Netanya, as guests prepare for a Passover meal. Nineteen are killed. The military wing of Hamas claims responsibility. On March 29, Israeli forces attack Arafat's Ramallah compound. The Palestinian leader is confined to the basement and vows that he would rather die than surrender. On April 9, thirteen Israeli soldiers are killed in a West Bank battle, the Israeli army's single biggest loss of life since the fighting began eighteen months previously. On April 12, U.S. secretary of state Colin Powell fails to secure an immediate withdrawal of Israeli forces from the West Bank after holding talks with Sharon. On April 13, Arafat condemns terrorism in a statement put out by a Palestinian news agency after meeting Powell. On April 15, the leader of the Palestinian Intifada, Marwan Barghuti, is seized by Israeli special forces from a house not far from Arafat's compound in Ramallah. Meanwhile journalists enter the Jenin refugee camp, seeing a "silent wasteland." On April 18, Israel gives its fullest account of its soldiers' conduct in Jenin, admitting 10 percent of the buildings in the city's refugee camp had been leveled during the fighting, but denying in the strongest terms that they had overseen a "massacre." On April 25, U.S.-Saudi talks begin in President Bush's Texas ranch. On April 30, Israel again refuses to cooperate with the UN inquiry into the fighting in the Jenin refugee camp. On May 2, Arafat emerges from confinement. On May 5, a deal to end the siege of the Church of the Nativity is brokered— the fighters will be released, with the allegedly most hardened going into exile and the others to Gaza. On May 7, a Palestinian suicide bomber kills fifteen people in an attack on a snooker hall near Tel Aviv. On May 8, Sharon renews his pledge to exile Arafat, who says he would rather die in the West Bank. On May 14, a report by an Israeli human rights group says Israel has secretly grabbed 42 percent of Palestinian land in the West Bank for illegal settlement activity. On May 31, Israeli troops enter the West Bank city of Nablus, while Arafat is reported to have signed a law reform package that is a framework for a Palestinian constitution. On June 18, at least twenty people are killed and more than forty wounded when a suicide bomber blows himself up on a crowded bus in Jerusalem. Israel says it will reoccupy Palestinian land on the West Bank and hold it indefinitely in reprisal for the bombing. On June 25, Israeli troops storm the Palestinian Authority headquarters in Hebron. The invasion brings the total of reoccupied cities to seven, leaving only Jericho, in the Jordan valley, under effective Palestinian control. On June 26, the Palestinian cabinet minister Saeb Erekat announces elections in January 2003 and details planned reforms to the Palestinian Authority. In June, Israel has begun the construction of a security fence along part of the western border of the West Bank to try to stop Palestinian terrorists crossing into its territory. Between September 28, 2000, and July 9, 2002, 1,662 Palestinians were killed by Israeli forces or settlers (SOURCE: Miftah). During the same period, at least 350 civilians, nearly all of whom were Israelis, were killed in 128 terrorist attacks (SOURCE: Amnesty International). On July 23, an Israeli fighter plane fires a missile into a crowded neighborhood in Gaza City, killing fifteen people, including nine children, and its target, the commander of the military wing of Hamas, Salah Shehada. International condemnation.

Notes

Introduction

EPIGRAPH: Franz Kafka, *The Castle*, trans. Mark Harman (New York: Schocken Books, 1998).

1. Dan Miron, "The Literary Image of the Shtetl," *Jewish Social Studies* 1, 3 (Spring 1995): 1–43.

2. Pierre-Vidal Naquet, *The Jews: History, Memory and the Present*, trans. and ed. David Ames Curtis (New York: Columbia University Press, 1996), p. 46.

Chapter 1

1. Quoted by R.J. Zwi Werblowsky, "Israël et Eretz Israël," *Les Temps modernes* 253 (1967): 372.

2. See, e.g., Lazarus Margulies, *The Right of the Jewish People to Palestine According to the Bible. Statement Presented to the Anglo-American Committee of Enquiry on Behalf of Italian Jewry* (n.p., 1946).

3. See W.D. Davies, *The Territorial Dimension of Judaism* (Berkeley and Los Angeles: University of California Press, 1982).

4. The Talmud, of which there are two versions, is a monumental compilation of the oral tradition produced by the rabbis of the schools of Palestine (between 220 and 375 C.E.) and of Babylonia (between 220 and 499 C.E.).

5. "It is hardly an exaggeration to assert that Zion is the central theme of the Bible," Abraham S. Halkin says, in id., ed., *Zion in Jewish Literature*, 2d ed. (Lanham, Md.: University Press of America, 1988), p. 18.

6. Gen. 1:1, 9–10, 12, 24, 28.

7. Gen. 2:5, 7, 9, 15, 23.

8. Cf. Gen. 1:11 and 4:25. The two meanings are associated in Hos. 2:23: "I will sow her in the land" (*u-zera'tiha li ba-arets*), a phrase evoking the replanting of Israel in the land.

9. Cf. Job 1:21: "Naked I came from my mother's womb, and naked I shall depart." See also Menahem Stein, "The Mother-Earth in Ancient Hebraic Literature," *Tarbiz* 9, 2 (Jan. 1938): 257–77 (in Hebrew).

10. Gen. 3:17–19, 23.

11. Zali Gurevitch and Gideon Aran, "On the Place (Israeli Anthropology)," *Alpayim* 4 (1991): 14 (in Hebrew).

12. Gen. 4:10–12.

13. Gen. 6:7; 11:8; 4:16; 11:2. See Seth Kunin, "Judaism," in Jean Holm and John Bowker, eds., *Sacred Place* (New York: Pinter Publishers, 1991), pp. 114–48.

14. Gen. 12:1.

15. Gen. 12:5–7.

16. See Harry M. Orlinsky, "The Biblical Concept of the Land of Israel: Cornerstone of the Covenant Between God and Israel," in Lawrence A. Hoffman, ed., *The Land of Israel: Jewish Perspectives* (Notre Dame, Ind.: University of Notre Dame Press, 1986), pp. 27–64.

17. Gen. 21:20–21; 36:6.

18. Gen. 15:13–16; 26:2–5, 35:11–12.

19. Gen. 13:17.

20. Gen. 23; 33:19–20; Josh. 24:32; 2 Sam. 24:15–25; 2 Chron. 3:1.

21. Gideon Biger, "The Names and Boundaries of Eretz-Israel (Palestine) as Reflections of Stages in its History," in Ruth Kark, ed., *The Land That Became Israel: Studies in Historical Geography* (New Haven, Conn.: Yale University Press; Jerusalem: Magnes Press, 1989), p. 4.

22. Gen. 15:18.

23. Gen. 14 and 34.

24. Gen. 24.

25. Gen. 26: 34–35; 28:1–9.

26. Gen. 10:5.

27. Gen. 10:19, 30.

28. Gen. 18:16–33.

29. Gen. 15:13–16.

30. Gen. 28:16–17.

31. Torah can also more broadly mean Jewish Law as a whole and the diverse corpora in which it is conveyed, including postbiblical writings and the commentaries on it.

32. Deut. 32:52; 34:4; Num. 14:28–32.

33. See Ilana Pardes, *The Biography of Ancient Israel: National Narratives in the Bible* (Berkeley and Los Angeles: University of California Press, 2000).

34. Exod. 16:3; Num. 11:5.

35. Num. 13:32.

36. Cf. Pardes, *Biography of Ancient Israel*, pp. 100–126. In the mouths of the rebels Dathan and Abiram, it is Egypt that is flowing with milk and honey (Num. 16:13)!

37. Exod. 3:5. The Hebraic phrase is *admat kodesh*, literally, "land of holiness."

38. Exod. 19:12, 23.

39. Jer. 2:2; Ezek. 20:33–38.

40. Josh. 24:2.

41. Deut. 26:5.

42. This usage is widely predominant and has been kept today in modern Hebrew, in which *ha-arets* continues to designate the land of Israel, in opposition to *huts la-arets*, "outside the land," meaning "abroad."

43. 1 Sam. 13:19.

44. Gen. 13:15; 2 Sam. 7:13, 15–16.

45. See Moshe Weinfeld, "To Inherit the Land—Right and Duty: The Conception of Promise in the Sources of the First and Second Temple Periods," *Zion* 49, 2 (1984): 115–37 (in Hebrew).

46. And thus very exactly on Exod. 12:2: "This month [that of Passover] shall mark for you the beginning of the months; it shall be the first of the months of the year for you."

47. Pss. 24:1–2; Deut. 32:8, 2:5, 9, 19.

48. Josh. 24:13.

49. Josh. 11:20.

50. Lev. 18: 25, 28.

51. Deut. 28:62.

52. Lev. 26:42.

53. Lev. 25:23.

54. On these prescriptions, see Lev. 25:2–7, 8–17 (sabbatical and jubilee years); Lev. 19:23–25 (harvesting of fruit); Deut. 26:1–10 (firstfruits); Num. 18:15–18 (firstlings of livestock); Num. 18:11 (*teruma*, "heave offerings"); Num. 18:24 (first tithe); Num. 15:17–20 (*hala*, share of bread reserved for priests).

55. Josh. 23:13; 13:1–7; Judg. 2:22.

56. Cf. Gen. 15:18–21; Exod. 23:31; and Deut. 1:7.

57. Ezek. 47:13–23.

58. Deut. 11:24: "Every spot on which your foot treads shall be yours."

59. Deut. 3:23–28. See also Deut. 4:21; 12:9–10.

60. Josh. 1:14–15.

61. Josh. 22. Yosi Nineve, "The Frontiers of the Land of Israel in the Bible," in Adam Doron, ed., *The State of Israel and the Land of Israel* (n.p.: Beit Berl, 1988), pp. 39–64 (in Hebrew).

62. 1 Kings 11:31.

63. Jer. 35.

64. Exod. 3:8; Num. 13:23; Deut. 8:8–9.

65. 1 Kings 4:20.

66. Zeph. 1:13; Jer. 4:26–27; Amos 9:13; Joel 4:18.

67. The Ark of the Covenant, containing the Tablets of the Law, was first placed in the heart of a mobile sanctuary in the desert and then in the Holy of Holies in the Temple at Jerusalem.

68. B. Dinaburg, "The Image of Zion and of Jerusalem in the Historical Consciousness of Israel," *Zion* 16, 1–2 (1951–52): 1–17 (in Hebrew).

69. F. E. Peters, *Jerusalem and Mecca: The Typology of the Holy City in the Near East* (New York: New York University Press, 1986), pp. 6–7.

70. 2 Sam. 7:5–6.

71. 1 Kings 8:27.

72. 1 Kings 18.

73. 2 Kings 5:15; 17.

74. "If I forget thee, O Jerusalem, may my right hand forget its skill, may my tongue cling to the roof of my mouth if I do not remember you, if I do not consider Jerusalem my highest joy" (Pss. 137: 5–6).

75. In Hebrew, "idle day, day of rest." The last day of the week in the Jewish calendar, beginning at sunset on Friday night and lasting until Saturday night.

76. 2 Chron, 36:21; Jer. 17:21–27; Isa. 58:13–14; Neh. 13:17–18. This idea would be taken up and developed by later rabbinical tradition, according to which it would be sufficient for Israel to observe two Sabbaths according the rules in order for her immediately to be delivered (Babylonian Talmud, Shabat 118b).

77. Lev. 18.

78. Exod. 34:15–16.

79. Esd. 9 and 10; Neh. 13:23–30.

80. Exod. 20:12; Deut. 25:15.

81. Jer. 7:7. See also Jer. 22:3–5.

82. Isa. 2:2–4; 56:7.

Chapter 2

1. *Av* is the month of the Hebraic calendar corresponding to July–August.

2. Mishnah, Ta'anit, 4:6.

3. Babylonian Talmud, Yoma 10a.

4. Shlomo Fischer, "Empire, conscience identitaire juive et relations internationales des Juifs à l'époque du Second Temple," in Shmuel Trigano, ed., *La Société juive à travers l'histoire* (Paris: Fayard, 1992–93), 3: 407–32.

5. Betsy Halpern Amaru, "Land Theology in Philo and Josephus," in Hoffman, ed., *Land of Israel*, pp. 65–93, and Shalom Rosenberg, "The Link to the Land of Israel in Jewish Thought: A Clash of Perspectives," in ibid., pp. 140–69.

6. Jer. 25:11–13; 29:10.

7. Esd. 4:1, 4; 9:2; 2 Kings 17:29; Esd. 4:2.

8. Betsalel Porten, "The Return from Babylon: Vision and Reality," *Cathedra* 4 (July 1977): 4–12; Efrayim Stern, "The State of Judea: Vision and Reality," ibid.: 13–24 (both in Hebrew).

9. 1 Macc. 3:43; emphasis added.

10. The name Zealots is applied to partisans of the armed revolt against Rome,

whose willingness to fight to the end would reach its extreme in the Jewish War of 66–74 C.E.

11. Peter Schäfer, *Histoire des juifs dans l'Antiquité*, trans. P. Schulte (Paris: Cerf, 1989), pp. 133–37.

12. Mireille Hadas-Lebel, *Jérusalem contre Rome* (Paris: Cerf, 1990), p. 180–81.

13. Weinfeld, "To Inherit the Land."

14. Richard S. Sarason, "The Significance of the Land of Israel in the Mishnah," in Hoffman, ed., *Land of Israel*, pp. 109–36; and "Land of Israel," in *The Talmudic Encyclopedia* (Jerusalem, 1973–84), 2: 199–235 (in Hebrew).

15. Judg. 1:27.

16. Pinhas Lederman, "The Land of Israel and the State of Israel in the Thought of Religious Movements—Past and Present," in Doron, ed., *State of Israel*, pp. 283–85.

17. Deut. 30:5; Neh. 1:9.

18. Zech. 2:16: "The Lord will take Judah to Himself as His portion in the Holy Land, and He will choose Jerusalem once more."

19. Ezek. 5:5; 38:12 (it is the Septuagint that translates the Hebrew *tabur*, of uncertain etymology, with the Greek *omphalos*, "navel"); Babylonian Talmud, Sanhedrin 37a. The Sanhedrin was a high court of justice, sitting in Jerusalem, whose authority extended beyond the geographical limits of Palestine.

20. Mishnah, Kelim 1:6–9. Yom Kippur, or "Great Pardon," is a 26-hour fast practiced in the autumn between the Jewish New Year and the Festival of Booths.

21. Babylonian Talmud, Kidushin 69a.

22. Yom-Tov Levinski, "How Was the Site of the Temple Fixed?" *Yeda-Am* 13, 33–34 (1968): 24–40 (in Hebrew).

23. Ephraim E. Urbach, "Center and Periphery in Jewish Historic Consciousness: Contemporary Implications," in Moshe Davis, ed., *World Jewry and the State of Israel* (New York: Arno Press, 1977), pp. 217–35.

24. Mishnah, Menahot 13:10.

25. S. Safrai et al., eds., *The Jewish People in the First Century: Historical Geography, Political History, Social, Cultural and Religious Life and Institutions* (Assen, Neth.: Van Gorcum, 1974–76), vol. 1, ch. 4, "Relations Between the Diaspora and the Land of Israel," pp. 184–215; Jackie Feldman, "Le Second Temple comme institution économique, sociale et politique," in Trigano, ed., *Société juive*, 2: 155–79.

26. The Jewish calendar is both lunar and solar. It is composed of twelve lunar months of twenty-nine or thirty days. But with biblical festivals being associated with the highlights of agricultural life, it is necessary to fill the gap that opens in the course of time between the lunar year and the solar year, which is eleven days longer. This is why a thirteenth month is periodically added in the spring of years called embolismic.

27. Jackie Feldman, "Les Pèlerinages au Second Temple," in Trigano, ed., *Société juive*, 4: 161–78.

28. See Deut. 11:13–15, and Avot de-Rabbi Natan A, 4.

29. The Pharisees were a current of Judaism active during the period of the Second Temple, from which rabbinical Judaism would emerge after 70 C.E.

30. The Sadducees were a political and religious grouping, consisting of the wealthiest elements of the population and tied to the sacerdotal aristocracy, active in Judea from the second century B.C.E. to the first century C.E.

31. Mishnah, Avot 1:2.

32. In Hebrew *mikdash meat*. See Ezech. 11:16 and Babylonian Talmud, Megila 29a.

33. Avot de-Rabi Natan A, 4.

34. Aelius was Hadrian's family name, and Capitolina evoked Jupiter Capitolinus.

35. Gerson D. Cohen, "Zion in Rabbinic Literature," in Halkin, ed., *Zion in Jewish Literature*, p. 56.

36. Mishnah, Hala 4:7–8.

37. Isadore Twersky, "Land of Israel and Exile in the Teaching of Maimonides," in Moshe Hallamish and Aviezer Ravitzky, eds., *The Land of Israel in Medieval Jewish Thought* (Jerusalem: Yad Yitshak Ben Zvi, 1991), pp. 90–122 (in Hebrew).

38. Babylonian Talmud, Yebamot 63a.

39. Jerusalem Talmud, Moed Katan 3:1; Avot de-Rabbi Natan A, 30.

40. Babylonian Talmud, Sota 14a. Charles Primus, "The Borders of Judaism: The Land of Israel in Early Rabbinic Judaism," in Hoffman, ed., *Land of Israel*, pp. 97–108.

41. 2 Bar. 85:3.

42. Sifrei, Ekev, 43. See Aviezer Ravitsky, "'Set Up Signposts' Toward Zion: History of an Idea," in Hallamish and Ravitzky, eds., *Land of Israel*, pp. 1–39 (in Hebrew).

43. We have used "signal" to render the Hebrew *tsiyun*, and "signals itself," meaning "excels in," to render the expression [*lihyot*] *metsuyan*.

44. Tefillin are small boxes with thongs allowing them to be attached to adult males during morning worship on working days, one on the forehead and the other on the arm, each containing calligraphy on parchment of verses from Deut. 6:4–9 and 11:13–21 and Exod. 13:1–16. A mezuzah is a small roll of parchment ritually fixed on the right door frame in Jewish houses, containing in calligraphy Deut. 6:4–9 and 11:13–21.

45. The *hala* is a deduction ritually taken from the loaf, a "tribute to the Lord" offered to the priests, following Num. 15:17–20.

46. Mishnah, Hala 2:1.

47. Cf. Gen. 15:19–21 and Deut. 7:1.

48. Num. 34:1–15.

49. Mishnah, Gitin 1:1–3.

50. Marvin Fox, "The Holiness of the Holy Land," in Jonathan Sacks, ed.,

Tradition and Transition: Essays Presented to Chief Rabbi Sir Emmanuel Jakobovits to Celebrate Twenty Years in Office (n.p.: Jews' College Publication, 1986), pp. 155–70.

51. Genesis Raba 68:9.

52. Deut. 11:11; Jer. 12:7.

53. Babylonian Talmud, Gitin 56b.

54. Leviticus Raba 13:2.

55. Mishneh Torah, Terumot 1:26.

56. B.M. Levin, "Vestiges of the *Geniza*," *Tarbiz* 2, 4 (1931): 396. The original Hebrew text plays on *Tsiyon* (Zion) and [*lihyot*] *metsuyan* ("to signal oneself," "to excel").

57. Yeshayahu Gafni, "The Transfer of the Cadaver for Burial in the Holy Land: Beginnings and Evolution of the Practice," *Cathedra* 4 (July 1977): 113–20 (in Hebrew).

Chapter 3

1. Twersky, "Land of Israel."

2. Jean-Christophe Attias, *Isaac Abravanel, la mémoire et l'espérance* (Paris, Cerf, 1992).

3. Shmuel Ettinger, "Le Peuple juif et Eretz Israël," *Les Temps modernes* 253bis (1967): 394.

4. Cohen, "Zion in Rabbinic Literature."

5. Avraham Melamed, "Land of Israel and Climate Theory in Jewish Thought," in Hallamish and Ravitzky, eds., *Land of Israel*, pp. 52–78 (in Hebrew).

6. Warren Zev Harvey, "R. Hasdai Crescas on the Uniqueness of the Land of Israel," in Hallamish and Ravitzky, eds., *Land of Israel*, pp. 151–65 (in Hebrew).

7. Judah Halevi, Kuzari 4:17. The expression "God of the land" appears in 2 Kings 17:26.

8. Gen. 35:2.

9. Dov Schwartz, "Land, Place, Star: The Status of the Land of Israel in Neoplatonic Thought of the Fourteenth Century," in Hallamish and Ravitzky, eds., *Land of Israel,* pp. 138–50 (in Hebrew).

10. Tanhuma, Ree 8. Berakha Zak, "Land and the Land of Israel in the *Zohar*," *Mehkerei Yerushalayim be-mahshevet Yisrael* 8 (1988–89): 239–53 (in Hebrew).

11. Kuzari 2:13–14.

12. Babylonian Talmud, Yoma 10a.

13. Aryeh Carmell, "The Mitzvah of Living in Eretz Yisrael: A Halakhic Survey," in H. Chaim Schimmel and Aryeh Carmell, eds., *Encounter: Essays on Torah and Modern Life* (Jerusalem and New York: Feldheim Publishers, 1989), p. 299.

14. Berakha Zak, "The Land of Israel in the Doctrine of R. Moses Cordovero," in Hallamish and Ravitzky, eds., *Land of Israel*, pp. 320–41 (in Hebrew).

15. Judah Halevi, Kuzari 2:14 (Schocken ed., p. 90).

16. According to an expression in the *Zohar*. Moshe Hallamish, "Characterizations of the Land of Israel in Kabbalistic Literature," in Hallamish and Ravitzky, eds., *Land of Israel*, p. 216 (in Hebrew).

17. Kuzari 2:14; emphasis added. See also 2:36.

18. This is the position of the Kabbalist Abraham Azoulai (ca. 1570–1643); see Rosenberg, "Link."

19. Stein, "Mother-Earth."

20. Mishnah Yoma, 5:2.

21. Babylonian Talmud, Sanhedrin 38a–b; Targum Yerushalmi on Gen. 2:7; Levinski, "How Was the Site of the Temple Fixed?" and Hayim Shwartzbaum, "Legendary Sources Regarding the Choice of a Site Suitable for Building the Temple of Jerusalem," *Yeda-Am* 13, 33–34 (1968): 41–45 (in Hebrew).

22. Moses Maimonides, Mishneh Torah, Beit Ha-Behira 2:2 and Targum Yonatan on Exod. 19:4.

23. Commentary on Lev. 26:16.

24. Amos 7:17; Hos. 9:3; Ezek. 7:17.

25. Eleazar Azikri (1533–1600) quoted by Yeshaya Halevi Horowitz (1565?–1630); see Hallamish, "Characterizations," p. 220.

26. Hasidism is a mystical current that appeared in eastern Europe in the eighteenth century and became a mass movement touching large sectors of the Jewish population.

27. Arthur Green, "The Zaddiq as Axis Mundi in Later Judaism," *Journal of the American Academy of Religion* 45 (1977): 327–47.

28. The theosophical Kabbalah aimed at theurgic action and adherence to the divine by means of a mystical and symbolic interpretation of Scripture, tradition, and the commandments of Jewish law, in contrast to the prophetic Kabbalah, which aimed at ecstasy and mystical union by means of spiritual experiences and specific techniques (such as the combination of letters).

29. *Zohar* 1:84b.

30. Moshe Idel, "*Erets Yisrael* dans la pensée juive," in Trigano, ed., *La Société juive à travers les âges*, 4: 77–105; id., "Jerusalem in Thirteenth-Century Jewish Thought," in Yehoshua Prawer and Haggai Ben-Shammai, eds., *The Book of Jerusalem: The Period of the Crusades and the Ayyubids 1099–1250* (Jerusalem: Yad Yitshak Ben-Zvi, 1990–91), pp. 264–86 (in Hebrew).

31. Depending on whether Jerusalem is spelled without *yod* (*yrushlm*) or with *yod* (*yrushlim*).

32. The Agent Intellect is a separate higher intellect with which the human intellect must unite in order to become active.

33. Idel, "*Erets Yisrael*," p. 103.

34. Chaim Z. Dimitrovsky, "Zion in Medieval Literature—I. Poetry," in Halkin, ed., *Zion in Jewish Literature*, pp. 65–82.

35. Ezra Spicehandler, "The Attitude Towards the Land of Israel in Spanish Hebrew Poetry," in Moshe Sheron, ed., *The Holy Land in History and Thought* (Leiden: E.J. Brill, 1988), pp. 117–39.

36. Efrayim Hazan, "The Presence of the Land of Israel in the Sacred and Profane Poetry of the Jews of North Africa," *Cathedra* 34 (Jan. 1985): 37–54 (in Hebrew).

37. Idel, "*Erets Yisrael*," pp. 87–77.

38. According to a homiletic interpretation of Gen. 28:10–19.

39. Quoted by Green, "Zaddiq."

40. In eastern Europe, a Jewish village was called a *shtetl* in Yiddish.

41. Miron, "Literary Image of the Shtetl."

42. R. Patai, "Earth Eating," in id., *On Jewish Folklore* (Detroit: Wayne State University Press, 1983), pp. 174–94.

43. See Avraham Yaari, *Voyages in the Land of Israel by Jewish Pilgrims from the Middle Ages to the Start of the Era of the Return to Zion*, 2d ed. (Tel Aviv: Modan, 1996) (in Hebrew).

44. On the metamorphoses of this myth in modern Yiddish and Hebrew literature, see Shmuel Verses, "Legends About the Ten Tribes and Sambation and Their Adaptations in Modern Literature," *Mehkerei Yerushalayim be-floklor yehudi* 7 (1985–86): 38–66 (in Hebrew).

Chapter 4

1. Babylonian Talmud, Bava Batra 60b.

2. The words of the famous pre-Zionist Moses Hess in *Rome and Jerusalem* (1862), trans. Meyer Waxman (1918; New York: Jewish Rabbinical Education Project, 1994), p. 32. Hess also mentions with emotion that his grandfather once showed him olives and dates, exclaiming "with beaming eyes, 'These were raised in *Eretz Yisroel.*'"

3. Karaism is a "deviant" current of Judaism, mainly characterized by its rejection of the oral tradition and by its exclusive attachment to the letter of Scripture.

4. Lawrence Hoffman, "Introduction: Land of Blessings and Blessings of the Land," in id., ed., *Land of Israel*, pp. 1–23.

5. Joseph Guttmann, "Return in Mercy to Zion: A Messianic Dream in Jewish Art," in Hoffman, ed., *Land of Israël*, pp. 234–60.

6. Kunin, "Judaism."

7. Cantique Raba 7:10; Babylonian Talmud, Megila 29a.

8. Yom-Tov Levinski, "The Jerusalems of the Diaspora," *Yeda-Am* 14, 35–36: 49–50 (in Hebrew).

9. Babylonian Talmud, Bava Batra 60b.

10. Twersky, "Land of Israel."

11. Yoel Bin-Nun, "The Obligation of Aliyah and the Prohibition of Leaving Israel in the Contemporary Era, According to the Opinion of Rambam (Maimonides)," in Chaim I. Waxman, ed., *Israel as a Religious Reality* (Northvale, N.J.: Jason Aronson, 1994), pp. 75–104; Lederman, "Land of Israel and the State of Israel."

12. Mishneh Torah, Melakhim 5:9.

13. Ibid., 5:12.

14. Babylonian Talmud, Ketubot 110a.

15. Babylonian Talmud, Ketubot, 110a. On the other hand, a wife who wants to move to the land of Israel has a right to require of her recalcitrant husband both a divorce and the payment of an indemnity stipulated in his marriage contract.

16. Marc Saperstein, "The Land of Israel in Pre-Modern Jewish Thought: A History of Two Rabbinic Statements," in Lawrence, ed., *Land of Israel*, pp. 188–209.

17. Shalom Bar Asher, "The Jews of North Africa and the Land of Israel in the Eighteenth and Nineteenth Centuries: The Reversal in Attitude toward Aliyah (Immigration to the Land) from 1770 to 1860," in Lawrence, ed., *Land of Israel*, pp. 297–315.

18. Babylonian Talmud, Ketubot 110b.

19. Commentaries on Gen. 17:8 and Lev. 25:38.

20. Hershel Schacter, "The Mitzvah of Yishuv Eretz Yisrael," in Shubert Spero and Yizchak Pessin, eds., *Religious Zionism After Forty Years of Statehood* (Jerusalem: Mesilot and World Zionist Organization, 1989), pp. 292–310; Carmell, "Mitzvah of Living in Eretz Yisrael." *Aliyah*, literally "going up," refers, according to context, to the pilgrimage or definitive immigration of a Jew to the Holy Land.

21. Ravitsky, "'Set Up Signposts' Toward Zion."

22. Yaakov Levinger, "The Specificity of the People of Israel, of Its Land, and of Its Language, According to Maimonides," *Milet* 2 (1983–84): 289–97 (in Hebrew).

23. Mishneh Torah, Melakhim 5:7–8.

24. Yitzhak F. Baer, *Galut*, trans. Robert Warshow (Lanham, Md.: University Press of America, 1988), pp. 14–15.

25. Babylonian Talmud, Megila 29a.

26. Isaac Luria Ashkenazi quoted by Idel, *"Erets Yisrael,"* p. 99. See also Shalom Rosenberg, "Exile and the Land of Israel in Sixteenth-Century Jewish Thought," in Hallamish and Ravitzky, eds., *Land of Israel*, pp. 166–92 (in Hebrew), and Jean-Christophe Attias, "Du judaïsme comme pensée de la dispersion," *Les Nouveaux Cahiers* 129 (Fall 1997): 5–12. On the fundamentally deterritorialized and spiritualized way in which the Hasidism of Gur understands Israel's mission in exile, see Yoram Yaakovson, "Exile and Redemption in the Hasidism of Gur," *Daat* 2–3 (1978): 175–215 (in Hebrew).

27. *Yeridah*, literally "descent," meaning the emigration of a Jew from the Holy Land, is the opposite of *aliyah*.

28. Moshe Gil, "*Aliyah* and Pilgrimage in the First Period of Muslim Occupation (634–1099)," *Cathedra* 8 (July 1978): 124–32 (in Hebrew).

29. Spicehandler, "Attitude Towards the Land of Israel in Spanish Hebrew Poetry."

30. Hasidim: literally, "pious" or "pietists"; adepts of Hasidism.

31. Yosef Salmon, "Les Émigrations traditionnelles vers la Palestine (1740–1880)," in Shmuel Trigano, ed., *La Société juive à travers l'histoire* (Paris: Fayard, 1992–93), 4: 123–38. The Perushim were disciples of the anti-Hasidic exegete and jurist Elijah ben Solomon Zalman, called "the Vilna Ga'on" (1720–97).

32. Raya Haran, "What Pushed the Disciples of the *Magid* to Go to the Land of Israel?" *Cathedra* 76 (July 1995): 77–95 (in Hebrew).

33. Yaakov Hasdai, "The Start of the Hasidic and *Mitnaged* Colonies in the Land of Israel—On *Aliyah* as Commandment and *Aliyah* as Mission," *Shalem* 4 (1983–84): 231–69 (in Hebrew).

34. Aviezer Ravitzky, "The Impact of the Three Oaths in Jewish History," in id., *Messianism, Zionism, and Jewish Religious Radicalism*, trans. Michael Swirsky and Jonathan Chipman (Chicago: University of Chicago Press, 1996), p. 217.

35. Ravitzky, *Messianism, Zionism, and Jewish Religious Radicalism*, p. 46.

36. Ein-Sof, "One without End," means God in His unknowableness, in contrast to the *sefirot*, emanations and manifestations of the Godhead.

37. Yehuda Liebes, "Sabbatean Messianism," *Pe'amim* 40 (1989): 4–20 (in Hebrew).

38. For example, Babylonian Talmud, Ketubot 111a.

39. Gérard Nahon, *La Terre sainte au temps des kabbalistes* (Paris: Albin Michel, 1997), p. 9.

40. Peters, *Jerusalem and Mecca*, pp. 15–16.

41. Israel Bartal, "Introduction," in id., *Exile Within the Country* (Jerusalem: Ha-sifria ha-tsionit, 1994) (in Hebrew).

42. Yisrael Heilperin, *Jews and Judaism in Eastern Europe* (Jerusalem: Magnes, 1968–69), p. 63 (in Hebrew).

43. Hasdai, "Start of the Hasidic and *Mitnaged* Colonies."

44. "Prince of the land of Israel": *Mara de-ar'a de-Yisrael* in Aramaic and *nesi erets Yisrael* in Hebrew.

45. Israel Bartal, "Les Émissaires de terre d'Israël: Entre la réalité d'un lien et l'abstraction d'une vision," in Trigano, *Société juive*, 4: 107–21.

46. Yaari, *Voyages in the Land of Israel;* Elhanan Reiner, *Pilgrims and Pilgrimages to the Land of Israel 1099–1517* (Ph.D. thesis, Hebrew University of Jerusalem, 1988) (in Hebrew); Jean Baumgarten, "Images du monde séfarade dans les récits de voyages vers la Terre sainte en langue yiddish (XVII–XVIII siècles)," in Esther Benbassa, ed., *Mémoires juives d'Espagne et du Portugal* (Paris: Publisud, 1996), pp. 223–37.

47. Nahum N. Glatzer, "Medieval Literature: II. Prose Works," in Halkin, ed., *Zion in Jewish Literature*, pp. 83–100.

48. S.Z. Kahan, "Tales of Pilgrimages to the Tombs of Saints and the Holy Sites in the Land of Israel," *Yeda-Am* 22, 50–51: 112–16; 23, 53–54: 36–49 (in Hebrew).

49. According to Law, a special blessing has to be recited at such places.

50. Genesis Raba 96:5.

51. Mark Verman, "*Aliyah* and Yeridah: The Journeys of the Besht and R. Nachman to Israel," in David R. Blumenthal, ed., *Approaches to Judaism in Medieval Times* (Atlanta: Scholars Press, 1988), 3: 159–71.

52. S. Klein, *History of the Study of the Land of Israel in Hebrew and General Literature* (Jerusalem: Mosad Bialik, 1936–37) (in Hebrew).

53. The three festivals of pilgrimage were, in fact, celebrated over two days in the Diaspora, and on a single day in the Holy Land.

54. Hayim Goren, "Knowledge of the Land of Israel in the Eighteenth Century: The *Sefer Yedei Moshe* of R. Moshe Yerushalmi," *Cathedra* 34 (Jan. 1985): 75–96 (in Hebrew).

55. Chone Shmeruk and Israel Bartal, "*Tela'ot Moshe*: The First Geography Book in Yiddish and the Description of the Land of Israel by Moshe bar Abraham the Proselyte," *Cathedra* 40 (July 1986): 121–37 (in Hebrew).

56. S.Y. Agnon, "Fable of the Goat," trans. Barney Rubin, in *A Book That Was Lost and Other Stories by S.Y. Agnon* (New York: Schocken Books, 1995), pp. 188–91.

Chapter 5

1. Arnold M. Eisen, "Off Center: The Concept of the Land of Israel in Modern Jewish Thought," in Hoffman, ed., *Land of Israel*, pp. 263–96.

2. Spinoza, *Theological-Political Treatise*, end of ch. 3.

3. Michael A. Meyer, *Response to Modernity: A History of the Reform Movement in Judaism* (New York: Oxford University Press, 1988).

4. The "science of Judaism" (in German, *Wissenschaft des Judentums*) was a current of thought that developed among German Jewish intellectuals in the nineteenth century in the wake of the Berlin Enlightenment, which sought scientifically, both inside and outside the Jewish community, to present aspects of the culture and history of Judaism most likely to aid in recognition of its values.

5. Heinrich Grätz, *The Structure of Jewish History, and Other Essays*, trans. and ed. Ismar Schorsch (New York: Jewish Theological Seminary of America, 1975).

6. B'nai Brith is a Jewish organization structured on the model of the Masonic orders into lodges and chapters, founded in the United States in 1843.

7. Ezra Mendelsohn, *On Modern Jewish Politics* (New York: Oxford University Press, 1993), p. 6, and passim for the rest of the ideas and concepts we discuss in the remainder of this chapter.

8. Quoted by Catherine Fhima, "Les Écrivains juifs français et le sionisme (1897–1930)," *Archives juives* 30, 2 (1997): 53.

9. Abbreviation for the Yiddish Algemayner Yidisher Arbeter Bund fun Lite, Poyln un Rusland (General Union of Jewish Workers in Lithuania, Poland and Russia). A socialist movement clandestinely created in Vilna in 1897.

10. Hillel Bavli, "Zion in Modern Literature: I. Hebrew Poetry," in Halkin, ed., *Zion in Jewish Literature*, pp. 101–20.

11. Glenda Abramson, "'Here' and 'There' in Modern Hebrew Poetry," in Sheron, ed., *Holy Land in History and Thought*, pp. 141–49.

12. In Greek and Latin bucolic poetry, Arcadia was the country of calm and serene happiness. Renaissance literature revived this fiction, which was continued in early modern works.

13. Ben Halpern, "Zion in Modern Literature. II. Hebrew Prose," in Halkin, ed., *Zion in Jewish Literature*, pp. 121–35.

14. *Yishuv* is Hebrew for "colony" or "settlement" and a term for the Jewish community in Palestine.

15. Yaakov Ariel, *On Behalf of Israel: American Fundamentalist Attitudes Toward Jews, Judaism, and Zionism* (Brooklyn, N.Y.: Carlson, 1991).

16. Steven Epperson, *Mormons and Jews: Early Mormon Theologies of Israel* (Salt Lake City: Signature Books, 1992).

17. Allan Arkush, "Revitalizing Nationalism: The Role of Klesmer in George Eliot's *Daniel Deronda*," *Jewish Social Studies* 3, 3 (1997): 61–73.

18. Catherine Nicault, "Missionaires, diplomates et savants en Terre sainte," *L'Histoire* 212 (July–Aug. 1997): 56–59.

19. Shmuel Almog, "People and Land in Modern Jewish Nationalism," in Jehuda Reinharz and Anita Shapira, eds., *Essential Papers on Zionism* (New York: New York University Press, 1996), pp. 46–62.

20. Yehoshua Ben-Arieh, *The Rediscovery of the Holy Land in the Nineteenth Century* (Jerusalem: Magnes Press; Detroit: Wayne State University Press, 1979); id., "Perceptions and Images of the Holy Land," in Ruth Kark, ed., *The Land That Became Israel: Studies in Historical Geography* (New Haven, Conn.: Yale University Press; Jerusalem: Magnes Press, 1989), pp. 37–53.

21. Israel Bartal, "'Old Yishuv' and 'New Yishuv': Image and Reality," *Jerusalem Cathedra*, 1981, pp. 215–31.

22. Shmuel Ettinger and Israel Bartal, "The First *Aliyah*: Ideological Roots and Practical Accomplishments," in Reinharz and Shapira, eds., *Essential Papers on Zionism*, pp. 63–93.

23. Israel Bartal, "Moses Montefiore and the Land of Israel," in id., *Exile Within the Country*, pp. 209–18.

24. Walter Lehn in association with Uri Davis, *The Jewish National Fund* (London: Kegan Paul International, 1988).

25. Jacob Katz, *Jewish Emancipation and Self-Emancipation* (Philadelphia: Jewish Publication Society, 1986).

26. The Alliance israélite universelle, a French Jewish organization, was created in 1860 by liberals inspired by the ideas of the French Revolution. Its mission was to defend the rights of persecuted Jews and work for their emancipation. After 1862, it devoted itself to educating the Jews of North Africa and the Middle East.

27. Moses Sofer (1762–1839) was called the Hatam Sofer, from the title of a collection of his responsa.

28. Georges Weill, "Charles Netter ou les Oranges de Jaffa," *Les Nouveaux Cahiers* 21 (Summer 1970): 2–36.

29. Yoram Mayorek, "Between East and West: Edmond de Rothschild and Palestine," in Georg Heuberger, ed., *The Rothschilds: Essays on the History of a European Family* (Sigmaringen, Germany: Thorbecke; Woodbridge, Suffolk, U.K.: Boydell & Brewer, 1994), pp. 129–45.

30. Hibbat Tsion, a movement founded in Romania and Russia after the 1880 pogroms, was active both in the Diaspora and in the colonization of Palestine.

31. Shlomo Avineri, *The Making of Modern Zionist Thought: Intellectual Origins of the Jewish State* (New York: Basic Books, 1981).

32. Esther Benbassa, "Les Relais nationalistes juifs dans les Balkans au XIXe siècle," in id., ed., *Transmission et passages en monde juif*, pp. 403–34 (Paris: Publisud, 1997).

33. Yigal Elam, "Gush Emunim: A False Messianism," *Jewish Quarterly* 1 (Autumn 1976): 60–69.

34. Jean-Marie Delmaire, "De Hibbat Zion au sionisme politique" (Ph.D. diss., 1990).

35. Jishoub Eretz Israel: in Hebrew, *yishuv erets Yisrael*, literally "settlement of the land of Israel."

36. "Bilu" derives from the initials of four words from Isa. 2:5: "Bet Yaakov lekhu ve-nelkha" ("O House of Jacob, come ye, and let us go").

37. S. Adler-Rudel, "Moritz Baron Hirsch: Profile of a Great Philanthropist," *Leo Baeck Year Book* 8 (1963): 29–69.

38. Joseph H. Udelson, *Dreamer of the Ghetto: The Life and Works of Israel Zangwill* (Tuscaloosa: University of Alabama Press, 1990).

39. Zeev Sternhell, *The Founding Myths of Israel: Nationalism, Socialism, and the Making of the Jewish State* (Princeton: Princeton University Press, 1998).

40. Alain Dieckhoff, "De Saint-Pétersbourg à Jérusalem: Les Empreintes du climate intellectuel russe sur le sionisme socialiste," in Benbassa, ed., *Transmission et passages*, pp. 434–50.

41. Matityahu Mintz, "Ber Borokhov," *Studies in Zionism* 5 (Apr. 1982): 33–53.

42. George L. Mosse, "Max Nordau, le libéralisme et le 'nouveau juif,'" in Delphine Bechtel et al., eds., *Max Nordau, 1849–1923* (Paris: Cerf, 1996), pp. 11–29.

43. Jacob B. Agus, *High Priest of Rebirth: The Life, Times, and Thought of Abraham Isaac Kuk* (New York: Bloch Publishing House, 1972).

44. Baruch Kimmerling, *Zionism and Territory: The Socio-Territorial Dimensions of Zionist Politics* (Berkeley: Institute of International Studies, University of California, 1983).

45. Baruch Kimmerling, "Academic History Caught in the Crossfire: The Case of Israeli-Jewish Historiography," *History and Memory* 7, 1 (Spring–Summer 1995): 41–65.

Chapter 6

1. Kimmerling, "Academic History."

2. Eliezer Schweid, *Homeland and Promised Land* (Tel Avid: Am Oved, 1979) (in Hebrew).

3. Kimmerling, *Zionism and Territory.*

4. Lehn and Davis, *Jewish National Fund.*

5. Biger, "Names and the Boundaries."

6. For figures in this chapter concerning the colonization, see Kimmerling, *Zionism and Territory*, pp. 17–19.

7. Aharon Kellerman, *Society and Settlement: Jewish Land in Israel in the Twentieth Century* (Albany: State University of New York Press, 1993).

8. Samuel Pohoryles, "Agricultural Transformation in Israel," *Jerusalem Quarterly* 33 (Fall 1984): 85–101.

9. Erik Cohen, "The City in Zionist Ideology," *Jerusalem Quarterly* 4 (Summer 1977): 126–44.

10. Yehoshua Kaniel, "The Terms 'Old Yishuv' and 'New Yishuv': Problems of Definition," *Jerusalem Cathedra*, 1981, pp. 232–45.

11. Bartal, *Exile Within the Country.*

12. Ettinger and Bartal, "First *Aliyah.*"

13. Y. Zerubavel, *Recovered Roots: Collective Memory and the Making of Israeli National Tradition* (Chicago: University of Chicago Press, 1995).

14. Anita Shapira, "The Origins of 'Jewish Labor' Ideology," *Studies in Zionism* 5 (Apr. 1982): 93–113.

15. Gershon Shaked, "Shall All Hopes Be Fulfilled? Genre and Anti-Genre in the Hebrew Literature of Palestine," in Reinharz and Shapira, eds., *Essential Papers on Zionism*, pp. 763–89.

16. Margalit Shilo, "The Women's Farm at Kinneret, 1911–1917: A Solution to the Problem of the Working Woman in the Second *Aliya*," in Deborah S. Bernstein, ed., *Pioneers and Homemakers: Jewish Women in Pre-State Israel* (Albany: State University of New York Press, 1992), pp. 119–43.

17. Yael Zerubavel, "The Forest as a National Icon: Literature, Politics and the Archaeology of Memory," *Israel Studies* 1, 1 (Spring 1996): 60–99.

18. Ibid., 97 n. 61.

19. Gurevitch and Aran, "On the Place."

20. Zeev Tzahor, "Ben Gurion's Mythopoetics," in Robert Wistrich and David Ohana, eds., *The Shaping of Israel* (London: Frank Cass, 1995), pp. 61–84.

21. Yossi Katz, "Document: The Hebrew Renaming of Places and Sites in the Negev in 1949–1950," *Iyunim bi-tekumat Israel* 5 (1995): 615–19 (in Hebrew).

22. Itamar Even-Zohar, "The Emergence of a Native Hebrew Culture in Palestine, 1882–1948," in Reinharz and Shapira, eds., *Essential Papers on Zionism*, pp. 727–44.

23. Almog, "People and Land."

24. Yaffa Berlovitz, "Literature by Women of the First *Aliyah*: The Aspiration for Women's Renaissance in Eretz Israel," in D.S. Bernstein, ed., *Pioneers and Homemakers*, pp. 49–73.

25. Delmaire, "De Hibbat Zion au sionisme politique," vol. 1.

26. Nurit Gertz, "Social Myths in Literary and Political Texts," *Poetics Today* 7, 4 (1986): 621–39.

27. Glenda Abramson, "Israeli Literature as an Emerging National Literature," in S. Ilan Troen and Noah Lucas, eds., *Israel: The First Decade of Independence* (Albany: State University of New York Press, 1995), pp. 331–53.

28. Nurit Gertz, "The Canaanites: Ideology vs. Literature," *Jerusalem Quarterly* 48 (Autumn 1988) 46–62; Yaacov Shavit, *The New Hebrew Nation: A Study in Israeli Heresy and Fantasy* (London: Frank Cass, 1987).

29. Dan Miron, "Songs of an Unseen and Unknown Land: The Place of Naomi Shemer in Our Life," *Igeret* 1 (1984): 173–206 (in Hebrew).

30. Orit Ben-David, "*Tiyul* (Hike) as an Act of Consecration of Space," in Eyal Ben-Ari and Yoram Bilu, eds., *Grasping Land: Space and Place in Contemporary Israeli Discourse and Experience* (Albany: State University of New York Press, 1997), pp. 129–45; see also the editor's introduction in the same book.

31. Palmah is an abbreviation for *plugot mahats*, the "shock troops" of the Hagana, the military organization of the Jewish community of Palestine at the time of the British Mandate and the kernel of the future army of the State of Israel.

32. Klein, *History of the Study of the Land of Israel*.

33. Yoram Bar-Gal, *Moledet and Geography over a Century of Zionist Education* (Tel Aviv: Am Oved, 1993) (in Hebrew).

34. Uri Ram, "Zionist Historiography and the Invention of Modern Jewish Nationhood: The Case of Ben Zion Dinur," *History and Memory* 7, 1 (Spring–Summer 1995): 91–124.

35. Ya'akov Shavit, "'The Truth will come out of the Ground'—The Development of Popular Interest in Archeology (until the 1930s)," *Cathedra* 44 (June 1987) 27–54 (in Hebrew).

36. Meron Benvenisti, *City of Stone: The Hidden History of Jerusalem*, trans. Maxine Kaufman Nunn (Berkeley and Los Angeles: University of California Press, 1996).

37. Igal Bursztyn, "Faces as Idea, Faces as Object: Cinematic History (1911–1967)," *Studies in Zionism* 10, 2 (1989): 139–54; Hillel Tryster, "*The Land of Promise* (1935): A Case Study in Zionist Film Propaganda," *Historical Journal of Film, Radio and Television* 15, 2 (June 1995): 187–217; Ella Shohat, *Israeli Cinema. East/West and the Politics of Representation* (Austin: University of Texas Press, 1989).

38. David N. Myers, *Re-Inventing the Jewish Past* (New York: Oxford University Press, 1995); Shmuel Almog, *Zionism and History: The Rise of a New Jewish Consciousness*, trans. I. Friedman (New York: St. Martin's Press; Jerusalem: Magnes Press, 1987; Kimmerling, "Academic History"; Ilan Pappe, "Critique and Agenda: The Post-Zionist Scholars in Israel," *History and Memory* 7, 1 (Spring–Summer 1995): 66–90.

39. The name Sicarii derives from the Latin *sica*, "curved dagger," evoking the combat tactic adopted by certain Jewish extremists under the Procurator Felix (52–60), consisting of striking their victims in the middle of crowds using small daggers that were easy to conceal under the cloak.

40. Biryonim, in Hebrew, "violent men, brigands," was the name given to a group of virulent opponents of Rome in the Second Temple period who also attacked moderate Jews.

41. Ruth Firer, *The Agents of Zionist Education* (Tel Aviv: Sifriyat Poalim, 1985) (in Hebrew); also quoted in Ram, "Zionist Historiography."

42. Dinaburg, "Image of Zion."

43. Literally, "Peace Alliance," a group active at the end of the 1920s and beginning of the 1930s.

44. Shalom Ratzaby, "The Polemic About the 'Negation of the Diaspora' in the 1930s and Its Roots," *Journal of Israeli History* 16, 1 (1995): 19–38.

45. S.H. Bergmann, "The Land and Exile," *She'ifotenu* 2, 8 (1932): 360 (in Hebrew), quoted by Ratzaby, "Polemic About the 'Negation of the Diaspora' in the 1930s," p. 30.

46. Tamar Katriel, "Remaking Place. Cultural Production in Israeli Pioneer Settlement Museums," in Ben-Ari and Bilu, eds., *Grasping Land*, pp. 147–75.

47. Baruch Zimmerling, "Boundaries and Frontiers of the Israeli Control System: Analytical Conclusions," in id., ed., *The Israeli State and Society: Boundaries and Frontiers* (Albany: State University of New York Press, 1989), pp. 265–84.

48. Dan Horowitz and Moshe Lissak, "The State of Israel at Forty," *Studies in Contemporary Jewry* 5 (1989): 3–24.

49. Yaakov Shavit, "Hebrews and Phoenicians: An Ancient Historical Image and Its Use," *Studies in Zionism* 5, 2 (1984): 157–80.

50. Ruth Kark, "Historical Sites—Perceptions and Land Purchase: The Case of Modi'in, 1882–1931," *Studies in Zionism* 9, 1 (1988): 1–17.

Chapter 7

1. Cohen, "City in Zionist Ideology."
2. Ibid., p. 129.
3. Derek J. Penslar, *Zionism and Technocracy: The Engineering of Jewish Settlement in Palestine, 1870–1918* (Bloomington: Indiana University Press, 1991).
4. Ibid., p. 4.
5. Shaked, "Shall All Hopes Be Fulfilled?"
6. Abramson, "'Here' and 'There.'"
7. Gurevitch and Aran, "On the Place."
8. Even-Zohar, "Emergence of a Native Hebrew Culture in Palestine."
9. Zilla Goldman, "Israel as Redemption in S.Y. Agnon's *A Guest for the Night*," in Sheron, ed., *Holy Land in History and Thought*, pp. 150–62.
10. André Levy, "To Morocco and Back: Tourism and Pilgrimage Among Moroccan-Born Israelis," in Ben-Ari and Bilu, *Grasping Land*, pp. 25–46, and the introduction.
11. *Yordim* (literally, "descendants") is a term used of Israelis who have deliberately chosen to live abroad.
12. Miriam Veinberger, "The Place of *Erets Yisrael* in the Work of Devorah Baron," *Be-emet*, 4–5 (1990–91): 61–76 (in Hebrew).
13. The *musar* (literally, "ethical") movement was initiated by Israel Lipkin Salanter (1810–83), whose educational establishments aimed not only at the intellectual improvement of students but also at their moral betterment.
14. Joseph Sherman, "The Gates of Zion and the Dwellings of Jacob: Zion and Zionism in the Work of Isaac Bashevis Singer," in Sheron, ed., *Holy Land in History and Thought*, pp. 163–72.
15. Mikhael Keren, "Literature and National Renaissance: The Reaction of Agnon to the Jewish State According to *The Book of the State*," *Iyunim bi-tekumat Yisrael* 5 (1995): 446–54 (in Hebrew).
16. Yehoshua Kohen, "Descriptions of Landscapes and Inhabited Places by the Writer Aharon Megged," *Erets Yisrael. Mehkarim biyedi'at ha'arets ve-atikoteiha* 22 (1990–91): 95–105 (in Hebrew).
17. Aviezer Ravitzky, "Exile in the Holy Land: The Dilemma of Haredi Jewry," *Studies in Contemporary Jewry* 5 (1989): 89–125; id., *Messianism, Zionism, and Jewish Religious Radicalism*.
18. *Haredim*, literally, "those who fear, those who tremble" (before God).
19. Menahem Friedman, "L'État d'Israël comme dilemme idéologique," *Pardès* 11 (1990): 15–65.
20. Claude Klein, *La Démocratie d'Israël* (Paris: Seuil, 1997).
21. Elam, "Gush Emunim: A False Messianism."
22. Erik Cohen, "Israel as a Post-Zionist Society," in Wistrich and Ohana, eds., *Shaping of Israeli Society*, pp. 203–13.

23. The Likkud, literally, "Union," is an Israeli coalition that since 1973 has gathered together several political factions of the center and right around the Herout party.

24. Ehud Sprinzak, "Gush Emunim: The Tip of the Iceberg," *Jewish Quarterly Review* 21 (Autumn 1981): 28–47; see also Alain Dieckhoff, "Le Gouch Emounim: Esquisse d'ethnographie politique," *Pardès* 11 (1990): 84–110.

25. Laurence J. Silberstein's book *The Postzionism Debates: Knowledge and Power in Israeli Culture* (New York: Routledge, 1999) gives an overview of this issue.

26. On these questions, see Tom Grier, "Reversed Diaspora: Russian Jewry, the Transition in Russia and the Migration to Israel," *Anthropology of Eastern Europe Review* 14, 1 (1996), and Danielle Storper Perez, *L'Intelligentsia russe en Israël: Rassurante étrangeté* (Paris: CNRS, 1998).

27. Ilan Pappe, "Critique and Agenda: The Post-Zionist Scholars in Israel," *History and Memory* 7, 1 (Spring–Summer 1995): 66–90.

28. Eliezer Schweid, "Beyond All That—Modernism, Zionism, Judaism," *Israel Studies* 1, 1 (Spring 1996): 224–46.

29. Moshe Lissak, "'Critical' Sociology and 'Establishment' Society in the Israeli Academic Community: Ideological Struggles or Academic Discourse," *Israeli Studies* 1, 1 (Spring 1996): 247–94.

30. Simha Flapan, *The Birth of Israel: Myths and Realities* (New York: Pantheon Books, 1987); Benny Morris, *The Birth of the Palestinian Refugee Problem 1947–1949* (New York: Cambridge University Press, 1987); Avi Shlaim, *Collusion Across the Jordan: King Abdullah, the Zionist Movement and the Partition of Palestine* (New York: Columbia University Press, 1988); Ilan Pappe, *Britain and the Arab-Israeli Conflict 1948–1951* (New York: St. Martin's Press, 1988).

31. Ram, *Changing Agenda of Israeli Society.*

32. Gershon Shafir, *Land, Labor and the Origins of the Israel-Palestinian Conflict, 1882–1941* (Cambridge: Cambridge University Press, 1989).

33. See Kimmerling, "Boundaries and Frontiers."

34. Ibid., p. 278.

35. Anita Shapira, "Politics and Collective Memory: The Debate over the 'New Historians' in Israel," *History and Memory* 7, 1 (Spring–Summer 1995): 9–40.

36. See Kimmerling, *Zionism and Territory.*

37. Ibid., p. 143.

38. Amnon Raz-Krakotzkin, "Exile in Sovereignty—Toward a Critique of the 'Negation of Exile' in Israeli Culture," *Teoria-u-vikoret* 4 (1993): 23–55; 5 (1994): 113–32 (in Hebrew); id., "Emptying the Empty Land," *Davar* 28 (June 1991) (in Hebrew).

39. Zvi Sobel, *Voyage to the Promised Land* (Tel Aviv: Am Oved, Sifriyat Ofakim, 1990) (in Hebrew). Extensively quoted by Sarit Shapira in *Routes of Wandering: Nomadism, Journeys and Transitions in Contemporary Israeli Art* (exhibition catalogue, Jerusalem: Museum of Israel, 1991) (in English and Hebrew).

40. Ehud Barak quoted by Ouri Nissan in *L'Arche*, no. 478 (Nov. 1997): 31–33.

41. Yael Zerubavel, "The 'Wandering Israeli' in Contemporary Israeli Literature," *Contemporary Jewry* 7, 1 (1986): 127–40.

42. Sarit Shapira, "Waymarks: Local Moves," in id., *Routes of Wandering*.

43. Gen. 12:1.

44. Gen. 12:7.

45. In Shapira, *Routes of Wandering*, pp. 246–56.

Epilogue

1. Galit Hasan-Rokem, "La Culture populaire juive en Israël: Dialogues et passages," in Benbassa, ed., *Transmission et passages*, pp. 137–49; Eyal Ben-Ari and Yoram Bilu, "Saints' Sanctuaries in Israeli Development Towns: On a Mechanism of Urban Transformation," in id., *Grasping Land*, pp. 61–83.

2. Levy, "To Morocco and Back"; Eyal Ben-Ari and Yoram Bilu, "Epilogue (Three Years Later)," in id., *Grasping Land*, pp. 231–35.

3. Erik Cohen, *L'Étude et l'éducation juive en France ou l'avenir d'une communauté* (Paris: Cerf, 1991) supplies precious data on these questions, but it does not cover French Jewry as a whole, as is typical of this type of study, all the more so because this one was commissioned by community organizations.

4. Theodore Solotaroff and Nessa Rapoport, eds., *Writing Our Home: Contemporary Stories by American Jewish Writers* (New York: Schocken Books, 1992, introduction, pp. xiii–xxvi; Andrew Furman, ed., *Israel Through the Jewish-American Imagination: A Survey of Jewish-American Literature on Israel, 1928–1995* (Albany: State University of New York Press, 1997), introduction, pp. 1–20; Mendelsohn, *On Modern Jewish Politics*.

Afterword

1. *Libération*, June 2, 2002.

2. Charles Enderlin, *Le Rêve brisé: Histoire de l'échec du processus de paix au Proche-Orient, 1995-2002* (Paris, Fayard, 2002), p. 264.

3. Ibid., p. 280.

4. Ibid., p. 282.

Select Bibliography

The following bibliography offers only a selection of titles useful to someone who wants to extend this study. Deliberately omitted are the customary titles, general histories of the Jewish people, syntheses of the history of Jewish thought, and the great books and grand authors of the rabbinical tradition. All the studies mentioned in the notes are cited here, with the exception of articles from collections bearing as a whole upon one or another of the major themes addressed in this book (in which case we reproduce only the titles of these collections). The articles and books preceded by an asterisk are in Hebrew. The titles are ordered alphabetically by the surnames of the authors, and then, for the same author, chronologically.

Abitbol, Michel. *Les Deux Terres promises: Les Juifs de France et le sionisme, 1897–1945*. Paris: Olivier Orban, 1989.

Adler, Elkan Nathan, ed. *Jewish Travellers in the Middle Ages: Nineteen Firsthand Accounts*. 1930. New ed. New York: Dover, 1987.

Adler-Rudel, S. "Moritz Baron Hirsch: Profile of a Great Philanthropist." *Leo Baeck Year Book* 8 (1963): 29–69.

Agnon, S.Y. *A Guest for the Night*. 1938–39. Translated by Misha Louvish. New York: Schocken Books, 1968.

——. "Fable of the Goat." Translated by Barney Rubin. In *A Book That Was Lost and Other Stories*, pp. 188–91. New York: Schocken Books, 1995.

Agus, Jacob B. *High Priest of Rebirth. The Life, Times, and Thought of Abraham Isaac Kuk*. New York: Bloch, 1972.

*Aharonson, Ran. "The Netter-Rothschild Program: The Start of Colonization Activity by the Baron in Palestine." *Cathedra* 44 (June 1987): 55–79.

Alcalay, Ammiel. *After Jews and Arabs: Remaking Levantine Culture*. Minneapolis: University of Minnesota Press, 1993.

Almog, Shmuel. *Zionism and History: The Rise of a New Jewish Consciousness*. Translated by Ina Friedman. New York: St. Martin's Press; Jerusalem: Magnes Press, The Hebrew University, 1987.

*—— "'The Land to Those Who Work It' and the Conversion of *Fellahs* to Judaism." In *A Nation and Its History*, pt. 2, pp. 165–75. Jerusalem: Zalman Shazar, 1993–94.

Aran, Gideon. *Israeli Visions and Divisions: Cultural Change and Political Conflict.* New Brunswick, N.J.: Transaction Books, 1989.

Ariel, Yaakov S. *On Behalf of Israel. American Fundamentalist Attitudes Toward Jews, Judaism, and Zionism, 1865–1945.* Brooklyn, N.Y.: Carlson, 1991.

Arkush, Allan. "Relativizing Nationalism: The Role of Klesmer in George Eliot's *Daniel Deronda.*" *Jewish Social Studies* 3, 3 (1997): 61–73.

*Arni, Efrayim. *The Land of Israel: History, Politics, Management and Development.* Jerusalem: Keren Kayemet le-Yisrael, 1979–80.

Aronoff, Myron J. "Development Towns in Israel." In Michael Curtis and Mordecai S. Chertoff, eds., *Israel: Social Structure and Change*, pp. 27–46. New Brunswick, N.J.: Transaction Books, 1973.

——. "Establishing Authority: The Memorialization of Jabotinsky and the Burial of the Bar Kochba Bones Under the Likud." In id., ed., *The Frailty of Authority*, pp. 105–30. New Brunswick, N.J., Transaction Books, 1986.

Attias, Jean-Christophe. *Isaac Abravanel, la mémoire et l'espérance.* Paris: Cerf, 1992.

——. "Du judaïsme comme pensée de la dispersion." *Les Nouveaux Cahiers* 129 (Fall 1997): 5–12.

Avineri, Shlomo. *The Making of Modern Zionism: The Intellectual Origins of the Jewish State.* New York: Basic Books, 1981.

*Avni, Haim. *Argentina, "Promised Land."* Jerusalem: Magnes Press, 1972–73.

*——. "Territorialism, Territorialist Colonization, and Zionist Colonization." *Yahadut Zmanenu* 1 (1993–94): 69–87.

*Azoulay, Ariella. "On the Possibility and Situation of Critical Art in Israel." *Teoria u-vikoret* 2 (1992): 89–118.

*——. "Open Doors: Museums of History in Israeli Public Space." *Teoria u-vikoret* 4 (1993): 79–95.

Baer, Yitzhak F. *Galut.* 1936. Translated by Robert Warshow. 1947. New ed. Lanham, Md.: University Press of America, 1988.

*Bar-Gal, Yoram. *Moledet and Geography over a Century of Zionist Education.* Tel Aviv: Am Oved, 1993.

Barnavi, Élie. *Une Histoire moderne d'Israël.* New ed. Paris: Flammarion, 1991.

Bartal, Israel. "'Old Yishuv' and 'New Yishuv': Image and Reality." *Jerusalem Cathedra*, 1981, pp. 215–31.

——. "Les Émissaires de terre d'Israël: Entre la réalité d'un lien et d'abstraction d'une vision." In Shmuel Trigano, ed., *La Société juive à travers l'histoire*, 4: 107–21. Paris: Fayard, 1992–93.

*——. *Exile Within the Country.* Jerusalem: Ha-Sifria ha-Tsionit, 1995.

*Bar-Yosef, Hamutal. "The Concept of Decadence in Brenner in the Context of the Idea of National Renaissance." *Iyunim bi-tekumat Yisrael* 1 (1991): 496–522.

Baumgarten, Jean. "Images du monde sépharade dans des récits de voyages vers la Terre sainte en langue yiddish (XVIIe–XVIIIe siècles)." In Esther Benbassa, ed., *Mémoires juives d'Espagne et du Portugal*, pp. 223–37. Paris: Publisud, 1996.

*Ben-Ami, Yisakhar. *The Popular Cult of Saints Among the Jews of Morocco.* Jerusalem: Magnes Press, 1984.

Ben-Ari, Eyal, and Yoram Bilu, eds. *Grasping Land: Space and Place in Contemporary Israeli Discourse and Experience.* Albany: State University of New York Press, 1997.

Ben-Arieh, Yehoshua. *The Rediscovery of the Holy Land in the Nineteenth Century.* Jerusalem: Magnes Press; Detroit: Wayne State University Press, 1979.

Benbassa, Esther. "Les Relais nationalistes juifs dans les Balkans au XIXe siècle." In id., ed., *Transmission et passages en monde juif*, pp. 403–34. Paris: Publisud, 1997.

Benbassa, Esther, and Alain Dieckhoff, eds. *Identités israéliennes: Modernité et mémoire d'une nation. Pardès* 18 (1993).

Ben Guigui, Jacques. *Israel Zangwill: Penseur et écrivain (1864–1926).* Toulouse: Imprimerie toulousaine, 1975.

Benvenisti, Meron. *City of Stone: The Hidden History of Jerusalem*, trans. Maxine Kaufman Nunn. Berkeley and Los Angeles: University of California Press, 1996. Published in French as *Jérusalem: Une Histoire politique*, trans. K. Werchowski and N. Weill (Arles: Actes Sud, 1996).

———. *Sacred Landscape: The Buried History of the Holy Land Since 1948.* Translated by Maxine Kaufman-Lacusta. Berkeley and Los Angeles: University of California Press, 2000.

Ben-Zadok, Efraim. "National Planning—The Critical Neglected Link: One Hundred Years of Jewish Settlement in Israel." *International Journal of Middle Eastern Studies* 17 (1985): 329–45.

Bernstein, S. Deborah. "Political Participation: New Immigrants and Veteran Parties in Israeli Society." *Plural Societies* 5 (1984): 13–32.

———. ed. *Pioneers and Homemakers: Jewish Women in Pre-State Israel.* Albany: State University of New York Press, 1992.

Bonfil, Roberto. "Gerusalemme 'Umbilicus Mundi.'" In Franco Cardini, ed., *La città e il sacro*, pp. 43–82. Milan: Libri Scheiwiller, 1994.

Bruner, Edward M., and Phyllis Gorfain. "Dialogic Narration and the Paradoxes of Masada." In Edward M. Bruner and Stuart Plattner, eds., *Text, Play and Story*, pp. 56–79. Washington, D.C.: American Ethnological Society, 1984.

Buber, Martin. *On Zion: The History of an Idea.* New ed. Translated from German by S. Godman. London: Horovitz Publishing, 1973.

Bursztyn, Igal. "Faces as Idea, Faces as Object: A Cinematic History (1911–1967)." *Studies in Zionism* 10, 2 (1989): 139–54.

Carmell, Aryeh. "The Mitzvah of Living in Eretz Yisael: A Halachic Survey." In H. Chaim Schimmel and Aryeh Carmell, eds., *Encounter: Essays on Torah and Modern Life*, pp. 292–310. New York: Feldheim Publishers, 1989.

Cohen, Erik. "Development Towns: The Social Dynamics of 'Planted' Urban Communities in Israel." In Shmuel N. Eisenstadt et al., eds., *Integration and Development in Israel*, pp. 587–617. Jerusalem: Israel Universities Press, 1970.

——. "The City in Zionist Ideology." *Jerusalem Quarterly* 4 (Summer 1977): 126–44.

——. *L'Étude et l'éducation juive en France ou l'avenir d'une communauté*. Paris: Cerf, 1991.

Cohen, Richard I. *The Return to the Land of Israel*. Jerusalem: World Zionist Organization/Zalman Shazar Center, 1986.

David, Abraham. *To Come to the Land: Immigration and Settlement in Sixteenth-Century Eretz-Israel*. Translated by Dena Orden. Tuscaloosa and London: University of Alabama Press, 1999.

Davies, W.D. *The Territorial Dimension of Judaism*. Berkeley and Los Angeles: University of California Press, 1982.

Delmaire, Jean-Marie. "De Hibbat Zion au sionisme politique." Ph.D. diss. 2 vols. Lille: Atelier national de reproduction des thèses, 1990.

——. *De Jaffa jusqu'en Galilée: Les Premiers Pionniers juifs (1882–1904)*. Villeneuve d'Ascq: Presses universitaires du Septentrion, 1999.

Deshen, Shlomo. "Social Organization and Politics in Israeli Urban Quarters." *Jerusalem Quarterly* 22 (Winter 1982): 21–37.

Dieckhoff, Alain. *Les Espaces d'Israël: Essai sur la stratégie territoriale israélienne*. 2d ed. Paris: Fondation pour les études de défense nationale/Presses de la Fondation nationale des sciences politiques, 1989.

——. "Les Trajectoires territoriales du sionisme." *Vingtième Siècle*, January–March 1989, pp. 29–43.

——. "Le Gouch Emounim: Esquisse d'ethnographie politique." *Pardès* 11 (1990): 84–110.

——. *L'Invention d'une nation: Israël et la modernité politique*. Paris: Gallimard, 1993.

——. *Israéliens et Palestiniens: L'Épreuve de la paix*. Paris: Aubier, 1996.

——. "De Saint-Pétersbourg à Jérusalem: Les Empreintes du climat intellectuel russe sur le sionisme socialiste." In E. Benbassa, ed., *Transmission et passages en monde juif*, pp. 434–50. Paris: Publisud, 1997.

*Dinaburg, B. "The Image of Zion and of Jerusalem in the Historical Consciousness of Israel." *Zion*, n.s., 16, 1–2 (1951–52): 1–17.

Dolev-Gandelman, Tsili. "The Symbolic Inscription of Zionist Ideology in the Space of Eretz Israel: Why the Native Israeli Is Called *Tsabar*." In Harvey

E. Goldberg, ed., *Judaism Viewed from Within and Without*, pp. 257–84. Albany: State University of New York Press, 1987.

*Doron, Adam, ed. *The State of Israel and the Land of Israel*. N.p.: Beit Berl, 1988.

*Dvir, Ori. *Where Shall We Walk This Week?* Tel Aviv: Levin Epstein, 1972.

*Efrat, Elisheva. *Geography and Politics in Israel*. Tel Aviv: Ahiasaf, 1984.

Efrati, Nathan, and Jossi Stern. *Homecoming*. Jerusalem: Israel Economist Publishing, 1982.

Eisen, Arnold. *Galut: Modern Jewish Reflections of Homelessness and Homecoming*, Bloomington: Indiana University Press, 1986.

Elam, Yigal. "Gush Emunim. A False Messianism." *Jerusalem Quarterly* 1 (Fall 1976): 60–69.

Encel, Fredéric. *Géopolitique de Jérusalem*. Paris: Flammarion, 1998.

——. *Le Moyen-Orient entre guerre et paix: Une Géopolitique du Golan*. Paris: Flammarion, 1999.

Enderlin, Charles. *Le Rêve brisé: Histoire de l'échec du processus de paix au Proche-Orient (1995–2002)*. Paris: Fayard, 2002.

Epperson, Steven. *Mormons and Jews: Early Mormon Theologies of Israel*. Salt Lake City: Signature Books, 1992.

Etkes, Immanuel. "Messianisme et politique en Israël: L'Histoire du *Gush Emunim*." In Jean-Christophe Attias, Pierre Gisel, and Lucie Kaennel, eds., *Messianismes: Variations sur une figure juive*, pp. 147–69. Geneva: Labor et Fides, 2000.

Ettinger, Shmuel. "Le Peuple juif et Eretz Israel." *Les Temps modernes* 253bis, *Dossier: Le Conflit israélo-arabe* (1967): 394–413.

Evron, Boaz. *Jewish State or Israeli Nation?* Bloomington: Indiana University Press, 1995.

Ezrahi, Sidra. "Our Homeland, the Text . . . Our Text, the Homeland: Exile and Homecoming in the Modern Jewish Imagination." *Michigan Quarterly Review* 31 (1992): 463–97.

Ezrahi, Sidra DeKoven. *Booking Passage: Exile and Homecoming in the Modern Jewish Imagination*. Berkeley and Los Angeles: University of California Press, 2000.

Feldman, Jackie. "Le Second Temple comme institution économique, sociale et politique." In Shmuel Trigano, ed., *La Société juive à travers l'histoire*, 2: 155–79. Paris: Fayard, 1992–93.

——. "Les Pèlerinages au Second Temple." In Shmuel Trigano, ed., *La Société juive à travers l'histoire*, 4: 161–78. Paris: Fayard, 1992–93.

*Firer, Ruth. *The Agents of Zionist Education*. Tel Aviv: Sifriyat Poalim, 1985.

Fischer, Shlomo. "Empire, conscience identitaire juive et relations internationales des Juifs à l'époque du Second Temple." In Shmuel Trigano, ed., *La Société juive à travers l'histoire*, 3: 407–32. Paris: Fayard, 1992–93.

Flapan, Simha. *The Birth of Israel: Myths and Realities.* New York: Pantheon Books, 1987.

Fox, Marvin. "The Holiness of the Holy Land." In Jonathan Sacks, ed., *Tradition and Transition: Essays Presented to Chief Rabbi Sir Immanuel Jakobovits to Celebrate Twenty Years in Office,* pp. 155–70. N.p.: Jews' College Publication, 1986.

Freudental, Gad. "Jérusalem ville sainte? La perspective maïmonidienne." *Revue de l'Histoire des Religions* 217, 4 (2000): 689–705.

Friedman, Menahem. "L'État d'Israël comme dilemme idéologique." *Pardès* 11 (1990): 15–65.

*Friesel, Evyatar. "Baron Edmond de Rothschild and the Zionists from 1918 to 1919." *Zion* 38 (1973): 117–36.

Furman, Andrew, ed. *Israel Through the Jewish American Imagination: A Survey of Jewish-American Literature on Israel, 1928–1995.* Albany: State University of New York Press, 1997.

*Gafni, Yeshayahu. "The Transfer of the Body for Burial in the Holy Land: Beginnings and Evolution of the Practice." *Cathedra* 4 (July 1977): 113–20.

Gafni, Isaiah. *Land, Center and Diaspora: Jewish Constructs in Late Antiquity.* Sheffield: Sheffield Academic Press, 1997.

*Ganuz, Yitshak. "Streetnames in the Towns of White Russia." *Yeda-Am* 17, 41–42 (1974): 69–71.

*Gelman, Yehuda. "Zion and Jerusalem—The Jewish State According to Rabbi Abraham Isaac Kook." *Iyunim bi-tekumat Yisrael* 4 (1994): 505–14.

Gertz, Nurit. "Social Myths in Literary and Political Texts." *Poetics Today* 7, 4 (1986): 621–39.

——. "The Canaanites: Ideology vs. Literature." *Jerusalem Quarterly* 48 (Autumn 1988): 46–62.

*Gil, Moshe. "*Aliyah* and Pilgrimage in the First Period of the Muslim Occupation (634–1099)." *Cathedra* 8 (July 1978): 124–32.

Golden, Deborah. "The Museum of the Jewish Diaspora Tells a Story." In Tom Selwyn ed., *The Tourist Image: Myths and Myth Making in Tourism,* pp. 223–50. New York: John Wiley & Sons, 1996.

*Gonen, Rivka. "Ancient Tombs and Holy Places—The Grotto of Makhpela and the Temple Mount." *Cathedra* 34 (January 1985): 3–14.

*Goren, Hayim. "Knowledge of the Land of Israel in the Eighteenth Century: The *Sefer Yedei Moshe* of R. Moshe Yerushalmi." *Cathedra* 34 (January 1985): 75–96.

Green, Arthur. "The Zaddiq as Axis Mundi in Later Judaism." *Journal of the American Academy of Religion* 45 (1977): 327–47.

Greilsammer, Ilan. *La Nouvelle Histoire d'Israël: Essai sur l'identité nationale.* Paris: Gallimard, 1998.

Grier, Tom. "Reversed Diaspora: Russian Jewry, the Transition in Russia and the Migration to Israel." *Anthropology of Eastern Europe Review* 14, 1 (1996).

Gurevitch, Zali. "The Land of Israel: Myth and Phenomenon." In Jonathan Frankel, ed., *Reshaping the Past: Jewish History and the Historians.* Studies in Contemporary Jewry, 10. New York: Oxford University Press for the Institute of Contemporary Jewry, Hebrew University of Jerusalem, 1994.

*Gurevitch, Zali, and Gideon Aran. "On the Place (Israeli Anthropology)." *Alpayim* 4 (1991): 9–44.

Habibi, Imil [Emile]. *The Secret Life of Saeed the Pessoptimist.* 1974. Translated by Salma Khadra Jayyusi and Trevor LeGassick. 1982. New York: Interlink Books, 2002.

*——. *Sarayah, Daughter of the Ghoul.* Translated by Anton Shammas. Tel Aviv: Ha-Sifriya Ha-Hadasha, 1993.

Hadas-Lebel, Mireille. *Jérusalem contre Rome.* Paris: Cerf, 1990.

——. *Massada: Histoire et symbole.* Paris: Albin Michel, 1995.

Halkin, Abraham S. *Zion in Jewish Literature.* 2d ed. Lanham, Md.: University Press of America, 1988.

Hall, Stuart. "Cultural Identity and Diaspora." In Jonathan Rutherford, ed., *Identity, Community, Culture, Difference*, pp. 222–37. London: Lawrence & Wishart, 1990.

*Hallamish, Moshe, and Aviezer Ravitzky, eds. *The Land of Israel in Medieval Jewish Thought.* Jerusalem: Yad Yitshak Ben Zvi, 1991.

Handelman, Don, and Lea Shamgar-Handelman. "Shaping Time: The Choice of the National Emblem of Israel." In Emiko Ohnuki-Tierney, ed., *Culture Through Time: Anthropological Approaches*, pp. 193–226. Stanford: Stanford University Press, 1990.

*Haran, Raya. "What Made the Disciples of the *Magid* Go to the Land of Israel?" *Cathedra* 76 (July 1995): 77–95.

*Harvey, W. Zeev, et al., eds. *Zion and Zionism Among Sephardi and Oriental Jews.* Jerusalem: Misgav Yerushalayim, 2002.

*Hasdai, Yaakov. "The Beginnings of the Hasidic and *Mitnaged* Colonies in the Land of Israel—*Aliyah* as Commandment and *Aliyah* as Mission." *Shalem* 4 (1983–84): 231–69.

Hasan-Rokem, Galit. "La Culture populaire juive en Israël: Dialogues et passages." In Esther Benbassa, ed., *Transmission et passages en monde juif*, pp. 137–49. Paris: Publisud, 1997.

Hasson, Shlomo. "Social and Spatial Conflicts: The Settlement Process in Israel During the 1950s and the 1960s." *L'Espace géographique* 3 (1981): 169–79.

——. "The Emergence of an Urban Social Movement in Israeli Society: An Integrated Approach." *International Journal of Urban and Regional Research* 7, 2 (1983): 157–74.

*Hazan, Efrayim. "The Presence of the Land of Israel in the Liturgical and Pro-
fane Poetry of the Jews of North Africa." *Cathedra* 34 (January 1985): 37–54.

*Heilperin, Yisrael. *Jews and Judaism in Eastern Europe.* Jerusalem: Magnes Press,
1968–69.

*Helfand, I. Jonathan. "Relations Between French Jewry and the Land of Israel."
Cathedra 36 (June 1985): 37–61.

Herzl, Theodor. *A Jewish State: An Attempt at a Modern Solution of the Jewish Question.* 3d ed., rev. Translated by Sylvia d'Avigdor. New York: Federation of
American Zionists, 1917. Originally published as *Der Judenstaat: Versuch
einer modernen Lösung der Judenfrage* (1896).

Hess, Moses. *The Revival of Israël. Rome and Jerusalem: The Last Nationalist Ques-
tion.* Translated and edited by Meyer Waxman. 1918. Lincoln: University of
Nebraska Press, 1995. Originally published as *Rom und Jerusalem: Die letzte
Nationalitätsfrage* (1862).

*Hever Hannan. "The Struggle over the Canon in Hebrew Literature." *Teoria u-
vikoret* 4 (1994): 55–78.

*——. "Women Poets of the War of Independence." *Teoria u-vikoret* 7 (1995):
99–123.

Heymann, Florence, and Michel Abitbol, eds. *L'Historiographie israélienne aujour-
d'hui.* Paris: CNRS, 1998.

History and Memory 7, 1, *Israeli Historiography Revisited* (Spring/Summer 1995).

Hoffmann, Lawrence A., ed. *The Land of Israel: Jewish Perspectives.* Notre Dame,
Ind.: University of Notre Dame Press, 1986.

*Idel, Moshe. "Jerusalem in Thirteenth-Century Jewish Thought." In Yehoshua
Prawer and Haggai Ben-Shammai, eds., *The Book of Jerusalem: The Period of
the Crusades and the Ayyubids, 1099–1250,* pp. 264–86. Jerusalem: Yad Yitshak
Ben-Zvi, 1990–91.

——. "*Erets Yisrael* dans la pensée juive." In Shmuel Trigano, ed., *La Société juive à
travers les âges,* 4: 77–105. Paris: Fayard, 1992–93.

Iogna-Prat, Dominique. "La terre sainte disputée." *Médiévales* 41 (Fall 2001): 83–112.

Ish-Shalom, Benjamin. *Rav Avraham Itzhak Hacohen Kook: Between Rationalism
and Mysticism.* Translated by O. Wiskind-Elper. Albany: State University of
New York Press, 1993.

Jackont, Amnon. *Borrowed Time: A Novel.* Translated by Dorothea Shefer-Vanson.
London: Hamish Hamilton, 1986. Originally published as *Pesek-zeman* (Tel
Aviv: Am Oved, 1982).

Jérusalem: Le Guide Autrement. Paris: Éditions Autrement, 1983.

*Kahan, S.Z. "Accounts of Pilgrimages on the Tombs of Saints and on Holy Sites
in the Land of Israel." *Yeda-Am* 22, 50–51: 112–16; 23, 53–54: 36–49.

Kaniel, Yehoshua. "The Terms 'Old Yishuv' and 'New Yishuv': Problems of Definition." *Jerusalem Cathedra,* 1981, pp. 232–45.

Kark, Ruth. "Agricultural Land in Palestine: Letters to Sir Moses Montefiore, 1839." *Jewish Historical Studies: Transactions of the Jewish Historical Society of England* 19 (1982–86): 207–30.

——. "Historical Sites—Perceptions and Land Purchase: The Case of Modi'in, 1882–1931." *Studies in Zionism* 9, 1 (1988): 1–17.

——, ed., *The Land That Became Israel. Studies in Historical Geography*. New Haven, Conn.: Yale University Press; Jerusalem: Magnes Press, 1989.

Karsh, Efraim. *Fabricating Israeli History: The "New Historians."* London: Frank Cass, 1997.

Katriel, Tamar, and Aharon Shenhar. "Tower and Stockage: Dialogic Narration in Israeli Settlement Ethos." *Quarterly Journal of Speech* 76, 4 (1990): 359–80.

Katz, Jacob. *Jewish Emancipation and Self-Emancipation*. Philadelphia: Jewish Publication Society, 1986.

*Katz, Yossi. "Document: The Hebrew Renaming of Places and Sites in the Negev in 1949–1950." *Iyunim bi-tekumat Yisrael* 5 (1995): 615–19.

*Katz, Yossi, and Shalom Reichman. "The Jewish Settlement of Goush-Etsion 1967–1970." *Iyunim bi-tekumat Yisrael* 3 (1993): 144–53.

Kellerman, Aharon. *Society and Settlement: Jewish Land of Israel in the Twentieth Century*. Albany: State University of New York Press, 1993.

*Keren, Mikhael, "Literature and National Renaissance: The Reaction of Agnon to the Jewish Nation-State According to *Sefer ha-Medina*." *Iyunim bi-tekumat Yisrael* 5 (1995): 446–54.

Kimmerling, Baruch. "Change and Continuity in Zionist Territorial Orientations and Politics." *Comparative Politics* 14, 2 (1982) 191–210.

——. *Zionism and Territory: The Socio-Territorial Dimensions of Zionist Politics*. Berkeley: Institute of International Studies, University of California, 1983.

——, ed. *The Israeli State and Society: Boundaries and Frontiers*. Albany: State University of New York Press, 1989.

Kimmerling, Baruch, and Joel Migdal, eds. *Palestinians: The Making of a People*. New York: Free Press, 1993.

Klein, Claude. *La Démocratie d'Israël*. Paris: Seuil, 1997.

*Klein, S. *History of the Study of the Land of Israel in Hebrew and General Literature*. Jerusalem: Mosad Bialik, 1936–37.

*Kohen, Yehoshua. "Descriptions of Landscapes and Inhabited Places in the Work of Aharon Megged." *Erets Yisrael. Mehkarim bi-yedi'at ha-arets ve-atikoteiha* 22 (1990–91): 95–105.

Kunin, Seth. "Judaism." In Jean Holm (with John Bowker), ed., *Sacred Place*, pp. 115–48. London: Pinter Publishers, 1994.

*"Land of Israel." In *The Talmudic Encyclopedia*, 2: 199–235. Jerusalem, 1973–84.

Laqueur, Walter. *A History of Zionism*. New York: Holt, Rinehart & Winston, 1972.

Lehn, Walter, in association with Uri Davis. *The Jewish National Fund*. London: Kegan Paul International, 1988.

*Levinger, Yaakov. "The Specificity of the People of Israel, of Its Land and Its Language According to Maimonides." *Milet* 2 (1983–84): 289–97.

*Levinski, Yom-Tov. "How Was the Site of the Temple Fixed?" *Yeda-Am* 13, 33–34 (1968): 24–40.

*———. "The Jerusalems of the Diaspora." *Yeda-Am* 14, 35–36: 49–50.

*Liebes, Yehuda. "Sabbatian Messianism." *Pe'amim* 40 (1989): 4–20.

Lissak, Moshe. "'Critical' Sociology and 'Establishment' Sociology in the Israeli Academic Community: Ideological Struggles or Academic Discourse." *Israel Studies* 1, 1 (Spring 1996): 247–94.

Lustick, Ian S. *For the Land and the Lord: Jewish Fundamentalism in Israel*. New York, Council on Foreign Relations, 1988.

Luz, Ehud. *Parallels Meet: Religion and Nationalism in the Early Zionist Movement, 1882–1904*. Translated by L. J. Schramm. Philadelphia: Jewish Publication Society, 1988.

Margulies, Lazarus. *The Right of the Jewish People to Palestine According to the Bible: Statement Presented to the Anglo-American Committee of Enquiry on Behalf of Italian Jewry*. N.p., 1946.

*Mayorek, Yoram. "Emile Meyerson and the Start of ICA Involvement in the Land of Israel." *Cathedra* 62 (December 1991): 67–79.

———. "Between East and West: Edmond de Rothschild and Palestine." In Georg Heuberger, ed., *The Rothschilds: Essays on the History of a European Family*, pp. 129–45. Sigmaringen, Germany: Thorbecke; Woodbridge, Suffolk, U.K.: Boydell & Brewer, 1994.

Medding, Peter Y., ed. *Israel: State and Society, 1948–1988*. Studies in Contemporary Jewry, 5. New York: Oxford University Press, 1989.

Medina, Joao Barromi Joel. "The Jewish Colonization Project in Angola." *Studies in Zionism* 12, 1 (1991): 1–16.

Megged, Aharon. *Masa' be-Av*. Tel Aviv: Am Oved, 1980.

Mehlman, Yosi. *The New Israelis: An Intimate Portrait of a Changing People*. New York: Birch Lane Press, 1992.

Mendelsohn, Ezra. *On Modern Jewish Politics*. New York: Oxford University Press, 1993.

*Merhavia, H. *Voices Calling upon Sion*. Jerusalem: Zalman Shazar Center, 1980.

*Michman, Dan, ed. *Post-Zionism and the Holocaust: The Role of the Holocaust in the Public Debate on Post-Zionism in Israel*. Research AIDS Series 8. Jerusalem: Bar Ilan University, 1997.

Mintz, Matityahu. "Ber Borokhov." *Studies in Zionism* 5 (1982): 33–53.

*Miron, Dan. "Songs of an Unseen and Unknown Land: The Place of Naomi Shemer in Our Life." *Igeret* 1 (1984): 173–206.

——. "The Literary Image of the Shtetl." *Jewish Social Studies* 1, 3 (Spring 1995): 1–43.

Morris, Benny. *The Birth of the Palestinian Refugee Problem, 1947–1949*. Cambridge, Cambridge University Press, 1987.

Mosse, George L. "Max Nordau, le libéralisme et le 'nouveau juif.'" In Delphine Bechtel, Dominique Bourel, and Jacques Le Rider, eds., *Max Nordau, 1849–1923*, pp. 11–29. Paris: Cerf, 1996.

Myers, David N. *Re-Inventing the Jewish Past*. New York: Oxford University Press, 1995.

Nahon, Gérard. *La Terre sainte au temps des kabbalistes*. Paris: Albin Michel, 1997.

Neher-Bernheim, Renée. *Jerusalem: Trois millénaires d'histoire. Du roi David à nos jours*. Paris: Albin Michel, 1997.

——. *La Vie juive en Terre sainte, 1517–1918*. Paris: Calmann-Lévy, 2001.

Nehorai, Micael Zvi. "The State of Israel in the Teachings of Rav Kook." *Daat* 2–3 (1978–79): 35–50.

Nicault, Catherine. *La France et le sionisme 1897–1948. Une rencontre manquée?* Paris: Calmann-Lévy, 1992.

——. ed. *Jérusalem, 1850–1948. Des Ottomans aux Anglais: Entre coexistence spirituelle et déchirure politique*. Collection Mémoires, 57. Paris: Éditions Autrement, 1999.

*Ofrat, Gideon. *Land, Man, Blood: The Myth of the Pioneer and the Cult of the Land in Colonial Drama*. Tel Aviv: Tsherikover, 1980.

Oz, Amos. *In the Land of Israel*. Translated by Maurie Goldberg-Bartura. San Diego: Harcourt Brace Jovanovich, 1983.

—— *A Perfect Peace*. Translated by Hillel Halkin. San Diego: Harcourt Brace Jovanovich, 1985. Originally published as *Menuhah nekhonah* (Tel Aviv: Am Oved, 1982).

La Palestine de Balfour à Bevin: Déclarations et documents. Translated by Maurice Moch. Paris: Éditions de la Terre retrouvée, 1946.

Pappe, Ilan. *Britain and the Arab-Israeli Conflict, 1948–1951*. New York: St Martin's Press, 1988.

——. "The New Historiography: Israel Confronts Its Past." *Tikkun*, November–December 1988, pp. 19–23, 99–102.

——. "The Eel and History: A Reply to Shabtai Teveth." *Tikkun*, March–April 1990, pp. 19–22, 79–86.

*——. "The New History of Zionism: The Academic and Public Confrontation." *Kivunim* 8, 45 (1995): 39–48.

*Pappe, Ilan, and Shlomo Swirski, eds. *The Intifada: An Inside View*. Tel Aviv: Mefaresh, 1992.

Pardes, Ilana. *The Biography of Ancient Israel: National Narratives in the Bible*. Berkeley and Los Angeles: University of California Press, 2000.

Patai, Raphael. "Earth Eating." In id., *On Jewish Folklore*, pp. 174–94. Detroit: Wayne State University Press, 1983.

Penslar, Derek J. *Zionism and Technocracy: The Engineering of Jewish Settlement in Palestine, 1870–1918*. Bloomington: Indiana University Press, 1991.

Peters, F.E. *Jerusalem and Mecca: The Typology of the Holy City in the Near East*. New York: New York University Press, 1986.

Picaudou, Nadine. *Les Palestiniens: Un siècle d'histoire*. Brussels: Complexe, 1997.

Pinsker, Leo [Lev Semenovich]. *Auto-Emancipation*. 1882. Translated by S. Blondheim and Arthur Saul Super. N.p.: Masada, Youth Zionist Organization of America, 1939.

*Piterberg, Gabi. "The Nation and Its Raconteurs: Orientalism and Nationalist Historiography." *Teoria u-vikoret* 6 (1995): 81–103.

Pohoryles, Samuel. "Agricultural Transformation in Israel." *Jerusalem Quarterly* 33 (Autumn 1984): 95–101.

*Porat, Hanina. *From the Desert to the Inhabited Land: Acquisition of Land and Colonization of the Negev 1930–1947*. Jerusalem: Yad Yitshak Ben-Zvi, 1996.

*Porten, Betsalel. "The Return from Babylon: Vision and Reality." *Cathedra* 4 (July 1977): 4–12.

Poznanski, Lucien. *La Chute du Temple de Jérusalem*. Brussels: Complexe, 1991.

*Ram, Uri, ed. *Israeli Society: Critical Perspectives*. Tel Aviv: Breirot, 1993.

——. *The Changing Agenda of Israeli Sociology*. Albany: State University of New York Press, 1995.

Ratzaby Shalom. "The Polemic about the 'Negation of the Diaspora' in the 1930s and Its Roots." *Journal of Israeli History* 16, 1 (1995): 19–38.

Ravitzky, Aviezer. *Messianism, Zionism, and Jewish Religious Radicalism*. Translated by Michael Swirsky and Jonathan Chipman. Chicago: University of Chicago Press, 1996.

*——, ed. *The Land of Israel in Modern Jewish Thought*. Jerusalem: Yad Yitshak Ben Zvi, 1998.

*Raz-Krakotzkin, Amnon. "Emptying the Empty Land." *Davar*, June 28, 1991.

*——. "Exile Within Sovereignty—Toward a Critique of the 'Negation of Exile' in Israeli Culture." *Teoria u-vikoret* 4 (1993): 23–55; 5 (1994): 113–32.

*——. "The Representation of Galut: Zionist Historiography and Medieval Jewry." Ph.D. diss., Tel Aviv University, 1996.

*Reiner, Elhanan. "Pilgrims and Pilgrimages in the Land of Israel, 1099–1517." Ph.D. diss., Hebrew University of Jerusalem, 1988.

Reinharz, Jehuda, and Anita Shapira, eds. *Essential Papers on Zionism*. New York: New York University Press, 1996.

Rosenblatt, Samuel. *This Is the Land*. New York: Mizrachi Organization of America, 1940.

Safrai, S., M. Stern, D. Flusser, and W.C. van Unnik. *The Jewish People in the First*

Century: Historical Geography, Political History, Social, Cultural and Religious Life and Institutions. Compendia rerum Iudaicarum ad Novum Testamentum. 2 vols. Assen, Neth.: Van Gorcum, 1974–76.

Safran, Alexandre. *Israël dans le temps et dans l'espace: Thèmes fondamentaux de la spiritualité juive.* Paris: Payot, 1980.

Said, Edward. *Orientalism.* New York: Vintage Books, 1989.

Salmon, Yosef. "Les Émigrations traditionnelles vers la Palestine (1740–1880)." In Shmuel Trigano, ed., *La Société juive à travers l'histoire,* 4: 123–38. Paris: Fayard, 1992–93.

Saltman, Michael, ed. *Land and Territoriality.* New York: Berg, 2002.

Schäfer, Peter. *Geschichte der Juden in der Antike: Die Juden Palästinas von Alexander dem Grossen bis zur arabischen Eroberung.* Stuttgart: Verlag Katholisches Bibelwerk; [Neukirchen-Vluyn]: Neukirchener Verlag, 1983. Translated by P. Schulte as *Histoire des juifs dans l'Antiquité* (Paris: Cerf, 1989). Translated by David Chowcat as *The History of the Jews in Antiquity: The Jews of Palestine from Alexander the Great to the Arab Conquest* (New York: Harwood Academic Publishers, 1995).

Schmidt, Francis. *La Pensée du Temple: De Jérusalem à Qûmran.* Paris: Seuil, 1994.

Schwartz, Barry, Yael Zerubavel, and Bernice Barnett. "The Recovery of Masada: A Study in Collective Memory." *Sociological Quarterly* 27, 2 (1986): 147–64.

*Schwartz, Dov. *One Faith at the Crossroads: Ideas and Acts in Religious Zionism.* Tel Aviv: Am Oved, 1996.

Schwartz, Regina M. *The Curse of Cain: The Violent Legacy of Monotheism.* Chicago: University of Chicago Press, 1997.

*Schwarzbaum, Hayim. "Legendary Sources Regarding the Choice of a Site Suitable for Building the Temple of Jerusalem." *Yeda-Am* 13, 33–34 (1968): 41–45.

*Schweid, Eliezer. *Homeland and Promised Land.* Tel Aviv: Am Oved, 1979.

——. "The Rejection of the Diaspora in Zionist Thought: Two Approaches." *Studies in Zionism* 5, 1 (1984): 43–70.

*——. "Nature and Background of Post-Zionism." *Gesher* 131 (Summer 1995): 18–26.

——. "'Beyond' All That—Modernism, Zionism, Judaism." *Israel Studies* 1, 1 (Spring 1996): 224–46.

Segev, Tom. *1949: The First Israelis.* New York: Free Press, 1986.

——. *The Seventh Million: The Israelis and the Holocaust.* New York: Hill & Wang, 1993.

——. *One Palestine, Complete: Jews and Arabs under the British Mandate.* Translated by Haim Watzman. New York: Metropolitan Books, 2000.

Selzer, Michael, ed. *Zionism Reconsidered: The Rejection of Jewish Normalcy.* London: Macmillan, 1970.

*Seri, Eyal, ed. *Days of Study on Torah and State: Anthology of Sources on the Land of Israel in the Bible, Thought, and the Halakhah.* Efrat: Mosdot Or Tora—Yeshivat Neve Shmuel, 1991–92.

Sha'altiel, Eli. "David Ben-Gourion on Partition, 1937." *Jerusalem Quarterly* 10 (Winter 1979): 38–59.

Shafir, Gershon. *Land, Labour, and the Israeli Palestinian Conflict, 1882–1920.* Cambridge: Cambridge University Press, 1989.

Shamgar-Handelman, Lea, and Don Handelman. "Holiday Celebrations in Israeli Kindergartens: Relationships between Representations of Collectivity and Family in the Nation-State." In Myron J. Aronoff, ed., *The Frailty of Authority*, pp. 71–103. New Brunswick, N.J., Transaction Books, 1986.

Shammas, Anton. *Arabesques: A Novel.* Translated Hebrew by Vivian Eden. New York: Harper & Row, 1988. Reprinted. Berkeley and Los Angeles: University of California Press, 2001.

Shapira, Anita. "The Origins of 'Jewish Labor' Ideology." *Studies in Zionism* 5 (April 1982): 93–113.

——. *Land and Power: The Zionist Resort to Force, 1881–1948.* Translated by William Templer. New York: Oxford University Press, 1992.

*——. *New Jews, Old Jews.* Tel Aviv: Am Oved, 1997.

*Shapira, Avraham. "Personal Ego and National Ego in the Thought of Aharon David Gordon." *Ha-Tsionut* 18 (1994): 39–54.

Shapira, Sarit. *Routes of Wandering: Nomadism, Journeys and Transitions in Contemporary Israeli Art.* Exhibition catalogue. Jerusalem: Museum of Israel, 1991. In English and Hebrew.

Shavit, Yaakov. "Hebrews and Phoenicians: An Ancient Historical Image and Its Use." *Studies in Zionism* 5, 2 (1984): 157–80.

*——. "'Truth will come out of the earth'—Development of Popular Interest in Archeology (up until the 1930s)." *Cathedra* 44 (June 1987): 27–54.

Sheron, Moshe, ed. *The Holy Land in History and Thought.* Leiden: E.J. Brill, 1988.

*Shiloah, Amnon. "The Poetry of *Aliyah* in Traditional Popular Literature in Israel." In Dov Noy and Yissakhar Ben-Ami, eds., *Studies from the Center for Research on Folklore*, 1: 349–68. Jerusalem: Magnes Press, 1969–70.

Shlaim, Avi. *Collusion Across the Jordan: King Abdullah, the Zionist Movement, and the Partition of Palestine.* New York: Columbia University Press, 1988.

*Shmeruk, Chone, and Israel Bartal. "*Telaot Moshe*: The First Geography Book in Yiddish and the Description of the Land of Israel by R. Moshe bar Abraham the Proselyte." *Cathedra* 40 (July 1986): 121–37.

Shohat, Ella. *Israeli Cinema: East/West and the Politics of Representation.* Austin: University of Texas Press, 1989.

Shokeid, Moshe. *Children of Circumstances: Israeli Immigrants in New York.* Ithaca, N.Y.: Cornell University Press, 1988.

Silberman, Neil Asher, and David Small, eds. *The Archaeology of Israel: Constructing the Past, Interpreting the Present.* Sheffield, U.K.: Sheffield Academic Press, 1997.

Silberstein, Laurence J. *The Postzionism Debates: Knowledge and Power in Israeli Culture.* New York: Routledge, 1999.

Silberstein, Laurence J., and Robert L. Cohn. *The Other in Jewish Thought and History: Constructions of Jewish Culture and Identity.* New York: New York University Press, 1994.

Singer, Isaac Bashevis. *The Family Moskat.* 1950. Translated by A.H. Gross. New York: Farrar, Straus & Giroux, 1978.

Solotaroff, Theodore, and Nessa Rapoport, eds. *Writing Our Home: Contemporary Stories by American Jewish Writers.* New York: Schocken Books, 1992.

Spero, Shubert, and Pessin, Yitzchak, eds. *Religious Zionism After Forty Years of Statehood.* Jerusalem: Mesilot and World Zionist Organization, 1989.

Sprinzak, Ehud. "Gush Emunim: The Tip of the Iceberg." *Jewish Quarterly Review* 21 (Autumn 1981): 28–47.

*Stein, Menahem. "The Mother-Land in Ancient Hebrew Literature." *Tarbiz* 9, 2 (January 1938): 257–77.

*Stern, Efrayim. "The State of Judea: Vision and Reality." *Cathedra* 4 (July 1977): 13–24.

Sternhell, Zeev. *The Founding Myths of Israel.* Translated by D. Maisel. Princeton, N.J., Princeton University Press, 1997.

Storper Perez, Danielle. *L'Intelligentsia russe en Israël: Rassurante étrangeté,* Cahiers du Centre de recherche français de Jérusalem. Paris: CNRS, 1998.

*Trachtenberg, Graciella. "The East and Israeli Society." In *To the East: Orientalism in the Arts in Israel,* pp. 33–45. Jerusalem: Israel Museum, 1998.

Trimbur, Dominique, and Ran Aaronsohn, eds. *De Bonaparte à Balfour: La France, l'Europe occidentale et la Palestine, 1799–1917.* Paris, CNRS, 2001.

*Troen, Ilan S. "A Turning Point in Zionist Policy: From the Rural Colony to Urban Organization." *Yahadut Zmanenu* 5 (1988–89): 217–40.

Troen, S. Ilan, and Noah Lucas, eds. *Israel: The First Decade of Independence.* Albany: State University of New York Press, 1995.

Tryster, Hillel. "*The Land of Promise* (1935): A Case Study in Zionist Film Propaganda." *Historical Journal of Film, Radio and Television* 15, 2 (June 1995): 187–217.

*Tuder, Shimon. "The Fruits of Jerusalem." *Yeda-Am* 14, 35–36: 43–45.

Udelson, Joseph H. *Dreamer of the Ghetto: The Life and Works of Israel Zangwill.* Tuscaloosa: University of Alabama Press, 1990.

Urbach, Ephraim E. "Center and Periphery in Jewish Historic Consciousness: Contemporary Implications." In Moshe Davis, ed., *World Jewry and the State of Israel,* pp. 217–35. New York: Arno Press, 1977.

Ussishkin, Anne. "The Jewish Colonisation Association and a Rothschild in Palestine." *Middle Eastern Studies* 9, 3 (October 1973): 347–57.

Veinberger, Miriam. "The Place of the Land of Israel in the Work of Dvora Baron." *Be-emet* 4–5 (1990–91): 61–76.

Verman, Mark. "*Aliyah* and *Yeridah*: The Journeys of the Besht and R. Nachman to Israel." In David R. Blumenthal, ed., *Approaches to Judaism in Medieval Times*, 3: 159–71. Atlanta: Scholars Press, 1988.

*Verses, Shmuel. "Legends About the Ten Tribes and About Sambation and Their Adaptations in Our Modern Literature." *Mehkerei Yerushalayim be-folklor yehudi* 7 (5746 [1985–86]): 38–66.

Vidal, Dominique, and Joseph Algazy. *Le Péché originel d'Israël: L'Expulsion des Palestiniens revisitée par les "nouveaux historiens" israéliens.* Paris: Éditions de l'Atelier, 1998.

Vidal-Naquet, Pierre. *The Jews: History, Memory and the Present.* Translated and edited by David Ames Curtis. New York: Columbia University Press, 1996.

Vince, Agnès. "Le Quartier juif: Comparaisons européennes." In Shmuel Trigano, ed., *La Société juive à travers l'histoire*, 2: 499–529. Paris: Fayard, 1992–93.

Vital, David. *The Future of the Jews.* Cambridge, Mass.: Harvard University Press, 1990.

Wasserstein, Bernard. *Divided Jerusalem: The Struggle for the Holy City.* New Haven, Conn.: Yale University Press, 2001.

Waxman, Chaim I. ed. *Israel as a Religious Reality.* Northvale, N.J.: Jason Aronson, 1994.

*Weinfeld, Moshe. "To Inherit the Land—A Right and a Duty: Conception of the Promise in Sources of the First and Second Temple Periods." *Zion* 49, 2 (1984): 115–37.

——. *The Promise of the Land: The Inheritance of the Land of Canaan by the Israelites.* Berkeley and Los Angeles: University of California Press, 1993.

*Weitz, Yehiam. *Between Vision and Revision.* Jerusalem: Merkaz Zalman Shazar, 1997.

Werblowsky, R.J. Zwi. "Israël et Eretz Israël." *Les Temps modernes* 253bis, *Dossier: Le Conflit israélo-arabe* (1967): 371–393.

Wilken, Robert L. *The Land Called Holy: Palestine in Christian History and Thought.* New Haven, Conn.: Yale University Press, 1993.

Wistrich, Robert, David Ohana, eds. *The Shaping of Israeli Society: Myth, Memory and Trauma.* London: Frank Cass, 1995.

Wohlgelernter, Maurice. *Israel Zangwill.* New York: Columbia University Press, 1964.

*Yaakovson, Yoram. "Exile and Redemption in the Hasidism of Gur." *Daat* 2–3 (1978): 175–215.

*Yaari, Abraham. *Letters from the Land of Israel.* Tel Aviv, 1950.

*——, ed. *Voyages to the Land of Israel by Jewish Pilgrims from the Middle Ages to the Start of the Return to Zion*. New ed. Tel Aviv: Modan, 1996.

Yehoshua, Abraham B. English. *A Late Divorce*. Translated by Hillel Halkin. Garden City, N.Y.: Doubleday, 1984. Originally published as *Gerushim me'uharim* (Tel Aviv: ha-Kibuts ha-me'uhad, 1982).

Yosef, Ovadia (Rav). "Ceding Territory of the Land of Israel in Order to Save Lives." *Crossroads: Halacha and the Modern World III*, pp. 11–18. Alon Shvut–Gush Etzion: Zomet Institute, n.d.

*Zak, Brachah. "Land and the Land of Israel in the Zohar." *Mehkerei Yerushalayim be-mahshevet Yisrael* 8 (5749 [1988–89]): 239–53.

Zerubavel, Yael. "The 'Wandering Israeli' in Contemporary Israeli Literature." *Contemporary Jewry* 7, 1 (1986): 127–40.

——. *Recovered Roots: Collective Memory and the Making of Israeli National Tradition*. Chicago: University of Chicago Press, 1995.

——. "The Forest as a National Icon: Literature, Politics, and the Archeology of Memory." *Israel Studies* 1, 1 (Spring 1996): 60–99.

The Authors

JEAN-CHRISTOPHE ATTIAS is professor of the History of Rabbinic Culture at the École Pratique des Hautes Études, Sorbonne, and a member of the Centre d'Études des Religions du Livre (Centre National de la Recherche Scientifique/EPHE). He is the author of *Le Commentaire biblique. Mordekhai Komtino ou l'herméneutique du dialogue* (1991) and of *Isaac Abravanel, la mémoire et l'espérance* (1992). He edited or coedited *De la Conversion* (1998), *Enseigner le judaïsme à l'Université* (1998), and *Messianismes: Variations autour d'une figure juive* (2000).

ESTHER BENBASSA is professor of Modern Jewish History at the École Pratique des Hautes Études, Sorbonne, and director of the Alberto Benveniste Center for Sephardic Studies and Culture (EPHE). Her books translated into English are *Haim Nahum: A Sephardic Chief Rabbi in Politics* (1995), *The Jews of France: A History from Antiquity to the Present* (1999), and, with Aron Rodrigue, *A Sephardi Life in Southeastern Europe* (1998) and *Sephardi Jewry: A History of the Judeo-Spanish Community, 14th–20th Centuries* (2000). She is also the author of *Une diaspora sépharade en transition (Istanbul, XIXe–XXe siècles)* (1993). She edited or coedited *Cultures juives méditerranéennes* (1985), *Mémoires juives d'Espagne et du Portugal* (1996), *Transmission et passages en monde juif* (1997), and *L'Europe et les Juifs* (2002).

JEAN-CHRISTOPHE ATTIAS and ESTHER BENBASSA already coauthored *Dictionnaire de civilisation juive* (1997), *Les Juifs ont-ils un avenir?* (2001), and *Le Juif et l'Autre* (2002), and edited *La Haine de soi: Difficiles identités* (2000).

Index of Names of Persons and Organizations

Index of Place-Names